Autonomic Steve

(motor)

(substant...)

**Basic
FORTRAN IV
Programming**

Cerebral Cortex
motor (tracts) Center
somesthetic
Enceplagraph- G
ideo motor area - fast snap
decisions
no storage

(Kinesthetic info.)

pre-motor & → physiolog

Basal Ganglia
caudate nuclea
Putamen
Red Nucleus — error control
Globus Pallidus
Amygdaloid
Calustrum

Anatom ical

Parkinson's ← Basal Ganglia - alcohol
1st treatment

Nitrogen freezing;

IRWIN-DORSEY
INFORMATION PROCESSING SERIES

EDITORS

ROBERT B. FETTER   RICHARD L. VAN HORN
Yale University   *Carnegie-Mellon University*

Basic FORTRAN IV Programming

DONALD H. FORD

Professor
College of Business and Public Administration
The University of North Dakota

1971
RICHARD D. IRWIN, INC.
and
THE DORSEY PRESS

HOMEWOOD, ILLINOIS

IRWIN-DORSEY LIMITED, GEORGETOWN, ONTARIO

First Printing, January, 1971
Second Printing, July, 1971
Third Printing, April, 1972

Library of Congress Catalog Card No. 70–135767

Printed in the United States of America

LEARNING SYSTEMS COMPANY—

a division of Richard D. Irwin, Inc. has developed a **PROGRAMMED LEARNING AID** to accompany texts in this subject area. Copies can be purchased through your bookstore or by writing **PLAIDS**, 1818 Ridge Road, Homewood, Illinois 60430

PREFACE

T HIS book has been designed for use as a text in a first course in computer programming. The only mathematical background required is a year of high school algebra. Special care has been taken to select problems which the student already understands so that only the art of communicating these problems to the computer need be learned. The materials have been used successfully with college students from a wide variety of academic disciplines and from freshman through graduate level. Survey readers and professionals who wish to learn FORTRAN as quickly as possible should find this book extremely valuable because it concentrates on teaching FORTRAN in particular rather than the art of programming in general.

The coverage is restricted to Basic FORTRAN IV, one of several versions of the FORTRAN language. Comparison of this version to other versions and to other languages, which tends to distract and confuse the beginning programmer, is avoided in this text. Basic FORTRAN IV is an ideal version for beginners to learn because it can be used on any IBM System/360 or/370 computer and, with a few minor adjustments, it can also be used on almost any other modern computer system commercially available in the United States. FORTRAN IV is the most current version of the most widely used of all programming languages. The version covered in this text equals or exceeds the minimum American National Standards Institute (ANSI) Standard X3.5–1966 on Basic FORTRAN, one of the two nationally accepted standard computer languages.

The order of presentation of each topic is that of a general introduction followed by a specific discussion and a series of to-the-point illustrations and examples. American National Standard Institute symbols are used in all flowchart illustrations. Whenever appropriate, previously presented material is briefly reviewed and compared to the topic under discussion. Programming problems have been carefully correlated with the text material and range from the easy to the difficult. Also, an adequate number of problems is provided so that the instructor can alternate program assignments.

Very elementary problems, which should be programmed and processed, are provided at an early point in the text to motivate the student. The purpose of a few easy programs is to develop confidence on the part of the student as well as to provide a background for more sophisticated problems. When the student receives his "first-run" output from the computer center, Appendix A should be a valuable aid. It explains the debugging process in general and illustrates with actual computer output almost every type of error the beginner will encounter. It explains what the error is, the probable cause, and how to correct it.

For the benefit of those students who punch their own program or correction cards, another Appendix explains the operation of a keypunch machine. IBM System/360 control cards and the composition of a typical elementary "job deck" are also briefly covered in an Appendix.

The first five chapters develop the required technical vocabulary and provide the background necessary to write a variety of complete elementary programs. Beginning in Chapter 5, the material is developed so that each succeeding chapter introduces new "short-cuts" as well as more sophisticated programming techniques. This approach should encourage students to read advanced chapters before they are assigned.

It is difficult for a beginning programmer to appreciate the real power of a computer unless he has had experience with arrays. Chapter 8 explains one-dimensional arrays in nontechnical terms and includes a series of illustrative array routines. Chapter 9 on two- and three-dimensional arrays is relatively short but includes enough information so the student can appreciate what they are, how they work, and when they should be used.

The final chapter deals at length with the four types of subprograms but purposely stays away from "high-powered" mathematics. Instead, the emphasis is on the purpose and power of subprograms, how they are written and used, and the fact that many are available to solve a wide variety of problems. A complete listing of the IBM built-in subprograms is included in an Appendix.

It is the intent of this book to teach FORTRAN as directly and quickly as possible and to whet the student's appetite for even more knowledge of the language. Anyone who has mastered the details of this book will be able to read and use the otherwise incomprehensible FORTRAN IV publications available from the various computer manufacturers.

The material in the text has been developed during the past few years from courses offered to undergraduate and graduate students at the University of North Dakota and to officers in the AFIT Minuteman Educational Program at the Grand Forks Air Force Base, North Dakota. To the many students who made helpful comments on an earlier draft of the text, I express my gratitude.

A special thanks is due to my secretary, Mrs. Kay Holte Pearson, for her careful and patient work on the manuscript and to Dr. Henry J. Tomasek for his early interest in, and continued encouragement of, this project.

Finally, because books are always hardest on an author's immediate family, this book is dedicated to Kay, Diane, and Paul.

January, 1971   DONALD H. FORD

CONTENTS

RØUTINE Subprograms. The CØMMØN Statement. The Power of Subprograms.

CHAPTER
1

INTRODUCTION

Computer programming can be defined as the art of preparing a plan to solve a problem and of reducing this plan to machine-sensible instructions.

Learning to program a computer can be compared to learning to ride a motorcycle. A new motorcyclist must learn to balance on the machine, to start, steer, and stop. He must acquire skill in the use of the various switches, pedals, and controls provided by the manufacturer. He must learn to communicate with the machine to use it as an effective means of transportation. But it is possible to become a skilled motorcyclist without understanding the principle of the internal-combustion engine or the technical aspects of the mechanical and electrical systems. Similarly, the beginning programmer need not understand the many technical concepts of computer design and electrical circuits; he must, however, learn to communicate with the machine to obtain the desired results. To communicate machine-sensible instructions, he must use a programming language.

This chapter provides an introduction to computer programming languages in general, a discussion of the punched card, and a brief description of a specific computer system.

COMPUTER LANGUAGES

A computer can perform various arithmetic computations such as addition, subtraction, multiplication, and division. It can perform various logical functions such as comparing two values and determining if the first value is less than, equal to, or greater than the second value, and such as dis-

1

tinguishing plus from minus and zero from nonzero. It can move data from one location in the computer to another. It can also read data and write results. It can do all these things, and more, at fantastic speeds but it cannot think. It is a robot. It must be told when to start, what data to use, what steps to take, what to do with the results, and when to stop. To perform a specific task, it must be given a detailed series of instructions, called a *program,* in a language which it is designed to read and obey.

Machine Languages

There are many ways to design a computer or machine to produce an optimum system for specific types of applications. As a result, with few exceptions, each make and model has its own internal coding system and each is designed to recognize or understand one unique language. Thus, a program written in the language of one machine cannot be processed by another.

The unique language which a computer is designed to recognize is called *machine language.* This language consists of machine-sensible instructions which usually take the form of long strings of numbers. These long strings of numbers may be in binary, decimal, octal, hexadecimal or some other representation depending upon the model of machine. For example, 2A0405 is a valid hexadecimal notation "add command" for an IBM/360 computer, 210042800857 is a valid decimal notation "add command" for an IBM 1620. Some machines are designed to use fixed-length instructions with each instruction requiring the same number of digits; others use instructions of variable length.

The basic characteristics of a machine language are:

1. It is specific in meaning. It is unlike human language where words and phrases may have different meanings in different contexts. With rare exceptions, if a single character in a machine-language instruction is changed, its entire meaning is changed.
2. It has a relatively small vocabulary. This is understandable when one considers the complex mathematical calculations which can be performed using combinations of only the four instructions for add, subtract, multiply, and divide.
3. It is concise. Lengthy human language verbal instructions can be reduced to a few digits.
4. It is machine-oriented rather than human-oriented. It has no relationship to the English language.

Programs written in machine language are called *object programs.* Writing object programs is difficult and tedious. Machine-language programmers must have a thorough knowledge of both the language and of the internal operations of the computer to be programmed.

Human-Oriented Languages

Suppose a Norwegian, who knew only his native tongue, wished to write two letters—one to a German and the other to a Japanese. How would he do it? Perhaps the most impractical approach would be to learn both the German and Japanese languages before he attempted to communicate. Obviously, a much faster and easier method would be to write both letters in Norwegian, then hire professional translators to convert the letters into the other languages.

A person wishing to write instructions to a computer may be faced with the same problem as the Norwegian. He knows how to express his instructions in the English language, but the machine language understood by the computer is foreign to him. He could, of course, employ a machine-language programmer to perform the translation, thus solving his communication problem. But, consider the advantages if he had a computer program which was designed to translate English language directly into machine language! In a sense, he could then literally "talk" to a computer.

Unfortunately, no computer programs exist which will translate ordinary English language into machine-language instructions. Attempts have been made to write such programs but not with complete success. These attempts, however, have resulted in translation routines which can make the programmer's job much easier. Human-oriented languages have been developed which are composed of letters, symbols, and numbers, grouped into various combinations to form a limited vocabulary of regular English and pseudo-English words and expressions. These languages are much easier to learn and to use than the machine language of the computer. The development of human-oriented languages has had a significant influence on the rapid advancement of computer technology.

Translators. A program written in a human-oriented language is called a source program. The *translator* is a special program, usually supplied by the manufacturer, which converts a human-oriented source program into a unique machine-language object program for the computer model on which it is translated. For example, source programs translated on an IBM 1620 computer result in 1620 object programs; source programs translated on an IBM/360 computer result in /360 object programs. This may appear to involve more work because a program must be written in one language, then translated into another language before it can be processed. It does involve more work, but the extra work is done by the computer at electronic speed. Use of a translation routine results in several advantages. First, the programmer may be required to learn only one language rather than a different language for each computer make and model used. Second, it is faster and easier to write programs in a human-oriented language.

Third, the translator writes better machine-language programs than most programmers can.

Currently, two broad classes of translators exist—one is called an assembler, the other a compiler.

Assemblers. An assembler is used to translate a low-level human-oriented language, called a *symbolic* language, into machine language. Symbolic languages generally use mnemonic (meaning *memory aid*) codes such as A for add, S for subtract, M for multiply, etc. An assembler is usually designed for a specific computer model. It generally converts symbolic language source programs into machine-language object programs on a one-for-one basis; that is, for each symbolic language instruction the assembler generates one corresponding machine-language instruction. This one-for-one translation makes it possible for the programmer, if he chooses, to match his symbolic language instructions to the translated machine-language instructions to see what occurred.

Compilers. A *compiler* is used to translate a high-level human-oriented language called a *problem-oriented language*. A compiler is more powerful than an assembler. It may generate or "compile" a list of many machine-language instructions for each problem-oriented language instruction. Thus, it is not an easy task to compare a series of high-level language instructions with the translated machine-language instructions; but, fortunately, such a comparison is rarely necessary. The use of high-level language does not require a thorough knowledge of the intricacies of the machine. Problem-oriented languages are not designed for a specific computer; they are designed to be used in solving a special class of problem. They are written in pseudo-English or in common algebraic notation rather than in mnemonic codes. Examples are: ADD A, B GIVING C and $C = A + B$.

FORTRAN

Many human-oriented languages are in existence. This book is concerned with the one developed by IBM and originally published in 1957. Called FORTRAN, an acronym for FORmula TRANslation, it is probably the most widely used problem-oriented language. It is often referred to as a "scientific language" and is designed to permit complex mathematical expressions to be stated similarly to regular algebraic notation. It has become an extremely popular language because of the ease with which it can be learned and because of the wide variety of applications for which it has been found suitable.

FORTRAN is not a dead language—it is subject to change. During its brief life-span, FORTRAN has been improved by modifications, additions, and deletions. As a result, FORTRAN, like ordinary human languages, suffers from the existence of several versions and dialects. This book uses a most current version called Basic FORTRAN IV, as used on IBM System/360.

The American National Standards Institute, Inc. (ANSI), has established a Basic FORTRAN IV standard (X3.10–1966) which is intended as a guide for manufacturers, consumers, and the general public. Conformance to this standard is not required; furthermore, there are many computer makes and models which differ both in size and in engineering design. Thus, some ANSI features are not present in all compilers whereas others go beyond the standard. But it should be noted that ANSI has had a major influence on the development of FORTRAN. As a result, any programmer who has mastered one current version of the language will find it relatively easy to learn the slight variations in other versions. Thus, in general, a FORTRAN programmer can communicate with any computer having a FORTRAN compiler. For this reason, FORTRAN is said to be machine-independent in that it may be written without regard for the specific make or model of machine on which it will be processed.

Programs written in FORTRAN must go through a "double run" on the computer. The first run is the *compilation* or translation run. This results in a FORTRAN source program being converted into a machine-language object program. The second run is the *execution* or computation run. This results in a machine-language object program processing data and producing the desired results. This can perhaps best be illustrated schematically. (See Figure 1–1.)

Large-scale computers, such as IBM System/360 and /370, can accept both a source program and problem data in one run. The intervening steps are handled automatically, but the logical procedures are the same as illustrated in Figure 1–1.

THE PUNCHED CARD

Various types of languages used to communicate with computers were explained in the previous section. Regardless of the programming language used, instructions must be prepared in machine-readable form. Just as humans may use various ways, such as telephones and letters, to communicate with each other, they may use various ways to communicate with computers. The punched card described in this section is a common medium of communication.

Description

A standard card (Figure 1–2) contains 80 vertical *columns* numbered 1 through 80 from left to right across the card. These can be compared to an 80–space line of printing. Each space on a printed page can contain only one letter, number, or special character if it is to be

FIGURE 1–1
Compiling a FORTRAN Source Program and
Executing the Object Program

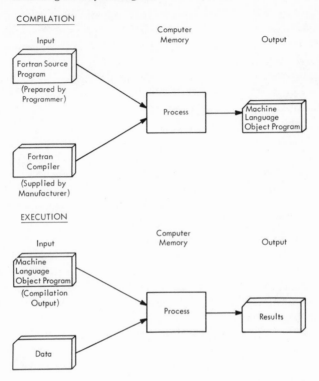

FIGURE 1–2
The IBM Card

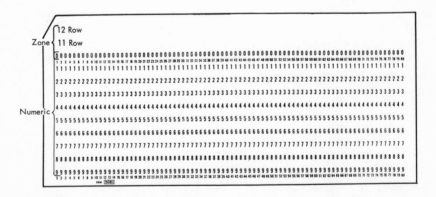

readable by humans. Likewise, each column on a card can contain only one number, letter, or special character if it is to be readable by the machine.

Each card contains 12 horizonal *rows* of punching positions. The first three rows from the top down are numbered 12, 11, and 0 respectively. The remaining nine rows are numbered sequentially 1 through 9. The card illustrated in Figure 1–2 has the numbers 0 through 9 printed in the lower 10 horizontal rows. Punches in these rows are called *numeric punches*. The 12 and 11 rows at the top of the card are not indicated by printed numbers. Punches in the 12, 11, and 0 rows are called *zone punches*. Note that the 0 punch is both a numeric and a zone punch. Various punches and combinations of punches within the 12 positions in each column are used to record, in machine-readable code, one number, alphabetic letter, or special character.

The top edge of an IBM punched card is referred to as the *12–edge*, the bottom as the *9–edge*, the left as the *1–edge*, and the right as the *80–edge*. Ordinarily, a card has printing on only one side, called the *face*. Cards are fed into specific devices in specific ways. For example, on the 2501 card reader—an input device used with IBM System/360—cards are processed 9–edge first, face down. It should be obvious that if cards are fed into this machine 12–edge first, instead of 9–edge first, the machine will "read" 12's as 9's, 11's as 8's, 0's as 7's, etc. Likewise, if the cards are fed 9–edge first, face-up instead of 9–edge first, face-down, the machine will "read" column 1 as column 80, 2 as 79, etc. Although the programmer may not actually operate the machine, this explanation should indicate the importance of properly arranging all cards before submitting a deck for processing. In referring to what happens when a computer is given invalid, inaccurate, or illogical input, programmers sometimes use the humorous but unofficial description, "garbage-in, garbage-out."

The Hollerith Code

Dr. Herman Hollerith designed the punched card and its machine-readable code during the 1880's. It may be unnecessary for programmers to memorize the *Hollerith Code*, but it is useful to have sufficient familiarity with this code to be able to distinguish between numbers, letters, and special characters. Fortunately, the code for numbers and letters is logical and easy to remember. The machine used to encode or punch cards is commonly called a "keypunch." An explanation of the operation of this machine is contained in Appendix C.

Numeric Characters. A numeric character is represented by a single punch in the appropriate numeric punching position (0 through 9) within a column. For example, to represent the digit 2 in any column, a punch is placed in the 2 row only in that column, a 3 is represented by a single 3 punch, etc. Only *one* punch is used within a column to record numeric information. (See Figure 1–3.)

FIGURE 1–3
Hollerith Code for Numbers and Letters

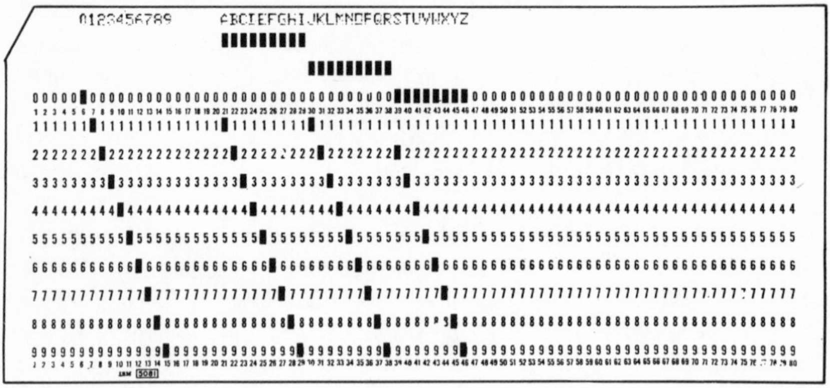

Alphabetic Characters. An alphabetic character is represented by *two* punches within a column; one *zone* punch is combined with one *numeric* punch in the 1 through 9 rows.

Codes for the first nine letters of the alphabet (A through I) use all nine combinations of one punch in the 12 row combined with a punch in one of the numeric rows 1 through 9. The letter A is represented by a 12 punch and a 1 punch, a B by a 12 and 2, C by a 12 and 3, etc.

Codes for the next nine letters (J through R) use all combinations of one 11 punch combined with a punch in one of the numeric rows 1 through 9. The letter J is represented by an 11 and 1, K by an 11 and 2, etc.

By combining one of three zone punches with one of nine numeric punches, there are 27 possible combinations of two punches with a column. But there are only 26 alphabetic letters so one of these combinations is not used. Dr. Hollerith chose to omit the 0 and 1 combination. Thus, the final series of eight letters begins with the letter S represented by 0 and 2 and ends with the letter Z represented by 0 and 9.

By remembering that the letter A is represented by a 12 and a 1 and that the combination of 0 and 1 is omitted in alphabetic coding, it is a simple matter to determine the code for any of the 26 letters even though the entire code is not memorized. *It should be especially noted that there is no code for lowercase letters, only uppercase (capitals).*

Special Characters. A special character is represented by no punch, one punch, or by various combinations of two or three punches within a column. The coding for special characters has no particular logic and is unnecessary to memorize. Codes for the special characters which are elements of the FORTRAN language are illustrated in Chapter 2.

Fields

A card *field* is a column or group of columns, generally in succession, reserved for a particular item of data or information. For example, the inventory data card illustrated in Figure 1–4 has several fields. These are used to indicate various types of information about one particular inventory item. (A similar card would normally be prepared for each item of inventory.) In the illustration, the first field on the left (columns 1 and 2) is a 2–column numeric field reserved for building number; columns 17 through 55 (a 39–column alphabetic field) are reserved for item description.

FIGURE 1–4
Illustration of Card Fields

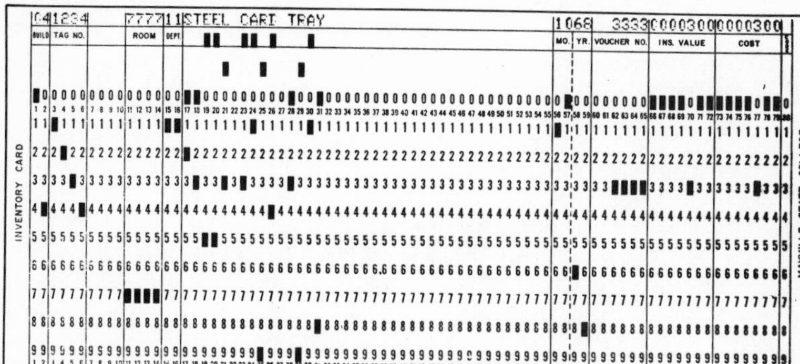

Numeric Fields. Normally, numeric fields are justified to the right. Any unused columns on the left or high-order side of a numeric field are filled in with zeros or simply spaced over and not punched. For example, refer to the data card illustrated in Figure 1–4. Building number 4 is indicated by a 0–punch in column 1 and a 4–punch in column 2; building number 40 would be indicated by a 4–punch in the first column of the field and a 0 in the second. Note that the voucher number field (columns 60 through 65) is an example in which punching is omitted to indicate zeros in the two high-order (leftmost) positions. Unpunched columns in a card are commonly called blank columns or simply *blanks*.

Alphabetic Fields.   Normally, alphabetic fields are "left justified." Note the item description field (columns 17 through 55) in Figure 1–4. Punching begins in the first column of the field (column 17) and continues, depending upon the data length, no further than the last column in the field (column 55). In contrast to numeric fields, alphabetic fields always contain blanks, never zeros, in any unused columns.

Field names, lengths, and locations can obviously vary depending upon the data to be recorded. This is a matter of card design. Once fields have been established for a particular record, it is mandatory that these established fields be strictly followed.

Records and Files

A punched card is commonly called an "external storage record." The term *external storage* pertains to a medium or device that is not an internal part of the computer and into which data can be placed, held, and later retrieved. Data is stored in a card by punching holes into the card in a machine-readable code. A *record* is defined as a collection of one or more related fields of data or information. A group of related records is called a *file*. Thus, a card file may contain many records, each record may contain many fields, and each field may contain many columns.

A COMPUTER SYSTEM

The two previous sections of this chapter covered computer languages in general and the punched card. This section describes what a computer looks like and how it works. As it is not the purpose of this book to consider the intricate details of various computer systems and designs, the discussion is limited to an elementary description of a specific computer system and selected devices.

Hardware

The physical equipment which makes up a computer system is called *hardware*. A minimum configuration of hardware consists of a central processing unit, one input device, and one output device. Generally speaking, the more input and output devices a computer system has, the more jobs it can do. This section describes a typical configuration of a popular model computer, the IBM System/360 Model 30.

Central Processing Unit (CPU). The CPU is the actual computer. It contains main storage (described in the next section of this chapter) and the logical and control circuitry. One end of the CPU has a control panel with various switches and dials for use in operating the machine. A light panel instantly indicates to the expert what the computer is doing or can be used to indicate the contents of any particular location within the computer.

Printer-Keyboard. This device, sometimes called the "console," has a standard typewriter keyboard and several special purpose switches. It can be used both as an input and output device but, because of its relatively low speed, it is generally used only for communication between the operator and the computer. Installations with a logging routine may use this device to print out information on all jobs processed on the computer.

FIGURE 1–5
IBM System/360 Model 30

Photo courtesy of IBM Corp.

Card Read-Punch. This combination input-output device is used to read cards and to punch or "write" cards. Many installations use separate devices for card reading and writing.

FIGURE 1–6
Card Read Punch Unit (IBM 2540)

Photo courtesy of IBM Corp.

Printer. The printer is a high-speed output device. The model illustrated has a maximum speed of 1,100 lines per minute.

FIGURE 1–7
IBM 1403 Printer

Photo courtesy of IBM Corp.

Disk Storage Drive. This high-capacity external storage device may be used for both input and output. The model pictured has removable disk packs. Each disk pack has a capacity of approximately 7¼ million characters. The FORTRAN compiler may be located on this device where it is almost instantly available to the computer.

FIGURE 1–8
IBM 2311 Disk Drive

Removable
Disk Pack

Photo courtesy of IBM Corp.

Internal Structure

To appreciate the difficulties of programming in machine language and the comparative ease of programming in FORTRAN, it is helpful to have at least a general understanding of the internal storage structure of a computer. *Internal storage* serves as a sort of filing cabinet into which data can be placed, held, and later retrieved in an orderly manner. A popular, glamorous, and somewhat sensational term for internal storage is "memory."

System/360 uses the most common type of internal storage medium which is *magnetic core*. A magnetic core is similar in shape to a tiny doughnut or ring. It is slightly smaller in diameter than the letter "o" on this printed page. It is metallic and may be magnetized in either a clockwise or counterclockwise direction. Internal storage contains many thousands of metallic cores which are strung on ultrafine wires arranged in the manner of a matrix. Electrical flow through these wires is used to establish or change the direction of magnetization or polarity and to "read" the direction of polarity. It is unnecessary to understand the many technical aspects of the electronic circuitry to realize that each core has but two possible states. It is often compared to an electric switch or to a light bulb, both of which have but two possible states, *off* and *on*. By convention, when a core has clockwise polarity it is considered to be *on* representing the binary value one; counterclockwise polarity indicates an *off* condition or the binary value zero.

The *binary* numbering system uses only two symbols (usually 0 and 1). To indicate a value greater than nine, using familiar decimal notations, two or more decimal digits are needed. Likewise, to indicate a value greater than one in binary, two or more binary digits are needed. Equivalent decimal and binary notations indicating the values zero through nine are:

Decimal	Binary
0	0
1	1
2	10
3	11
4	100
5	101
6	110
7	111
8	1000
9	1001

Data stored in magnetic core are called "bits." The word *bit* is a contraction of the two words binary digit.

System/360 storage is divided into groups of bits called *bytes*. Each byte consists of one parity-check bit and eight data bits. The parity-check bit is used by the computer, each time internal data is manipulated, to determine if any bits within a byte have accidentally changed or "flipped" from zero to one or vice versa. This is an automatic feature of the computer. A System/360 byte contains nine bits but because one (parity-check bit) is not under programmer control, it is commonly referred to as an eight-bit byte. These eight bits provide the possibility of 512 different combinations of zeros and ones (representing the binary values 00000000 through 11111111 or the hexadecimal values 00 through FF). Various combinations of *off* and *on* cores are used to represent a single number, letter, or special character within one byte. For example, the letter *R* might be internally represented by the bit combination 10111001.

Each byte has an *address* to indicate its specific location. Computer memory is sometimes compared to a post office. Numbers may be used to identify and to indicate locations of mail boxes. The post-office box number corresponds to the address of a byte. The contents of a post-office box may be cards, letters, packages, etc. These correspond to the contents of a computer storage location which may be one number, letter, or special character represented by a coded combination of *on* and *off* cores. The difference between the *contents* and *address* of a location is crucial to the understanding of computing. The contents is a character (numeric, alphabetic, or special). The address is an identification of a specific place within storage where a character is located.

> Address 0 1 2 3 4 5 6 7 8 9
> Contents R A 1 7 2 0 7 9 3 5

An instruction does not ordinarily *tell* a computer, for example, to add one specific numeric value to another. Instead of specifying numeric values in an instruction, the programmer specifies the addresses where these values are located. Stated another way, the instruction tells the computer to add the contents of one address to the contents of another address.

Byte addresses are consecutively numbered starting with zero. How many addresses a machine has depends upon the model and size of the computer. For example, a System/360 Model F30 is referred to as a "65K" machine, indicating it has approximately 65,000 addressable storage locations.

FORTRAN Programming

A machine-language programmer must have a *detailed* knowledge of the internal structure of a computer, but a FORTRAN programmer does not. This section briefly illustrates why. Subsequent chapters cover the details of FORTRAN programming.

Suppose an input card contains two numeric data fields. One field indicates the hours worked by an employee on Monday, the other the hours worked on Friday. The data are to be read into the computer and stored for later processing. If a programmer decided to write a machine-language program to perform this task, he would be required to indicate the specific addresses or locations chosen for the storage of each input data field. These addresses, in machine language, are in the form of long strings of numbers. Data cannot be located just anywhere—there are certain restrictions. For example, the beginning address of internal data fields must be evenly divisible by two, four, or eight, depending upon the type of data to be stored. In addition to instructing the computer where each data field begins, the programmer must indicate where each ends. If a machine-language program was written, all of the foregoing indicated information would be contained in instructions consisting of long strings of numbers.

Suppose, however, that the programmer decided to communicate in FORTRAN. To tell the computer to read the data card, instead of a numeric code, he would use the descriptive English word READ. Instead of numeric addresses, he would use descriptive names to indicate *symbolic addresses*. A symbolic address is expressed in symbols convenient to the programmer. For example, the READ instruction could direct the computer to store the data at the symbolic addresses MØNDAY and FRIDAY.[1] Another pseudo-English instruction would describe the type, length, and location of each input card field. The compiler would then perform the task of translating these instructions into machine language. Valid addresses would automatically be assigned based on the programmer's description of the input card. In most cases the FORTRAN programmer need not be concerned with numeric addresses of internal data fields. To process the data, he simply calls for it by the descriptive symbolic addresses MØNDAY and FRIDAY.

It should now be apparent why it is difficult, tedious, and time consuming to communicate with a computer in machine language and why human-oriented languages are so popular. The reader should now begin to appreciate some of the wonders of FORTRAN!

REVIEW QUESTIONS

1. Define the following terms:

   A. Machine language
   B. Symbolic language
   C. Problem-oriented language
   D. FORTRAN
   E. Assembler
   F. Compiler
   G. Source program
   H. Object program
   I. Internal storage
   J. Hardware

2. Distinguish between:

   A. Column, field, record, and file
   B. Core, bit, and byte
   C. Contents and address
   D. Compilation and execution

3. The Hollerith Code requires how many punches within a column to represent:

   A. A number?
   B. An uppercase letter?
   C. A lowercase letter?
   D. A special symbol?

---

[1] Note that, throughout this text, zeros and Capital O's will be distinguished in commands by a diagonal slash through the capital O (Ø). Likewise a horizontal bar will distinguish the letter Capital Z (Ƶ) from the figure 2.

4. Indicate whether the following devices can be used for input, for output, or both:

A. Printer-keyboard or "console"   C. High-speed printer

B. Card read-punch   D. Disk storage drive

5. What is meant by the expression: "32K machine?"

6. Why might a beginning programmer prefer to learn FORTRAN rather than a machine language?

7. Interpret the Hollerith Code punched in this card:

CHAPTER
2

GENERAL DESCRIPTION OF BASIC FORTRAN IV

Because this chapter provides only an overview of FORTRAN programming, it is not intended that the reader comprehend all the details presented. Its purpose is to acquaint the reader with only a general understanding of FORTRAN programming. Following chapters cover the detailed rules for writing the language. Stated another way, this chapter covers "the forest," later chapters, "the trees."

THE CHARACTER SET

FORTRAN IV is written with a basic set of 48 characters consisting of 27 letters (the dollar sign is considered to be a letter), 10 numbers, and 11 special characters. All FORTRAN elements must be formed from these characters only. Fortunately, the valid FORTRAN characters are all familiar to the reader.

Alphabetic Letters

As previously indicated, the dollar sign is a letter, not a special character. The 27 FORTRAN letters are:

ABCDEFGHIJKLMNØPQRSTUVWXYZ and $

Numbers

The valid FORTRAN numbers are the familiar decimal digits:

0123456789

Special Characters

The 11 valid special characters are:

Blank	
Plus	+
Minus	—
Asterisk	*
Slash	/
Equal	=
Decimal point or period	.
Comma	,
Apostrophe	'
Open parenthesis	(
Close parenthesis	)

One special character, the *blank*, deserves special comment. Card columns without punches are called "blanks." The keypunch operator, like the typist, indicates a blank by striking the space bar. The blank—that is, the absence of a character—is considered to be a special character by the FORTRAN compiler. In some FORTRAN statements a specific number of blanks is required.

FIGURE 2–1
The Valid FORTRAN IV Characters

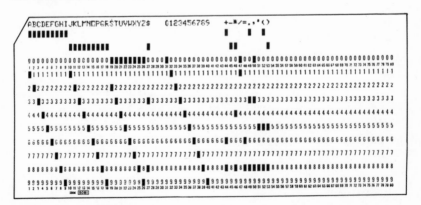

STATEMENT TYPES

A program consists of a series of instructions which directs the computer to perform a certain task. Each instruction in a FORTRAN program is called a *statement*. Statements may be classified into four basic categories: input/output, arithmetic, control, and nonexecutable. It is important to note again that FORTRAN statements cannot be executed; the machine-language instructions into which these statements are translated by the compiler can be executed. But, because "executable statement" is a conventional phrase, it will be used in all subsequent discussions.

Input/Output

I/O statements direct the computer to READ or WRITE a record, indicate the device to be used (such as card reader, card punch, printer, etc.), and reference a nonexecutable statement which describes the record.

Arithmetic

One major function of an arithmetic statement is to direct the computer to perform certain arithmetic calculations and to indicate where and how the results are to be stored. Arithmetic statements constitute the "heart" of most FORTRAN programs.

Control *IF ; GØTØ ; DØ*

Ordinarily, statements are executed in the order in which they appear in the source program. Control statements can be used to instruct the computer to change this normal order of execution. For example, control statements can be used to cause the computer to repeat an instruction or series of instructions a specific number of times, or to execute certain instructions only under specified conditions. Control statements can be used not only to govern the sequence in which instructions are executed, but also to terminate program execution.

executable — control, arith., I/Ø

Nonexecutable

There are several types of nonexecutable statements, but all are used to give the computer information it will need to execute other statements. For example, one type of nonexecutable statement is called a FØRMAT statement. It describes the length and location of each field on a record as well as the type of data contained in each field. The purpose of a FØRMAT statement is to provide descriptive information about the record which is to be read or written when an I/O statement is executed.

Input/output, arithmetic, and control statements are called *executable* statements because they indicate a specific action the computer is to take. The FORTRAN compiler translates each executable statement into one or more equivalent machine-language instructions. On the other hand, nonexecutable statements merely provide descriptive information to the FOR-

nonexec. — 1) Housekeeper ; type, dimension, common, data, equivalence 2) Format — input/output

at beginning of program

TRAN compiler. Equivalent machine-language instructions are *not* prepared. This is an important distinction which should be remembered.

STATEMENT COMPOSITION

FORTRAN statements are composed of various combinations of key words, variable names, numbers or constants, expressions, and codes.

Key Words

Key words have a special meaning in FORTRAN. When used in proper context, they identify operations designated by statements or indicate the type of information contained in statements. An alphabetized list of these key words is given in Figure 2–2.

FIGURE 2–2
The Key Words Used in Basic FORTRAN IV

ABS	END	IF
	ENDFILE	IFIX
BACKSPACE	EQUIVALENCE	INTEGER
	EXIT	ISIGN
CALL	EXTERNAL	
CØMMØN		PAUSE
CØNTINUE	FIND	
	FLØAT	READ
DABS	FØRMAT	REAL
DBLE	FUNCTIØN	RETURN
DEFINE		REWIND
DIM	GØ	
DIMENSIØN	GØTØ	SIGN
DFLØAT		SNGL
DØ	IABS	STØP
DØUBLE PRECISIØN	IDIM	SUBRØUTINE
DSIGN		WRITE

Variable Names

A *variable name* is a symbolic address selected by the programmer in accordance with the rules of FORTRAN. Although the address or location remains constant, it is called a variable name because the data contained at the symbolic address may be repeatedly changed during execution of a program.

It is emphasized again that the difference between the *address* and *contents* of an internal storage location is crucial to the understanding of computing. A variable name (symbolic address) is an identification of a storage location. In FORTRAN, the contents of each variable name is not limited to one character but may have many.

Numbers or Constants

There are two distinct kinds of numbers which everyone uses in daily life, perhaps without realizing they are quite different. These two kinds of numbers are sometimes called measuring numbers and counting numbers.

A measuring number must be capable of expressing fractional precision. In ordinary arithmetical notation, it is called a decimal fraction and is written with a decimal point. The diameter of a circle, for example, may be expressed as 1,357.086 feet, 1,357.09 feet, or as 1,357.1 feet depending upon the precision desired. In FORTRAN, measuring numbers are also written with a decimal point but no embedded commas are allowed. They are called "real numbers," "real constants," "floating point numbers," or "floating point constants." This book generally uses the latter term.

Counting numbers are whole numbers which have no fractional part. In FORTRAN, they are always written *without* a decimal point to distinguish such numbers from floating point constants. They are called "integer numbers" or "integer constants." This book uses the latter term. As in the case of floating point constants, embedded commas are not allowed. Beginning programmers are cautioned that the results of arithmetic calculations performed in integer mode are always integer. Stated another way, results are always whole numbers with no fractional parts. Integer mode arithmetic does not present a problem when one whole number is added to, deducted from, or multiplied by another whole number because no fractional part can be expected. However, when division is performed, fractional parts may be expected but cannot be computed. Thus, in integer arithmetic:

4/5 is 0   5/4 is 1   500/4 is 125

If fractional precision is desired, arithmetic calculations *must* be performed in floating point rather than integer mode.

Expressions

The only type of expression provided in Basic FORTRAN IV is the *arithmetic expression*. It can consist of a single variable name, a single constant, or a combination of variable names and/or constants separated by arithmetic operators (sometimes called operational signs or operational symbols). Variable names, floating point constants, and integer constants have previously been defined. An example of an arithmetic operator is "+." The plus sign in FORTRAN, as in regular mathematical notation, is used to indicate addition. The use of expressions and operational signs is covered in detail in Chapters 3 and 4.

Codes

The FORTRAN language includes various alphabetic and numeric codes. For example, the letters I or F are used to specify that a record contains integer or floating point data. Similarly, numeric codes are used to designate specific input/output devices.

ILLUSTRATIVE PROGRAM

The several steps generally required in FORTRAN programming may be stated as follows:

1. Problem definition
2. Flowcharting
3. Coding
4. Compilation and debugging
5. Testing and execution

This section briefly explains each of these steps by use of an illustrative example.

Problem Definition

This step involves the preparation of a clear statement of the problem and a determination of the input and output requirements for solution. To enable the reader to devote his major efforts to learning FORTRAN rather than to defining problems, all problems presented in this book have been defined. However, in actual practice this is always the first (and sometimes the most time-consuming) step in FORTRAN programming. To illustrate this programming step, consider the following introductory problem:

Southern Sales Corporation has an electrical appliance division which stocks only irons, knives, and mixers. They have prepared one punched card with three numeric data fields indicating the current inventory quantities of each type of electrical appliance. The card has the following format:

Card Columns	Indicates Quantity of
1 through 3	Irons
4 through 5	Knives
6 through 9	Mixers

Management has decided to expand their electrical appliance division and has issued a purchase order for 220 electric toothbrushes. They desire to know the total number of items in their electrical appliance division inventory including the 220 electric toothbrushes on order.

It is decided to write a FORTRAN program to solve their problem. The output is to be one card with the total number of items punched in the first five columns.

Flowcharting

Now that the problem has been defined and the available input and desired output has been established, the next step is preparation of a *flow-chart*.

A flowchart (sometimes called a block diagram) may be defined as a graphic representation of the various steps to be taken by the computer, structured to indicate the sequence of these steps. Stated another way, a flowchart is a program outline which serves the programmer as a visual aid and guide for composing FORTRAN statements. It is composed of various symbols (usually connected by lines with arrowheads to indicate step sequence) and of brief explanatory remarks.

Flowcharting may be defined as an art rather than an exact science because a problem can be flowcharted in a variety of ways. The sequence of steps, the detail in which steps are indicated, the extent of explanatory remarks, and the set of symbols used are some ways in which a flowchart of a specific problem can vary. Over the years, various sets of symbols have been used, but the standard set of symbols established by the American National Standards Institute, Inc. (X3.5–1968) has become increasingly popular. Only ANSI standard symbols, illustrated and explained in Appendix B, are used in this book.

A flowchart for the illustrative problem is illustrated in Figure 2–3.

FIGURE 2–3
Illustrative
Flowchart

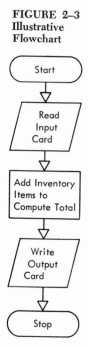

Coding

Now that the flowchart is completed, the next step leading to a solution of the problem is *coding*. Coding is the process of reducing a flowchart to a series of FORTRAN statements. There is no statement which directs the computer to start. (This task is handled by the computer operator and by "system control statements" discussed in Appendix D.) All other symbols in the illustrative flowchart require one executable statement. Several nonexecutable statements, not indicated by flowchart symbols, are also required.

Coding is usually done in pencil on a special FORTRAN coding form. The purpose of a coding form is to indicate the specific number, letter, or special symbol which is to appear in each column of the FORTRAN statement cards. A detailed explanation of the use of coding forms appears in Chapter 3 of this book, but a few comments are appropriate at this time to get the beginning programmer off to a good start.

Always use block style capital letters; lowercase and script must be avoided because these cannot be punched in Hollerith Code. Use only the best of penmanship—the importance of neatness in coding cannot be overemphasized. The coding sheet serves as a means of communication with the keypunch operator. If coding is misinterpreted, the program will not produce the desired results. The few extra minutes required to do a good job of coding will be more than offset by the savings in debugging time. Extreme care must be taken when coding numbers, letters, and characters which are similar in appearance. A classic example is the letter "O" and the digit zero. To distinguish between these two "look-alikes" a "slash" is used. Unfortunately, some computer centers slash the letters whereas others slash the number. Most FORTRAN statements contain more zeros than letter O's, but some other high-level languages use more O's than zeros. As a matter of convenience, programmers prefer to put the slash on the lesser population. As previously noted, in this text, commands will be written with a slash through the letter O and a bar through the letter Z. At computer centers where key punch operators must punch program cards written in various languages, confusion can obviously result unless a local shop rule on slashes is adopted. To avoid any misinterpretations, the reader is cautioned to check the requirements of his particular computer center.

Beginning programmers are particularly cautioned to distinguish between:

1. The letter Ø and the number 0
2. The letter I, the number 1, the slash /, and apostrophe '
3. The letter Z and the number 2
4. The letter G and the number 6
5. The letter S and the number 5

6. The letter C and the open parenthesis (
7. The letter T and the plus sign +
8. The comma , and the apostrophe '

Coding for the illustrative program could appear as illustrated in Figure 2–4.

FIGURE 2–4
Coded FORTRAN Program

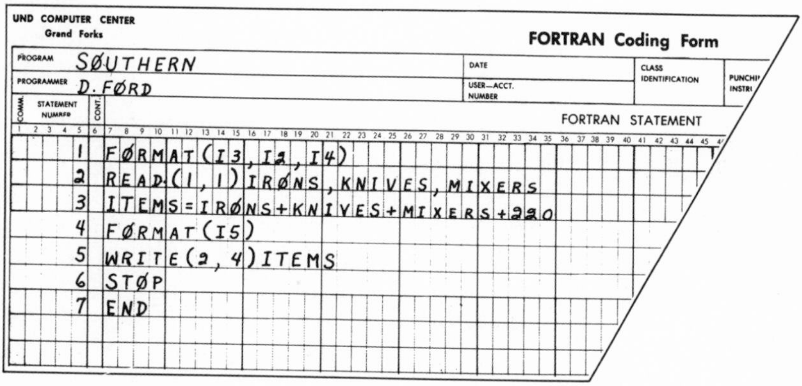

Keypunching from the coding sheet should result in a "source program deck" as illustrated in Figure 2–5.

FIGURE 2–5
Illustrative Source Program Deck

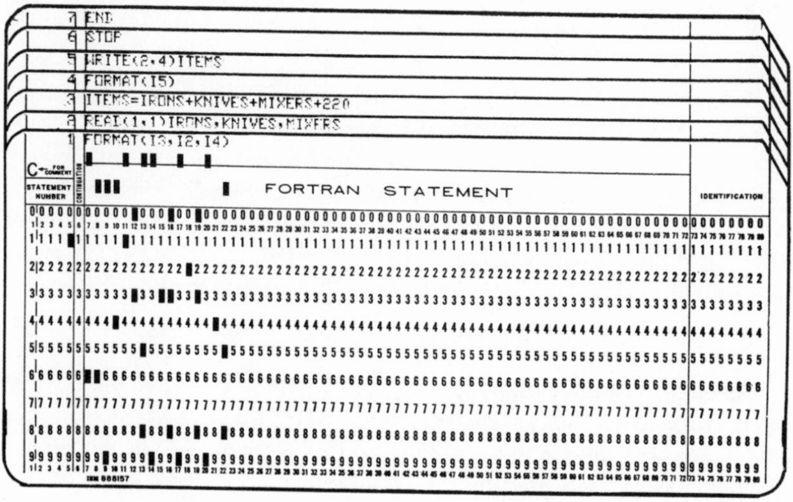

Note that each coded FORTRAN statement in Figures 2–4 and 2–5 is preceded by a number. Statement numbers may be arbitrarily chosen by the programmer and need not appear in any particular sequence. There are two major restrictions. First, the number may not exceed five decimal digits in length. This is because the card format, which must be followed, provides only a five-column field for the statement number. The second restriction is that each number must be unique; that is, two or more statements may not be assigned an identical number. The purpose of statement numbers is to permit reference to a particular statement within the program. Obviously this would not be possible if more than one statement was identified by the same number. Statements which are not referenced need not be numbered. Statement numbers in the illustrative program were chosen for convenience only.

Now, a cursory examination of each statement will be made to give "the feel" of the FORTRAN language.

1 FØRMAT(I3,I2,I4)

Statement 1 is a nonexecutable statement. FØRMAT is a key word (see Figure 2–2) which tells the compiler that this statement describes an input or output record. The parenthetical notation describes the record by indicating the number of fields, the length and location of each field, and the type of data contained in each field. It obviously does all this in much less space and with much less effort than is required to describe it in human language. The three codes within parentheses: I3, I2, and I4, tell the compiler that the record contains three data fields. The first element, I3, indicates that the first field contains integer data and is three columns in length. Because it is the first field specified, these three columns are necessarily the first three columns in the card. I2 indicates the next two columns constitute another field of integer data. I4 similarly describes the last field.

2 READ(1,1)IRØNS,KNIVES,MIXERS

Statement 2 is an I/O statement. READ is a key word instructing the computer to read a record. The first number within the parentheses is a code that indicates which input device the computer is to read the record from; in this case the code 1 specifies a card reader. The second number is a code that references the nonexecutable statement which describes the record. The three variable names IRØNS, KNIVES, and MIXERS indicate the symbolic addresses where the input data is to be stored.

3 ITEMS=IRØNS+KNIVES+MIXERS+220

Statement 3 is an arithmetic statement. It indicates that the data contained at the symbolic addresses IRØNS, KNIVES, and MIXERS and the integer constant 220 are to be added and that the sum is to be stored at the symbolic address indicated by the variable name ITEMS.

4 FØRMAT(I5)

Statement 4 is a nonexecutable statement which describes the output. Although the actual input data is unknown, the size of the input fields (I3,I2,I4) indicates that the largest possible sum in this case would be five digits in length (999 + 99 + 9999 + 220). Thus, the output field is specified to be five columns long (I5).

5 WRITE (2,4) ITEMS

Statement 5 is an I/O statement. WRITE is a key word. The code 2 indicates output is to be on a card punch, and the code 4 references the nonexecutable statement which describes the output record. The variable name ITEMS indicates the symbolic address where the sum was stored by statement number 3 and where it is now available for output.

6 STØP

Statement 6 is a control statement which causes the computer to halt rather than to continue executing statements. Because this is an executable rather than a nonexecutable statement, it causes the compiler to generate an equivalent machine-language instruction.

7 END

Statement 7 is a nonexecutable statement. *The END statement must always be the final statement in any FORTRAN program.* It *does not* cause any machine-language instruction to be generated by the compiler. The purpose of this statement is to indicate to the compiler that this is the terminal point, or end, of the program. It is extremely important that the programmer understand the different functions served by the END statement and by the STØP statement. To repeat—the END statement gives an instruction to the FORTRAN compiler; the STØP statement gives an instruction to the computer when the program is executed.

Compilation and Debugging

If no syntax or logic errors have been made in preparing the FORTRAN statements which constitute the source program, most of the manual work has been completed. Most of the work in the remaining two steps will be done by the computer.

The next step is to compile and debug the program. If the FORTRAN statements contain syntax errors; that is, if any rules of the language have been violated, compilation will terminate because the compiler cannot translate invalid statements. The programmer would then debug his program; that is, search out all errors and make necessary corrections. Debugging techniques which will be useful to beginning programmers are described in Appendix A. Because there are no errors in the illustrative program, it will require no debugging.

When the program is compiled, a printed copy of the source program, called a *computer listing,* can be prepared on a high-speed printer as illustrated in Figure 2–6.

FIGURE 2–6
Computer Listing of Illustrative Program

```
1  FORMAT(I3,I2,I4)
2  READ(1,1)IRONS,KNIVES,MIXERS
3  ITEMS=IRONS+KNIVES+MIXERS+220
4  FORMAT(I5)
5  WRITE(2,4)ITEMS
6  STOP
7  END
```

Testing and Execution

The final step in arriving at a solution to the problem is to execute the machine-language program generated by the compiler from the FORTRAN statements. To do this, the program is loaded (stored). The data card indicating the number of irons, knives, and mixers, is placed in an input device which, in this case, is the card reader. The computer is then started, and it executes the program which consists of reading the input, processing the data, and writing the results. But, before this final step is taken, the programmer would normally perform a series of test runs to assure the effectiveness of the program. To test the illustrative program, several input cards could be prepared which contain known data for which the solutions have been determined in advance. These cards would be processed by the program and the results compared to the predetermined solutions. If the computer output agrees with the predetermined solutions, the program would be considered free of errors.

FIGURE 2–7
Input Card for Illustrative Program

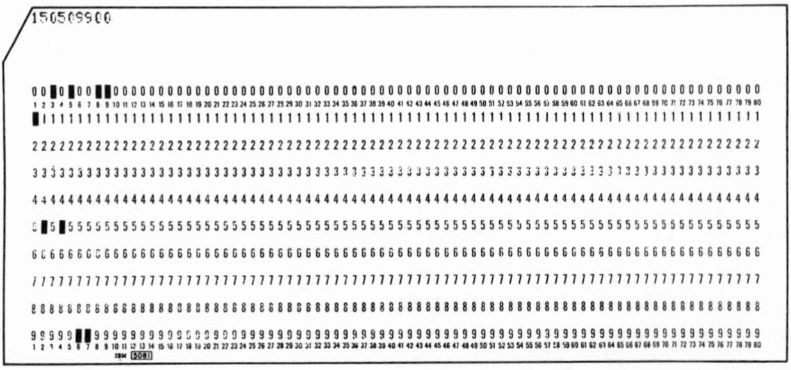

The illustrative program is designed to compute the total of 220 plus the sum of IRØNS, KNIVES, and MIXERS as indicated in the input data card. The output is to be one punched card with the computed total punched in the first five columns. Assuming the input data are 150, 50, and 9900 (Figure 2–7), the output card will contain the computed total 10320 (Figure 2–8).

FIGURE 2–8
Output Card for Illustrative Program

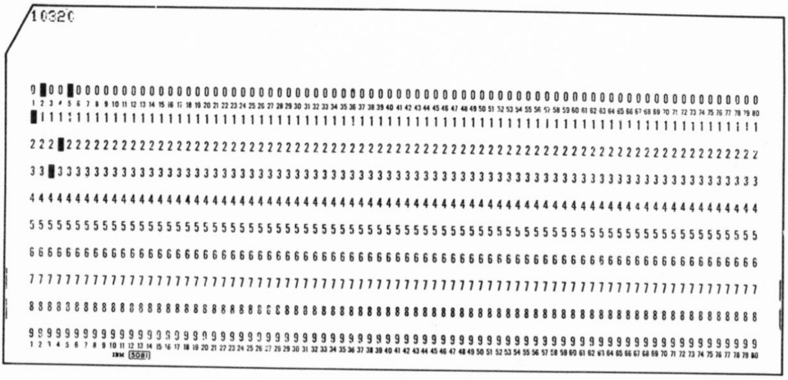

REVIEW QUESTIONS

1. The FORTRAN IV language is composed of how many:
   a) Numbers?
   b) Letters?
   c) Special characters?

2. What are the four basic types of FORTRAN statements?

3. What is the difference between a FORTRAN statement that is executable and one that is nonexecutable?

4. Give two examples of a key word.

5. Name two types of FORTRAN constants and give an example of each.

6. Give an example of an arithmetic operator.

7. Name the several steps generally required in FORTRAN programming.

8. What is the purpose of a flowchart or "block diagram?"

9. What statement must always appear last in any FORTRAN program?

10. Distinguish between the STØP and END statements.

11. Give some examples of numbers, letters, and special characters which are similar in appearance.

12. What is the purpose of numbering a FORTRAN statement?

13. Why must all statement numbers be unique?

CHAPTER
3

ELEMENTS OF FORTRAN STATEMENTS

THE first section of this chapter describes the general form required for all types of FORTRAN statements. Later sections explain and illustrate the essential elements which comprise the basic framework for arithmetic statements. The following chapter deals with various methods of combining these elements to form complete arithmetic statements.

STATEMENT FORM

FORTRAN programs must be composed of statements but, if desired, may also include comments. All statements and comments must be written on the coding form so as to exactly correspond to the card format illustrated in Figure 3–1. *No more than one statement may be written on one line of the coding form or punched in one card.*

Statement Number Field

This field is located in the first five columns of the card as illustrated in Figure 3–1. A statement number, also called a label, should be right justified in the field. It should contain no embedded blanks; but, as a matter of convenience, high-order zeros are normally omitted. For example, to indi-

FIGURE 3–1
Required Card Format for FORTRAN Statements and Comments

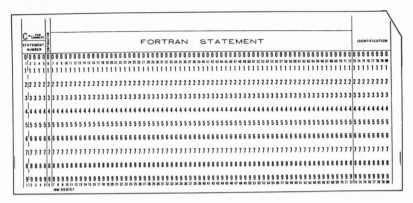

cate statement number 72, the 7 should be punched in column 4, the 2 in column 5, and the first three columns left blank.

Statement numbers do not affect the order in which statements are executed; therefore, the programmer may number the statements in any desired sequence. Numbers may be used for all statements but are required only for those statements which are referenced in the program. All numbers must be unique; that is, two or more statements must not be identified by the same number.

Comment Cards.   Only decimal digits and blank spaces are permitted in the statement number field with one exception. Column 1 may be punched with the letter C to designate that the card contains a *comment* rather than a statement. The purpose of a comment card is to provide program *documentation*; that is, to make a program easier to read. It is usually desirable to cause a high-speed printer to generate a *program listing* which contains one printed line for each card in the source program deck. It is permissible to punch the letter C in column 1 and leave the other columns blank. A "blank comment" may be used to provide a blank line (except for the letter C) in a program listing. A comment may precede any statement in the program or may follow any statement except the END statement. The programmer need not be concerned with any rules or restrictions when composing a comment. It may be written in "free form" and may appear anywhere in the comment field which extends from column 2 through 80. Because a comment is not a statement, it is ignored in the translation process. There is no limit to the number of comments which may be included in a program except as dictated by the capacity of the computer. Furthermore, comments may be composed of any character compatible to the computer system; special characters which are not included in the FORTRAN character set may be included in a comment.

Continuation Field

Column 6 (Figure 3–1) is a one-column continuation field. Quite often even beginning programmers compose statements which are too long to be contained in one card. It is permissible to continue a statement on as many as 19 additional successive cards. To indicate to the compiler that a card is a continuation of a statement, rather than the beginning of a new statement, column 6 is punched with a *continuation character*. A continuation character may be any valid FORTRAN number, letter, or special character except a zero or a blank. This distinguishes continuation cards from the first card of any statement which *must* contain a zero or blank in this field. As a matter of convenience, most programmers leave column 6 blank on all cards except continuation cards. It should be noted that continuation cards should not contain a statement number because it is invalid to reference a partial statement.

Statement Field

The statement field, illustrated in Figure 3–1, extends from column 7 through 72. All statements must be confined to this field. If a statement requires more than the 66 columns provided in this field, it must be continued in the same field on successive cards. A common error of some beginning programmers is to write part of a statement outside the boundaries of this field.

Identification Field

The rightmost field, illustrated in Figure 3–1, extends from columns 73 through 80 and is called the identification field. It is ignored by the compiler during translation, but anything written in this field will appear in a program listing providing the characters used are available on the printing mechanisms. The identification field may be used at the programmer's discretion for free form notations, for numeric sequencing, for program or programmer identification, etc. It is often left blank.

CONSTANTS

A constant is a known numeric value written in the source program. As the term "constant" implies, the value cannot be changed. It is always composed of one or more decimal digits. It may be positive, zero, or negative. It may be signed or unsigned; if written without a sign, it is assumed to be positive. If signed, the sign must precede the first digit. Embedded commas are not permitted. Two types of constants are recognized in FORTRAN, *integer* and *floating point*.

Integer Constants

An integer constant is a whole number with no fractional part. It must be written without a decimal point. Integer constants are usually used for counting and form a minor part of most FORTRAN programs.

Maximum magnitude of an integer constant on System/360 is 2147483647. It may seem strange that with 10 decimal digits the maximum is not 9999999999. The reason for this limitation is because of the way integer data is stored.

All integer constants are stored in a fixed-length format of 32 contiguous bits. One is used to indicate whether the data is positive or negative leaving 31 bits to represent the integer constant. The maximum binary value which can be represented with a string of 31 "on" or "1" bits $(2^{31}-1)$ is equivalent to the decimal value 2147483647.

It is not necessary to memorize this number because no problems in this book, and few in actual practice, exceed this magnitude. It is important, however, to recognize that all makes and models of machines have specific magnitude limitations. Programmers should keep in mind at least the general limitations of the specific computer they will use to process their programs.

Valid Integer Constants	*Invalid Integer Constants*	
0000	56+	(sign must precede digits)
+4	73.	(decimal point not allowed)
8	487,564	(embedded comma not allowed)
−7	8123456789	(exceeds maximum magnitude)
587459		

Floating Point Constants

Most constants used in FORTRAN programs are in floating point mode (form) rather than integer mode. A floating point constant is a number expressing decimal fractional precision. It is stored without a decimal point and in an entirely different manner than an integer constant. How does the computer know where the decimal point is located if it is not in storage? Stated simply, a floating point constant is stored in two parts; one part contains the number, and the other indicates where the decimal point is implied to be located. To simplify the explanation, a hypothetical computer will be used as an illustration.

Hypothetical Computer. A decimal number is stored in two parts, each containing signed decimal digits. One part is called the *fraction* or characteristic which is four digits in length and signed to indicate whether the number is positive or negative. The number is "normalized," meaning the first digit is not zero and, although it has no actual decimal point, the assumed decimal point always precedes the first significant digit. Thus, the positive decimal values 25.7 and .0257 will both be stored as $+2570$ with an implied decimal point preceding the first digit.

The second part is called the *exponent* or mantissa which is one digit in length and is also signed. The exponent is used to indicate where the actual decimal point in the fraction is located, relative to its implied position. A positive exponent tells the computer the actual decimal point is located to the right of its implied position—a negative exponent indicates it is to the left. The digit in the exponent indicates the number of positions the decimal point is located from its implied position. For example:

Decimal Values	Internal Representation	
	Exponent	Fraction
$+25.7$	$+2$	$+2570$
$+.0257$	-1	$+2570$
$-.257$	$+0$	-2570
		$\uparrow$
		implied decimal point

The exponent actually represents a one-digit power of 10. The first datum above can be stated as .2570 times 10^2, the second as .2570 times 10^{-1} and the last as .2570 times 10^0.

Because this hypothetical computer uses only a four-decimal digit fraction, it can accommodate numbers only in the range of 0000 through 9999. It uses only a one-decimal digit exponent so it can move the decimal point only a maximum of nine positions from its implied location. Thus, the largest value that can be stored is 999900000 (which is the product of the fraction .9999 and 10 raised to the power of the exponent 9). Note that a maximum of four significant digits can be stored, but the exponent makes it possible to represent a value consisting of any four decimal digits followed by five zeros or preceded by nine zeros.

System/360. This computer is considerably more sophisticated and powerful than the hypothetical computer previously described. A floating point number is stored in System/360 in either 32 or 64 contiguous bits depending upon the precision required. Eight bits are used to represent the sign of the fraction and, in effect, the signed exponent; the other 24 or 56 bits represent the fraction. The bits represent hexadecimal (a numbering system having 16 symbols) instead of decimal digits. The fraction contains a radix point to the left of the high-order digit. (It is not called a decimal point because the data is not in decimal notation.) The decimal value equivalent is the product of the fraction and 16 raised to the power of the exponent.

Fortunately, it is not necessary for a FORTRAN programmer to understand hexadecimal notation because the computer always does the conversion for him. Furthermore, it is not necessary to understand the exact manner in which a constant is actually stored. But it is important to realize that a floating point constant is stored in an entirely different manner than an integer constant. An integer constant, unlike a floating point constant, is stored with no provision for indicating a decimal point location. Thus, integer arithmetic can produce only integer results, but floating point arithmetic can produce results with fractional precision.

Single-Precision Floating Point Constants.   There are two methods of writing single-precision floating point constants in a FORTRAN program. One is called ordinary *decimal form,* the other, *exponential form.* Regardless of which method is used by the programmer, the computer automatically converts and stores the constant internally as a signed hexadecimal fraction with a signed exponent as previously described.

Single-Precision Decimal Form.   This type of constant must contain from one to seven decimal digits and a decimal point. Thus, .0000001 through 9999999. is the magnitude range of positive single-precision constants. If unsigned, it is assumed to be positive. If signed, the sign must precede the first digit. Embedded commas are not allowed.

Some examples of valid single-precision floating point constants in ordinary decimal form are:

$$+1. \qquad -.31416 \qquad 587.82$$

Some invalid examples are:

100	(decimal point omitted)
37,416.52	(contains embedded comma)
$51.07	(contains alphabetic letter)
1234567.8	(exceeds seven digits)

Single-Precision Exponential Form.   The programmer may elect to write a constant in exponential form rather than in ordinary decimal form. Exponential form provides a means of increasing the magnitude range to approximately 10^{-78} through 10^{75} (the exact magnitude is 16^{-64} through 16^{63}). An example of this form of constant is:

$$.257E-5$$

An exponential form constant contains three elements. The first is a one- to seven-digit number called the *fraction* (or characteristic) which may be signed or unsigned. If unsigned, it is assumed to be positive. If signed, the sign must appear in the first (leftmost) position. The fraction usually includes a decimal point; but, if none is indicated, a whole number is assumed; that is, a decimal point is implied to follow the low-order (rightmost) digit.

The second element is the letter E which indicates to the computer that the constant is in exponential form.

The third element is called the *exponent* (or mantissa). It must be either a one- or two-digit whole number. No decimal point or comma is allowed. The exponent may be either signed or unsigned. If unsigned, it is assumed to be positive. If signed, the sign must precede the first digit. The decimal equivalent of an exponential form constant is the product of the fraction and 10 raised to the power of the exponent.

Following are some examples of valid exponential form constants:

Exponential Form Constant	*Decimal Equivalent*
.50E4	$+5000.$
$-.00005E+8$	$-5000.$
$+500.E\ 1$	$+5000.$ (embedded blank permitted)
$-50000E-1$	$-5000.$
1234567.E4	$+12345670000.$
$-.1234567E-6$	$-.0000001234567$

Note that the sign of the fraction indicates whether the value is positive or negative; the sign of the exponent indicates, in effect, which way to move the decimal point from its actual or implied position in the fraction.

Following are some examples of invalid exponential form constants:

Invalid Constant	*Reason Invalid*
$2.2+12$	Letter E omitted
50.E	Exponent not indicated; zero is *not* assumed
50.E4.1	Exponent contains decimal point
1,234.75E3	Fraction contains embedded comma
1.2E+127	Exponent exceeds maximum magnitude of $+75$ and also contains more than two digits

Exponential form is particularly useful to express very large or very small decimal fractions. Not only is it more powerful than ordinary decimal form, but it is also more convenient for both the programmer to write and the keypunch operator to punch 1.E17, for example, rather than 100000000000000000.

Double-Precision Floating Point Constants. As covered previously, a single-precision constant is represented in storage by 32 contiguous bits which are divided into two parts. Eight bits represent the sign of the fraction and, in effect, a signed exponent. The other 24 bits represent the fraction.

Twice as much storage area is required for a double-precision constant. It is represented in storage by 64 contiguous bits (instead of 32) which are also divided into two parts. One part requires the same amount of storage area as a single-precision constant. That is, eight bits represent the sign of the fraction and, in effect, a signed exponent. Thus, the precision is not doubled but remains 10^{-78} through 10^{75}. The other part of a double-precision constant is 56 bits which represent the fraction. Note that the storage area required for this fraction (56 bits) is more than twice the size of the area required to store the fraction of a single-precision constant (24 bits). For this reason, a double-precision constant can have a maximum of 16 decimal digits which is more than double the maximum of 7 allowed in single-precision.

In summary, a double-precision constant can have a maximum of 16 decimal digits with a precision of 10^{-78} through 10^{75} and requires twice as much storage area as a single-precision constant.

Double-precision constants, like single, may be written in either ordinary *decimal form* or in *exponential form*.

Double-Precision Decimal Form. If an ordinary decimal form constant contains from one to seven digits, it is considered to be a single-precision floating point constant. But if it contains from 8 to 16 digits, it is considered to be a *double-precision* floating point constant and will automatically be handled accordingly by the computer. If unsigned, it is assumed to be positive. If signed, the sign must precede the first digit. Embedded commas are not allowed.

Double-Precision Exponential Form. This type of floating point constant is similar to single-precision exponential form, but it differs in two important ways. First, the fraction may contain as many as 16 decimal digits instead of a maximum of 7; and second, the letter D (indicating double precision) replaces the letter E preceding the exponent.

Following are some valid examples of both types of double-precision floating point constants:

Floating Point Constant	Decimal Equivalent
-1234.5678	-1234.5678
1234567890.123456	$+1234567890.123456$
$1234567890.123456D-11$	$+.01234567890123456$
$-18.D4$	$-180000.$

If a programmer elects to use double-precision rather than single-precision constants, arithmetic operations will require more processing time. Also, as discussed earlier, double-precision constants require twice as much storage area. For these reasons, double precision should not be used unless the extra "power" it provides is required by the problem to be solved.

VARIABLE NAMES

A variable name is the symbolic address of an internal storage location. It is called "variable" because the contents of this address may be changed repeatedly during the execution of the program. A variable name is composed by the programmer but must follow the rules of FORTRAN.

1. It must begin with one of the 27 alphabetic letters. (Remember, the dollar sign is considered to be a letter.)
2. If desired, it may contain up to a maximum of five additional letters and/or numbers which may appear in any sequence.
3. The only special character allowed is the blank. Embedded blanks, if any, are ignored by the compiler. In rare cases, an embedded blank may improve readability; but, in most cases, it can cause confusion and should be avoided.

The first letter of a variable name has special significance because it implies whether the particular mode of data stored at this address is integer or floating point. This is a convention of FORTRAN called *implicit definition of mode*. Chapter 8 includes an explanation of how to override this implicit definition of mode by use of a nonexecutable statement called an explicit specification statement.

Integer Variable Names

If integer data are to be stored, locations are indicated by variable names which must begin with one of the following six letters:

$$I J K L M N$$

An easy way to learn this rule is to remember that one of the letters I through N is used to begin an INteger variable name.

Numeric data stored at locations indicated by integer variable names are represented internally in the same manner as integer constants. Thus, only whole numbers with a maximum value of 2147483647 are allowed.

Floating Point Variable Names

The compiler does not use the variable name to distinguish between single-precision (sometimes called real) and double-precision floating point data. Either type can be stored at locations indicated by variable names which begin with a letter other than I through N.

Numeric data stored at locations indicated by floating point variable names are represented internally in the same manner as floating point constants. Thus, the same restrictions as to maximum values apply.

Following are some selected examples of variable names:

Valid Variable Names	Mode
X	Floating point
$ALES	Floating point
RATE	Floating point
DATA3	Floating point
HØURS	Floating point
PAYNET	Floating point
NETPAY	Integer
J23456	Integer
NUMBER	Integer
MIXERS	Integer
KNIVES	Integer

Invalid Variable Names	Reason Invalid
2ND	First character is not alphabetic
ITEM-2	Hyphen is an invalid character
TØØTHBRUSHES	Exceeds six letters in length

The programmer should make a special effort to compose variable names which are as descriptive as possible within the rules. For example, a program to compute payroll might include the variable names HØURS, RATE, and PAY. These names are obviously more descriptive than H, R, and P or (worse yet) X, W, and Z. The use of descriptive variable names documents the program; that is, makes it easier to read not only by the programmer, but by others.

Because the first letter of the variable name implies the mode and because the name cannot exceed six letters and/or numbers in length, the programmer will often find it necessary to misspell and/or abbreviate. For example, a program designed to count the input cards processed might include the integer variable name KØUNT rather than a floating point variable name such as CØUNT. Likewise, a program designed to compute interest on a loan might include the floating point variable name ZINT. In this case, INTEREST could not be used as a variable name for two reasons. First, it exceeds the maximum allowable length (six numbers and/or letters). Second, the implied mode is integer which is not designed to be used with decimal values.

It is important that the programmer be aware of what the computer does when told to store a decimal value at an integer variable name. It will *truncate* (cut off without rounding) the fractional portion to the right of the decimal point and store only the whole number. Thus, if an attempt is made to store 100.99 at the integer variable name NETPAY, only 100 will be stored. Of course, the fractional portion is retained if a floating point variable name such as PAYNET is used.

Substituting variable names such as KØUNT and KØDE for CØUNT and CØDE is one way to stay within the rules when the most descriptive name begins with a forbidden letter. Another "trick of the trade" takes advantage of the fact that few descriptive names begin with the letter Z. When composing a floating point variable name, some programmers develop the habit of preceding a forbidden descriptive name with the letter Z. To illustrate, ZMEAN, ZMØDE, and ZINT might be used as variable names for mean, mode, and interest.

ARITHMETIC OPERATORS

Arithmetic operators are symbols used to designate arithmetic operations. They are:

Operators	Meaning
+	Add
−	Subtract
/	Divide
*	Multiply
**	Raise to the power of

The add, subtract, and divide operators used in FORTRAN are identical to those used in regular mathematical notation. The asterisk is used to indicate multiplication rather than X because the computer always interprets X as an alphabetic letter. The double asterisk is used to designate exponentiation because input and output devices are not designed to handle the superscripts used in regular mathematical notation.

Only the operators illustrated are valid; no other symbols are allowed.

DELIMITERS

Delimiters are used to separate FORTRAN statements and the various elements within a FORTRAN statement. Stated another way, they are used to tell the computer where one statement or one element ends and the next begins. On this printed page, blank spaces are used to separate the elements (such as words and numbers) in a sentence. In FORTRAN, blanks cannot be used to separate elements because the language not only allows as many blanks to be written between the elements as are necessary to improve the readability of a statement, but it also permits embedded blanks within some elements.

The rules of FORTRAN require that in each statement (*a*) every constant, (*b*) every variable name, (*c*) every code, and (*d*) almost every key word be followed by one or more appropriate delimiters. The delimiters are the following 10 special characters:

$$+ - / * = . , ( ) '$$

and column 73 in the statement card. If one statement is written on more than one card, column 73 is assumed to be a delimiter only on the last card of the statement. It should be noted that the only FORTRAN special character which is not a delimiter is the blank. Thus, embedded blanks in variable names and in key words are ignored by the compiler.

The uses of these FORTRAN delimiters are illustrated in following chapters which describe and illustrate complete statements.

REVIEW QUESTIONS

1. What is the maximum number of statements allowed on one card?

2. What is the maximum number of cards that can be used to contain one statement?

3. Continuation cards cannot be numbered ("labeled"). Why?

4. Where can comments appear in a program?

5. How many comments may appear in any one program?

6. What characters are allowed in comments?

7. What distinguishes a continuation card from the first card in a statement?

8. What distinguishes a second continuation card from a first continuation card?

9. Is it permissible for a relatively short statement which could be punched in one card to be punched in two or more cards by use of continuation cards?

10. Which characters are allowed in a statement?

11. What happens if a programmer extends a statement beyond column 72?

12. Which characters are allowed in the identification field of a statement?

13. Write the numerical value 7 as:
   a) An integer constant
   b) A floating point constant in
       (1) single-precision decimal form (2) single-precision exponential form (3) double-precision exponential form.

14. Which characters are allowed in a variable name?

15. What is meant by "implicit definition of mode"?

EXERCISES

On a separate sheet of paper classify the numbered items listed below as one of the following: Integer or Floating Point Valid Constant; Integer or Floating Point Valid Variable Name; or, Invalid. If invalid, briefly indicate why.

1. 345	10. NUM	19. A(154
2. PAYROLL	11. $170	20. L3A7
3. 3.	12. .104E−88	21. 73.4E−3
4. 32D7.4	13. WRITE	22. $2.86
5. UNITS	14. 37.4+E4	23. 12345678.0
6. Data	15. 47	24. ITEM−3
7. −7.70	16. E 3	25. MAXIMUM
8. X	17. 859.D17	
9. −32E+7	18. 3,875.22	

CHAPTER
4

ARITHMETIC STATEMENTS

AN arithmetic statement can tell the computer where to store a constant or where to store the data contained at a symbolic address. It can also tell the computer to perform certain arithmetic calculations and indicate where and how the results are to be stored. This chapter explains how the previously presented constants, variable names, and arithmetic operators are combined to form arithmetic statements. To assist the reader to visualize the format, card columns are indicated in all statement illustrations.

" $=$ " -is replaced by ;

GENERAL FORM

The general form of an arithmetic statement is:

```
|12345|6|7
 nnnnn    vn=ae
```

Legend:

nnnnn   A statement *number* which is required only if the statement is referenced elsewhere in the program but may always be used at the programmer's option.

=   A required separator between the two parts of an arithmetic statement.

vn   A *variable name* in either integer or floating point mode.

ae   An *arithmetic expression* which may consist of one constant, one variable name, or a combination of constants and/or variable names separated by one or more delimiters.

vn ← ae

46

An arithmetic statement has the same general form but not the same meaning as a regular algebraic equation. The equal sign, separating the two basic components of an arithmetic statement, does not mean equivalence. The equal sign means "store." In effect, the arithmetic statement tells the computer to store the numeric value indicated by the expression on the right of the equal sign at the symbolic address represented by the variable name on the left.

For example, the arithmetic statement:

|12345|6|7

   N=1

directs the computer to store the integer constant 1 at symbolic address N.

Regardless of what was stored at N before this instruction was executed, it will be replaced with the integer constant 1. Furthermore, N will continue to have a "current value" of 1 no matter how many times it is used in the program unless or until it is changed by another statement. This is sometimes referred to as "destructive read-in and nondestructive read-out." In this respect, a computer can be compared to a tape recorder. If a popular song, for example, is located on a certain area of tape, it can be repeatedly played back or read-out. But if a speech is recorded or read-in on the same area of the tape, the song is lost and is replaced by the speech.

To illustrate this point, suppose a program contains four arithmetic statements which will be executed in sequence:

|12345|6|7

   1   N=7
   2   I=N
   3   J=I
   4   N=8

After statement number 1 is executed, N will have a current value of 7. Statement 2 directs the computer to store the current value of N at I. At this point in the program, both N and I have a current value of 7. After the execution of statement number 3, N, I, and J all have a current value of 7. Statement 4 changes the current value of N to 8 but does not affect the current values of I and J.

ARITHMETIC EXPRESSIONS

As previously indicated, an arithmetic expression is that portion of an arithmetic statement to the right of the equal sign. It may contain a single constant or a single variable name, as illustrated earlier. It may also contain combinations of constants and/or variable names. This latter type of expression is more complex and requires strict compliance with certain rules.

Rules for Writing Arithmetic Expressions

The following rules must be followed when writing arithmetic expressions which contain two or more constants and/or variable names:

Separation of Constants and Variable Names. Each constant and/or variable name must be separated by an operational sign to explicitly indicate the desired computation. Arithmetic operations are never implied in FORTRAN. For example, in regular mathematical notation, to indicate "X times Y," it is common to write:

$$XY$$

However, XY does not mean "X times Y" in FORTRAN. In fact, XY is not two variable names; but rather it is one variable name containing two valid characters. To indicate "X times Y" in FORTRAN, the programmer must write:

$$X*Y \text{ or } Y*X$$

Likewise, to indicate "12 times K" instead of the regular mathematical notation:

$$12K$$

either of the following notations must be used:

$$12*K \text{ or } K*12$$

Separation of Arithmetic Operators. Two or more arithmetic operators can never appear in sequence in an arithmetic expression. For example, to tell the computer to multiply "A times the negative value -12.5," the expression cannot be written as follows:

$$A*-12.5$$

It is valid, however, to write:

$$A*(-12.5)$$

The preceding expression illustrates how parentheses can be used to separate arithmetic operators. Other uses of parentheses are discussed in a later rule.

Order of Computation. The computer evaluates some arithmetic expressions from left to right and others from right to left. The evaluation of more complex expressions may begin in about the middle, then go to the right, back to the left, back to the right again, etc. If the programmer avoids mixed mode expressions (discussed in the following section), it is not necessary to comprehend the intricate sequence of steps the computer actually goes through when evaluating a complex expression. It is only necessary to understand the effects of these steps, which are described next.

If an expression contains two or more arithmetic operators, computation is performed from left to right according to the hierarchy:

Hierarchy	Operation
1st	Parenthetical expressions
2nd	Exponentiation
3rd	Multiplication and division
4th	Addition and subtraction

Observe that the hierarchy goes from what might be considered the most difficult to the least difficult.

All operations in a given level of hierarchy are performed before going to the next lower level. To illustrate the effects of the steps taken in the evaluation of an arithmetic expression, consider the following:

$$A*B-C/D*7.00+G**2.$$

The computer would first scan the expression from left to right looking for parenthetical expressions. Finding none, it would return to the left.

Next, it would scan from left to right again until it gets to the exponential operator. It would then calculate $G**2$. If the result of this calculation is called "W," the expression would now appear as follows:

$$A*B-C/D*7.00+W$$

On the third scan, it would look for multiplication and division operators. As these are on the same level of hierarchy, it would handle each in order as they appear from left to right. First, $A*B$ would be calculated (call the result "X"). Next, it would calculate C/D (call the result "Y"). Finally, it would calculate $Y*7.00$ (call the result "Z"). The expression would now look like this:

$$X-Z+W$$

On the final scan, Z would be subtracted from X and then the difference would be added to W. This would complete the evaluation.

Use of Parentheses. Parentheses may be used to avoid two sequential operational signs, as already indicated. Parentheses may also be used to specify the order in which calculations are to be performed. In effect, they may be used to alter the lower three levels of hierarchy.

To illustrate the flexibility and convenience the use of parentheses provides, suppose the programmer desires to add A to B to C and then double the sum. Instead of writing the following series of statements:

| 12345 | 6 | 7 |

```
        X=A*2.
        Y=B*2.
        Z=C*2.
        ANS=X+Y+Z
```

or one long statement such as:

> ⌈12345⌈6⌈7‾‾
>   ANS=A*2.+B*2.+C*2.

he could write:

> ⌈12345⌈6⌈7‾‾
>   ANS=(A+B+C)*2.

Because parenthetical expressions are evaluated first, the computer would first compute the sum, then multiply.

For another example, the expression:

$$(A+B)**(7.5*C)$$

will cause the computer to first add, then multiply, and finally to exponentiate. Note that the use of parentheses, in effect, reversed the lower three levels of hierarchy.

Hierarchy always applies within a parenthetical expression. To illustrate:

$$A/(B+C*D)$$

The computer would first multiply C times D, then add the product to B. Finally, the sum of the latter calculation would be divided into A.

If "nested" parentheses are used, the innermost parenthetical expression is evaluated first. For example:

$$A=B+(C*(G-4.5))$$

The order of calculation would be: $G-4.5$ (call this "X"), $C*X$ (call this "Y"), and finally $B+Y$.

If beginning programmers have any doubt as to whether parentheses are required in a particular arithmetic expression, it is suggested parentheses be used. The computer can handle unnecessary parentheses in a fraction of the time required to debug a program in which required parentheses are omitted.

Mixed Mode Expressions

If the constants and the numeric values associated with variable names are not all integer, or all single-precision floating point, or all double-precision floating point, the expression is said to be in *mixed mode*.

Most versions of FORTRAN do not permit mixed mode arithmetic expressions; but FORTRAN IV, as used on System/360, does. The programmer must be familiar with the exact sequence of steps the computer actually goes through when evaluating a complex expression if he wishes to use mixed mode. The net effect of these steps, discussed in the preceding section, does not apply to mixed mode expressions which are for the expert and should be avoided by beginning programmers. However, because mixed mode expressions are accepted by the computer and sometimes unintentionally written by beginning programmers, the following brief explanation is given.

The final result of calculations indicated by an arithmetic expression is determined by the hierarchy:

Hierarchy	Final Result
1st	Double precision
2nd	Single precision
3rd	Integer

If a mixed mode expression contains only integer and single-precision floating point values, the final result will be in single precision. If it contains one or more double-precision values, the final result will be in double precision.

The type of calculation changes at different stages of the evaluation. Thus, depending upon the values associated with the variable names, the result of the expressions M/N*B and B*M/N may not be the same.

MIXED MODE STATEMENTS *don't mix integer + floating point.*

A mixed mode statement is one in which the variable name to the left of an equal sign and the arithmetic expression to the right are not in the same mode. Mixed mode *expressions* should be avoided, but mixed mode *statements* are not only permissible, but often required.

To illustrate, assume that a routine to compute the dollars and cents VALUE of a particular class of inventory (number of ITEMS times unit price) is to be added to an existing program. Further assume that the existing program has already stored the number of ITEMS in integer mode, but the unit price of $9.25 has not been stored so it must be written into the program as a constant. If a mixed mode expression is to be avoided, the following statement cannot be used because it contains an integer variable name and a floating point constant:

1 2 3 4 5	6	7

```
        VALUE=ITEMS*9.25
```

The programmer can, however, use the following statements:

1 2 3 4 5	6	7

```
        UNITS=ITEMS
        VALUE=UNITS*9.25
```

The first statement will cause the computer to convert the integer value, stored at ITEMS, to floating point mode and then store it at UNITS. The second statement completes the routine and solves the problem without using a mixed mode expression.

Mixed mode statements are sometimes required but are sometimes optional. For example, the integer value 257 could be stored at NUMBER by either of the following two arithmetic statements:

```
|12345|6|7
         NUMBER=257
```

or

```
|12345|6|7
         NUMBER=257.00
```

The latter example above is a mixed mode statement which requires extra machine-language instructions to be generated by the compiler because the floating point constant must be converted to integer mode before it is stored. It thus requires a larger storage area for the object program as well as more compilation and execution time.

Truncation of Decimal Fractions

In an arithmetic statement, the mode of the variable names and/or constants to the right of the equal sign determines the mode in which the expression will be evaluated. The mode of the variable name to the left of the equal sign governs the mode in which the results of the expression evaluated will be stored. The idea may be illustrated in this manner:

Answer Mode=Arithmetic Mode

Caution must be exercised with mixed mode statements or the computer may not furnish the desired results. To illustrate what can happen, assume that the following series of statements are executed sequentially in an attempt to determine the exact amount of interest on a one-year bank loan (interest equals principal times annual rate):

```
|12345|6|7
         PRINC=3500.00
         RATE=.0725
         INT=PRINC*RATE
```

The first two statements establish the current value of PRINC and RATE. The expression in the last statement is evaluated in floating point mode; and the result, in this case, is 253.75. However, when this result is converted to integer mode and stored at INT, the decimal fraction is truncated (dropped without rounding) and only the integer 253 is stored at

INT. If the floating point variable name ZINT had been used, instead of the integer variable name INT, the entire amount would have been retained.

To further illustrate, assume that the following arithmetic statements are executed in the order in which they appear:

```
|12345|6|7
    1   I=5
    2   J=4
    3   K=I/J
    4   X=I/J
```

When statement number 3 is evaluated, the result will be the integer value 1 which will be stored at K. (Remember, results of integer arithmetic are always integer; if floating point variable names had been used, the result would have been 1.25.) The result of the evaluation of statement number 4 will also be 1, but it will be converted to the floating point value 1.0 before it is stored at X.

Now consider the following series of arithmetic statements:

```
|12345|6|7
    1   R=5
    2   S=4
    3   T=R/S
    4   L=R/S
```

When statement number 3 is executed, the expression R/S will be evaluated as 1.25; and this value will then be stored at T. The evaluation of the expression in statement number 4 will be the same, but the fraction .25 will be truncated, and only the integer 1 will be stored at L.

Programmers should be aware that fractional portions can be lost in two ways: First, if the computer is told to store a floating point value at a location identified by an integer variable name, and second, if it is told to evaluate an arithmetic expression in integer mode.

As previously indicated, the equal sign does not have the same meaning in FORTRAN as it does in regular algebraic notation. The following two statements emphasize this difference:

```
|12345|6|7
        N=2
        N=N+1
```

The first statement tells the computer to store 2 at N. The second statement is obviously not correct algebraically, but it is a valid FORTRAN statement. It tells the computer to add 1 to the current value of N and then to store the sum at N. Following execution of both statements, N will have a current value of 3.

INITIALIZATION OF VARIABLE NAMES

The computer "knows" the value of each constant because it is told directly by the arithmetic statement in which it appears. But how does the computer know the value of variable names? It doesn't, unless it has been told either by the statement being executed or by some previous statement.

It should be obvious that unless the computer knows the value of J and K it is impossible to solve the following arithmetic statement:

```
|12345|6|7
     I=(J+K)**2
```

There are two ways to set up or *initialize* the values of variable names. One is via an arithmetic statement, the other is via an input statement which is covered in the next chapter. The following series of statements show how variable names can be initialized via arithmetic statements:

```
|12345|6|7
  1   J=3
  2   K=5
  3   I=(J+K)**2
```

In the above illustration, statement number 1 establishes the initial value of J as 3; statement number 2 initializes K to the value of 5. The numeric value 64, resulting from the evaluation of the arithmetic expression in statement number 3, is stored at the variable name to the left of the equal sign, thus initializing I. Statement number 2 could precede 1, but obviously both must precede 3.

UNNECESSARY BLANKS

The compiler ignores embedded blanks in key words and variable names because a blank is not a delimiter. Likewise, blanks separating variable names, constants, codes, and delimiters are also ignored by the compiler. Thus, each of the following three statements would be interpreted in the same manner by the compiler (the last two lines are continuations of statement number 44):

```
|12345|6|7
  22   N=(M-3)*L
  33   N= (M-3)   *L
  44   N
     1  =
     1 (M-3)    *L
```

Although one or more blanks separating the various elements of a statement are always permissible, they are never required. The omission of unnecessary blanks obviously permits longer statements to be written on one card and is thus a convenience to both the programmer and the key punch operator. For this reason, most programmers develop the habit of avoiding unnecessary blanks.

EXERCISES

1. Are the following valid *arithmetic expressions*? On a separate sheet identify those that are valid as either integer or floating point expressions. Assume that mixed mode expressions are invalid. Rewrite all invalid expressions correctly.

1. RADIUS*RADIUS
2. +1234
3. LENGTH*WIDTH/2.0
4. X+Y
5. L*(M+(N−2))
6. ITEM−3/i
7. BASE*HEIGHT/2
8. XY
9. I²+N²
10. 2N*7
11. A+(N−7)*2
12. L+−N
13. 12.34E+3**R
14. 12.34+3E**R
15. PRINC*RATE*(DAYS/365)
16. C(−D)
17. R*π*2.
18. A**12.0
19. 1234−NØRTH
20. −1234+1234
21. NØRTH*1234
22. NØRTH**NØRTH
23. 4A+2.
24. N+
25. ((A*B)+(C/D))

2. On a separate sheet indicate whether the following *arithmetic statements* are valid or invalid. All valid variable names represent integer or single-precision values. If the statement is invalid, rewrite it correctly. Assume that mixed mode *expressions* are invalid.

1. ZINT=PRT
2. NETPAY=GRØSS−DED'NS
3. ENDBAL=BEGBAL+PURCH−PAYMTS
4. ANSWER=PI*RADIUS**2
5. 147=140+7
6. J=(L+(N*2)
7. TØTAL=(NUMBER−1)+(NUM2−2)
8. ASSETS+LIAB=NETWØRTH
9. KØUNT=0
10. X=3Y
11. AMØUNT=$40500
12. ITEMS=IRØNS+KNIVES+MIXERS
13. INTEREST=PRIN*RATE*TIME/365.
14. I*N/M
15. X=X*.12E−4
16. PAY=SALARY+CØMISH
17. SIX=5.0

18. INCØME=REVN−EXP
19. ANS=A+(B−(C*D)**2.
20. GRØSS=HØURS*RATE
21. I=N*M
22. VALUE=ITEMS*2.17
23. PI=3.141593
24. I=M(N*J/K)
25. FINTØT=FINTØT+SUBTØT

3. On a separate sheet evaluate each arithmetic expression and indicate the numeric value which would be stored at the variable name to the left of the equal sign when the following arithmetic statements are executed:

1. A=3.0*4.00−1.5
2. I=(3.0*4.00)−1.5
3. B=3.0*(4.0−1.5)
4. J=(3.0*(4.0−1.5))
5. C=(3.0+(4.)*1.5)

6. K=(3.0)+(4.0*1.5)
7. D=(3.0+4.0)*1.5
8. E=8/3*3**2
9. M=3*((2+2*5/2)+4)
10. R=18/4−3+2**2

4. On a separate sheet write the equivalent FORTRAN arithmetic statement for each of the following algebraic equations. Avoid mixed mode expressions. Include parentheses only if required.

1. L=I+J−3
2. K=5N+2M
3. $5+\dfrac{X}{2}-Y=R$
4. $A=\dfrac{\pi R^2 H}{3}$
5. $D=\dfrac{X}{Y+4}$

6. $E=\left(18+\dfrac{X}{3}\right)^Y$
7. $F=\dfrac{X-4}{Y+Z}$
8. $G=\left(\dfrac{5X}{2Y}\right)^{Z+2}$
9. $H=\dfrac{1}{2}\left(\dfrac{6X}{B-2}\right)$
10. $A=\sqrt{B^2+C^2}$

CHAPTER
5

INPUT/OUTPUT STATEMENTS

Chapter 4 covered arithmetic statements which are used to process data and which might be considered the middle part of a program. This chapter covers the statements necessary to get data into and out of the computer.

The computer must be supplied not only with the *statements* required to solve the particular problem but also with the specific *data* to be processed when these statements are executed. It is often possible, but not necessarily convenient, to supply all data directly in the program by including constants in one or more arithmetic statements. When this method is used, the program might be called self-operational because the program supplies the data as well as the instructions to process it. But many programs require that the data be supplied from one or more records which are not a part of the program. The input section of this chapter explains and illustrates the statements used to describe and read data from punched cards.

After the data has been processed and the computed results have been internally stored, these results must be returned to the programmer in an acceptable form. The output section of this chapter explains and illustrates the statements required to accomplish this task.

This chapter completes the presentation of all essential information required to write elementary programs. After studying this chapter, the reader should be ready to communicate to a computer.

INPUT

Input statements are used to transmit information from an external medium into computer storage. Many types of external media including magnetic tape, magnetic disk, punched paper tape, and punched cards may be used for transmission. Attention in this book will center upon the statements required to read information from punched cards via an external device called a card reader.

Data Card Input

Each unit of input, such as a card, is sometimes called a record. Because an input card contains data to be processed, it is often called a *data card*. A group of related data cards is called a file, a data set, or simply a data deck. Each data card is divided into fields containing one or more columns of information. The form of numeric information in a data card is similar to that of constants in a *statement* card. If the data are composed of only one or more decimal digits, it is in integer form; if it is composed of only one or more decimal digits and a decimal point, it is in ordinary decimal form; if it is composed of only a fraction, the letter D or E, and an exponent, it is in exponential form. As in the case of constants, high-order signs are optional and embedded commas are prohibited.

It is important to distinguish between *input data cards*, which provide information to be processed, and *program statement cards*, which give instructions to the computer. The exact format required for all statement cards, as described in Chapter 3, is specified by the rules of FORTRAN and cannot be changed by the programmer. If a statement is not written in prescribed form, it is invalid. The programmer does not describe statement cards to the computer because the format is implied.

On the other hand, there are no rules restricting the format of *data cards*. The number and sequence of fields and the type of data punched in each field is designed to fit the requirements of the problem and the convenience of the programmer and/or keypunch operator. Because the data card format is optional, it cannot be implied. It must be explicitly described to the computer via a nonexecutable statement called a FØRMAT statement.

The FØRMAT Statement

A FØRMAT statement is nonexecutable. Its purpose is to tell the computer where and how data will be found in a data record. It explicitly describes each data field as to type, size, and location. FØRMAT statements may appear anywhere in the source program before the END statement, but most programmers develop the habit of placing them all together either at the beginning or end of the program or of placing each immediately preceding or following the I/O statement by which they are referenced.

The general form of a FØRMAT statement is:

$$\overline{\rule{0pt}{1.4ex}12345|6|7}$$

nnnnn   FØRMAT($c_1,c_2,c_3, \ldots c_m$)

Legend:

nnnnn	Any unique one- to five-digit integer which specifies the statement *number*. It is required so that this statement may be referenced by an I/O statement.
FØRMAT	A key word which identifies the type of statement.
$c_1, \ldots c_m$	Indicates one or more format *codes* which must be contained within parentheses and ordinarily separated by commas. The sequence in which they appear must correspond to the sequence of the fields on the data records which they describe. The code specifies the type of data contained in the field, the length of the field in columns, and the position of the decimal point, if any. It may also specify that a field is to be ignored.

Several of the available format codes used to describe input data cards are illustrated and discussed in the following sections.

Integer Format Code.   The code used to describe an integer data field is:

$$rIl$$

Legend:

r	An integer number which specifies the number of times the format code is to be *repeated*. It is optional with the programmer and is omitted if the code is used only once.
I	Specifies that the field contains *integer* data.
l	An integer number which indicates the *length* of the field in card columns.

To illustrate, the following four-field data card:

$$\overline{\rule{0pt}{1.4ex}\begin{array}{ll|l|l|l}123|456|&78|9&\\ +12|913|&-7|&78\end{array}}$$

could be described either as:

$$\overline{\rule{0pt}{1.4ex}12345|6|7}$$

FØRMAT(I3,I3,I2,I3)

or as:

$$\overline{\rule{0pt}{1.4ex}12345|6|7}$$

FØRMAT(2I3,I2,I3)

Note that the preceding data card contains three I3 fields but cannot be described as 3I3 because the format codes must appear in the same sequence as the card fields. Note also that the FØRMAT statement only specifies the contents of the first 11 columns. Any data punched in column 12 through 80 will be ignored. It is permissible to describe a card as containing less than 80 columns but in no case can it be described as containing more than 80.

Floating Point Format Codes. There are two basic types of floating point data—ordinary decimal form and exponential form. The format codes are different so each will be discussed separately.

Ordinary Decimal Form. The code to describe *both single- and double-precision* floating point fields which contain ordinary decimal form data is:

$$rFl.d$$

Legend:

r	An integer which specifies the number of times the format code is to be *repeated*. It is optional with the programmer and is omitted if the code is used only once.
F	Specifies that the field contains *floating point* data in ordinary decimal form.
l	An integer number which indicates the *length* of the data field in card columns.
.d	A decimal point followed by an integer which specifies the number of *decimal point positions*. If the input data field contains a decimal point, this specification is ignored by the compiler; but it cannot be omitted by the programmer.

To review integer format codes and also to illustrate floating point format codes, consider the following six-field data card:

```
12 3456 78 9
27|+2.7|+8|2.12|−.12|257.567
```

The FØRMAT statement to describe the above card could be either:

```
12345|6|7
```

FØRMAT(I2,F4.1,I2,F4.2,F4.2,F7.3)

or the two contiguous F4.2 fields (the 4th and 5th) could be coded as 2F4.2 at the programmer's option.

Chapter 3 called attention to the rule that *constants* written in ordinary decimal form *must* contain a decimal point. The rule for *constants* written in a FORTRAN statement does not apply to decimal *data* punched in a data card; decimal data may be punched in a data card either with or without a decimal point. If a decimal point is not punched in a data field, the compiler automatically assumes a decimal point in the position indicated by the format code. Thus, the data card:

```
123 4567
357|
```

could be coded as F3.0 to indicate the decimal datum 357. or coded F3.2, for example, to indicate 3.57 as the decimal datum.

What if the card contained the following datum:

```
┌─────────┬──
│123456│78
│+127.7│
```

and the format code specified F6.3 instead of F6.1? FORTRAN IV provides that in event of a conflict, the decimal point punched in the card overrides the decimal point specified by the format code. In other words, the computer assumes that the data card is correct and ignores the programmer's specification.

This provision of FORTRAN allows some flexibility in placement of data within a field if the data contains a decimal point. For example, assume that a data field is located in the first nine columns in a card. Data is usually punched right-justified in a field as follows:

```
┌─────────┬──
│123456789│
│    12.45│
```

It is not necessary to punch zeros in the high-order (leftmost) position in a field because the computer always assumes each blank preceding the first significant digit to be zero. Likewise, each blank following the last significant digit is also always assumed to be a zero. Thus, the decimal value 12.45 could be punched in the field in several ways including:

```
┌─────────┬──
│123456789│
│    12.45│
│00012.450│
│  12.45  │
```

The format code must describe this field as floating point with a field length of nine; but because the location of an actual decimal point overrides the format code specification, it could be described several ways such as:

$$F9.0 \qquad F9.2 \qquad F9.6$$

Stated simply, floating point data containing a decimal point may be punched anywhere in the field because leading and trailing zeros do not change the value.

However, if the data field does not contain a decimal point, it must be punched to agree with the format code because trailing zeros do change the value. For example, to indicate 12.45 with an implied rather than an actual decimal point in a field described as F9.2, it must be right-justified because if it is punched as follows:

```
┌─────────┬──
│123456789│
│  1245   │
```

the trailing blank will cause the computer to assume 124.50 as the value.

Thus, floating point data with an implied decimal point, like integer data, must agree with the corresponding format code.

The ability of the compiler to allow decimal points to be implied and to allow actual decimal points to override format code specifications can be useful to the programmer. However, to avoid the difficulties inherent in discussion of several methods of representation of floating point data at the same time, *future illustrations in this book will always show decimal datum with a decimal point. This will readily distinguish it from integer datum in which a decimal point is never allowed.*

Exponential Form. Two format codes are provided for describing fields containing exponential form data. One specifies single precision, the other, double precision. The general forms are:

rEl.d and rDl.d

Legend:

r An integer which specifies the number of times the format code is to be *repeated*. It is optional with the programmer and is omitted if the code is used only once.

E Specifies that the field contains single-precision data in *exponential* form.

D Specifies that the field contains *double-precision* exponential form data.

l An integer number which indicates the *length* of the data field in card columns.

.d A decimal point followed by a one- or two-digit integer which specifies the number of *decimal positions* in the fraction preceding the letter E or D. If the number following the decimal point is omitted, the code is invalid (the computer does *not* assume a zero). If the input data field contains a decimal point, this specification is ignored by the compiler; but it cannot be omitted by the programmer.

For example, the following data card:

```
|123456|789  |
 .47E−4|58.E6|+.0374D+22
```

would be described as:

```
|12345|6|7
     FØRMAT(E6.2,E5.0,D10.4)
```

X Format Code. This code, sometimes called the blank or skip format code, specifies that an input field is to be ignored. The general form is:

1X

Legend:

l An integer number greater than zero which specifies the *length* of the field to be skipped when reading an input card. If this number is omitted, the code is invalid (the compiler does not assume a field length of one).

X Specifies that the field is to be ignored.

To illustrate, the following FØRMAT statement:

⌐12345|6|7
            FØRMAT(4X,I2,1X,I3)

will cause the first and third fields on the following data card to be ignored:

⌐1234|56|7|89 ¯
+2.4|37| |256|

In effect, the above FØRMAT statement indirectly tells the computer that the first data field (I2) begins in column 5 because it specifies that the first four columns are to be ignored. Similarly, it indirectly indicates the next field (I3) begins in column 8 because column 7 is to be ignored. It should be emphasized that the field length must *precede* the letter X; in all other format codes discussed thus far, the field length must follow the letter which specifies the type of format code.

T Format Code. This code, sometimes called the tabulator, or tab code, specifies directly, rather than indirectly, where reading is to begin. Two or more T format codes are not allowed to appear in sequence. The general form is:

Tc

Legend:
T   Identifies the type of format code.
c   An integer number greater than zero which indicates the specific card
        column where the data field described by the following format code begins.

To illustrate, the following FØRMAT statement:

⌐12345|6|7
            FØRMAT(T5,I2,T8,I3)

will ignore the first and third fields of the data card illustrated below:

⌐1234|56|7|89 ¯
+2.4|37| |256|

The T5 specification tells the computer that reading is to begin with column 5; likewise, T8 specifies the next field begins in column 8. This illustration should be compared to the one given in the preceding section describing the X format code.

Neither the T or X format codes have a provision for indicating the number of times the code is to be repeated. The basic difference between the T and X format codes is that the former indicates directly where the next field begins, the latter indirectly. Both codes tell the computer to ignore one or more fields so either may be used to accomplish the same task. The programmer can select the one which is more convenient under the circumstances.

The READ Statement

Two statements are required to read data from an input record into internal storage. One is the nonexecutable FØRMAT statement previously described, the other is the executable READ statement covered in this section. The READ statement is an executable I/O statement which can direct the computer to read one or more data cards from a card reader device. The READ statement can also be used with other types of input records; but this book, as indicated previously, is concerned only with punched cards as input media.

General Form and Functions. The READ statement tells the computer what to read, specifies the input device where the record is located, and references a FØRMAT statement which describes the record. The general form is:

$\overline{|12345|6|7}$

nnnnn   READ(dc,fn)vn$_1$,vn$_2$, . . . vn$_m$

Legend:

nnnnn	Any unique one- to five-digit integer which specifies the statement *number*. It is required only if the statement is referenced by another statement in the program.
READ	A key word specifying the operation to be performed.
dc	An integer number, or an integer variable name, which specifies the *device code*. The standard FORTRAN IV device code number to specify a card reader is 1 and is used throughout this book, but the reader is cautioned to determine the code number used at the installation where his programs will be processed.
fn	An integer *FØRMAT statement number* which references the statement that describes the input record. Note that "dc" and "fn" must be separated by a comma, enclosed in parentheses, and appear in the order indicated.
vn$_1$, . . . vn$_m$	Represents one or more optional *variable names* separated by delimiters. All variable names listed must agree both in mode and sequence with the format codes specified in the referenced FØRMAT statement.

A READ statement can reference a FØRMAT statement only by an integer number. But, it can reference an input device either by an integer number or by an integer variable name which has been initialized to a numeric value by some other statement in the program. The integer variable name option can be particularly convenient if the program is to be processed at two or more installations which use different device codes.

To illustrate, suppose a program contains 20 READ statements which each include the integer number 1 to reference the card input device. Before it can be processed at an installation using some other device code, all 20 READ statements must be changed.

But, suppose the programmer had used the variable name INCARD to reference the input device and had initialized INCARD to 1 by this arithmetic statement:

$\overline{|12345|6|7}$

        INCARD=1

In this case, the device code referenced by each of the 20 READ statements could automatically be changed by simply changing the integer constant in the arithmetic statement illustrated above.

Equal Number of Variable Names and Available Data Fields. Regardless of how many fields a card contains, only those specified by a FØRMAT statement are available for reading. To illustrate this point, assume that a data card contains two integer fields followed by two floating point fields:

$\overline{|12|345|6789|}$
 11|222|3.33|.444

If all data in the above card is required for the problem to be solved, each of the four fields must be described by a FØRMAT statement. To illustrate:

$\overline{|12345|6|7}$

  55   FØRMAT(I2,I3,F4.2,F4.3)

Of course, it is not necessary to store data which is not required for the problem to be solved. Data fields which are not described in a FØRMAT statement are not available for reading. Thus, if only the first field (columns 1 and 2) is to be processed, the data field card could be described as follows:

$\overline{|12345|6|7}$

  66   FØRMAT(I2)

When a READ statement is executed, the available data is stored at locations indicated by the list of variable names. To illustrate, assume the following data card:

$\overline{|12|34|56789|}$
 24|75|17.45|.333|.281

The following two statements will cause the above data card to be read, and the data in all but the fourth field will be stored:

$\overline{|12345|6|7}$

  77   FØRMAT(I2,I2,F5.2,4X,F4.3)
        READ(1,77)I,N,A,B

Four available data fields are specified by the format codes (the X field is ignored), and an equal number of variable names appear in the READ list. Note, particularly, how the implied mode of the variable names listed in

the READ statement agrees sequentially with the mode of the data specified by the codes in the FØRMAT statement. After the above READ
statement is executed, the variable names listed will be initialized to the
following values:

I	24
N	75
A	17.45
B	.281

The READ statement is only one way to initialize the values of variable
names. As discussed previously, arithmetic statements can also be used. I,
N, A, and B could have been initialized to the same values as in the preceding illustration by these four statements:

| $\overline{12345|6|7}$ |
| I=24 |
| N=75 |
| A=17.45 |
| B=.281 |

It should be noted that constants are *fixed* values which cannot be
changed during execution of a program. Thus, if all data are supplied directly in the program as constants, each time the program is executed it will
compute the same results. On the other hand, if data are supplied from
cards which are not a part of the source program, the computed results will
vary according to the data values supplied. Thus, a program which includes
one or more READ statements can be supplied with *variable* data.

Many programs which include READ statements also include constants.
For example, a payroll program may include the social security rate as a
constant, but the number of hours and rate of pay would ordinarily be supplied from an outside source such as a data card. This approach would
make it possible to use the same program, but different data cards, each
payroll period. Only a change in the problem, such as the social security
rate or I/O requirements, would require a change in the program. Compared to the alternative of supplying all data as constants, this approach
would be much more practical. It would save compilation time as well as
programming time because the program would not have to be recompiled
unless it was changed.

The list of variable names in a READ statement must agree in mode
and sequence with the available data fields specified by the format codes,
but it is not necessary for the *number* of names to agree with the number of
available data fields. The READ list may contain fewer variable names
than the number of format codes specified in the FØRMAT statement, or it
may contain more as illustrated in the following two sections.

Fewer Variable Names Than Available Data Fields. If the list contains fewer variable names than the number of available data fields specified by the format codes, reading stops when the list is satisfied; additional data fields specified by format codes are ignored. In other words, it is the READ statement that determines how many fields will be read, not the FØRMAT statement which only describes the fields and indicates how many are available.

To illustrate, assume the following two input data cards, each containing six fields:

```
12 345 678 9
27 123 856 12 17.32 867.18
```

```
12 345 678 9
44 555 666 77 88.88 999.99
```

As a result of the following statements:

```
12345 6 7
   22    FØRMAT(I2,T6,I3,2X,F5.2,F6.2)
         READ(1,22)M,N,R
```

only the first of the two input data cards will be read; and M, N, and R will be initialized to the current value of 27, 856, and 17.32 respectively. The T6 and 2X format codes specify that two of the six data fields are to be ignored leaving four data fields (I2,I3,F5.2, and F6.2) available for reading. But the READ list contains only three variable names. Because reading stops when the list is satisfied, the last field available for reading (F6.2) is ignored.

Each time a READ statement is executed, one record is read. To further illustrate, the following series of statements:

```
12345 6 7
   1    FØRMAT(I2,T6,I3,2X,F5.2,F6.2)
        READ(1,1)M
        READ(1,1)N
```

will cause the computer to read the first data field in each of the two input data cards, and M and N will be initialized to 27 and 44 respectively. To reiterate, the READ statement determines the number of fields to be read, not the FØRMAT statement. If the same variable name had been used in both READ statements, it would have a current value of 27 after execution of the first and 44 after execution of the second. Remember, read-in is destructive.

More Variable Names Than Available Data Fields. The READ list may contain more variable names than the number of available data fields specified by the format codes. If so, what occurs is slightly more complex and requires a more lengthy explanation.

The number of variable names listed in the READ statement determines the number of data fields to be read; reading continues until the list is satisfied. The format codes enclosed in parentheses describe one card; the computer automatically assumes the end of the record has been reached when it gets to the close (rightmost) parenthesis. Thus, if the list contains more variable names than the number of fields specified by the FØRMAT statement, two or more cards are required to satisfy the list. Exactly how does the computer handle this situation? Whenever it reaches the close (rightmost) parenthesis of the FØRMAT statement, it automatically reads another card, transfers back to the open (leftmost) parenthesis, and reuses the same format codes in sequence until the list is satisfied.

To illustrate what happens when there are five variable names in the list but only three format codes specifying data available for reading, assume the following two data cards:

```
┌12345│67│89│       │
 11.11│66│22│333│77.77
```

```
┌12345│67│89│       │
 45.67│55│89│012│88.88
```

and the following statements:

```
┌12345│6│7
   6   FØRMAT(F5.2,2X,I2,I3)
       READ(1,6)B,I,J,A,K
```

After execution of the above statements, the following values will be stored:

Variable Name	Value Stored
B	11.11
I	22
J	333
A	45.67
K	89

The data cards each contain five fields, but the format codes only specify three to be available for reading. The second field is ignored because of the X format code, and the last is ignored because it is not specified. It should be noted that if the last two variable names in the list had not been in floating point and integer mode, respectively, the program would fail. The variable names and the corresponding format codes *must* be consistent in mode.

One final point—the programmer could have written two READ statements instead of one:

⌐12345|6|7
```
6    FØRMAT(F5.2,2X,I2,I3)
     READ(1,6)B,I,J
     READ(1,6)A,K
```

and the values stored at B, I, J, A, and K would be the same as previously indicated. This latter series of statements requires more time to write, to keypunch, and to execute. It also results in more machine-language instructions, so more storage area is required for the object program.

Selective Reading. Designing a READ statement which includes more variable names than the number of corresponding format codes or includes more than one READ statement in the program are only two of the many techniques that can be used to cause the computer to read more than one input data card. One more technique will be discussed in this section; following chapters will cover more advanced methods.

To understand selective reading, it is necessary to realize the sequence of what happens to an input card when a READ statement is executed. The execution of a READ statement always causes one card to be fed from the hopper of the card reader into what is called the "reading station." The reading station is designed to detect the presence or absence of holes in the various punching positions in the card. Only the card located at the reading station can be read, and a card must always be fed before it can be read. Only one card can be located at this station at any one time. The card located at the reading station is automatically ejected into a stacker, where it is no longer available for reading, whenever another card is fed into this station.

Figure 5–1 illustrates this sequence of steps.

FIGURE 5–1
Schematic of the Card Path through a Card Reader Device

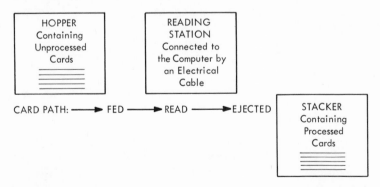

It was pointed out earlier in this chapter that the close (rightmost) parenthesis of the FØRMAT statement indicates the end of the record. If the READ list contains more variable names than the number of data fields available according to the format codes specified, another card is automatically fed into the reading station. The computer then returns to the open (leftmost) parenthesis and reads the new card, reusing the same format codes, until the READ list is satisfied.

A slash (/) within the parentheses of a FØRMAT statement also indicates the end of a record and causes a new card to be fed. But instead of returning to the open (leftmost) parenthesis and reusing the format codes, the computer continues rightward using any remaining available format codes until the READ list is satisfied or the close (rightmost) parenthesis is encountered. Each slash encountered during the execution of a READ statement causes the card at the reading station to be ejected into the stacker and another card to be fed into position for reading.

To illustrate, assume the following statements:

$\overline{|12345|6|7}$

```
33   FØRMAT(I4/I3)
     READ(1,33)M,N
```

Execution of the READ statement will cause the computer to feed one card. (Remember, this statement *always* causes a card to be fed to begin the operation.) Next, the integer data contained in the first four columns (I4) will be read and stored at M. Next, the slash will cause another card to be fed into the reading station. Finally, the integer data contained in the *first* three columns (I3) of the second card will be read and stored at N. Because the list is satisfied before the close (rightmost) parenthesis is reached, no more cards will be fed or read. A close examination of the FØRMAT statement will reveal that the slash takes the place of the comma which is usually required as a delimiter to separate the format codes.

Note that the preceding two statements have the same effect as the following four:

$\overline{|12345|6|7}$

```
11   FØRMAT(I4)
22   FØRMAT(I3)
     READ(1,11)M
     READ(1,22)N
```

There are usually several ways to read data into internal storage, some of which are more convenient than others. To illustrate, assume a program is to be written which will process the following two data cards:

$\overline{|12345|6789}$
|27.00|

$\overline{|12345|6789}$
|11.50|

This series of four statements illustrates one way to transfer data from the above cards into internal storage:

```
|12345|6|7
    4   FØRMAT(F5.2)
    5   FØRMAT(F5.2)
        READ(1,4)DATA1
        READ(1,5)DATA2
```

Because both data cards, in this case, can be described with the same format code, it is unnecessary to use two FØRMAT statements. Instead, both READ statements can reference the same FØRMAT statement. The following series of three statements illustrate a second way to read in the two data cards:

```
|12345|6|7
    6   FØRMAT(F5.2)
        READ(1,6)DATA1
        READ(1,6)DATA2
```

In this particular problem, it is unnecessary to use two READ statements; the following two statements illustrate a third way to do the same job:

```
|12345|6|7
    7   FØRMAT(F5.2)
        READ(1,7)DATA1,DATA2
```

A fourth way, illustrated below, is to use a slash in the FØRMAT statement:

```
|12345|6|7
    8   FØRMAT(F5.2/F5.2)
        READ(1,8)DATA1,DATA2
```

Of the four ways to store data, illustrated in the preceding examples, the third is the most convenient because less coding is required. But, this method cannot be used unless both data fields can be described by the same format code. To illustrate, assume the data in the following two cards is to be read into internal storage:

```
|12|3456789
 27|
```

```
|12345|6789
 11.50|
```

In this case, the two cards contain different types of data as well as different field lengths, so the same format code cannot be used to describe both fields.

The following four statements illustrate an inconvenient way to read in the two data cards:

```
|12345|6|7‾‾
    9   FØRMAT(I2)
   10   FØRMAT(F5.2)
        READ(1,9)NDATA1
        READ(1,10)DATA2
```

The following two statements, which can be used instead of the preceding four, illustrate the convenience of a slash:

```
|12345|6|7‾‾
   11   FØRMAT(I2/F5.2)
        READ(1,11)NDATA1,DATA2
```

For another example, suppose a program is to be written which will compute the total amount of sales for one of the many products sold by a company. There are two data cards for each product, and each contains two fields. The first field on each card indicates the product identification number. The second indicates the amount of sales; one card indicates year-to-date sales prior to the current month, and the other indicates sales for the current month only. Following are the two data cards for product number 6666:

```
|1234|56789‾‾
 6666|12345.78
```
```
|1234|56789‾‾
 6666|222.22
```

If a slash is used, one FØRMAT statement can describe both data cards. The following statements tell the computer to store the data from each of the four fields:

```
|12345|6|7‾‾
   38   FØRMAT(I4,F8.2/I4,F6.2)
        READ(1,38)IDNUMB,YR2DAT,IDNUMB,CURENT
```

Data is stored at the variable names in the same sequence in which these names appear in the READ list from left to right. Thus, the computer will store 6666 from the first card at IDNUMB, but later it will replace this value with the identification number from the second card which, in this case, is also 6666. This is not a recommended technique, but it is illustrated to show what happens when a variable name appears more than once in a READ statement.

The following statements tell the computer to store the identification number from only the first card:

⌐12345⌐6⌐7
```
 39   FØRMAT(I4,F8.2/4X,F6.2)
      READ(1,39)IDNUMB,YR2DAT,CURENT
```

In this case, only three fields are available for reading; so the READ list includes only three variable names. The same results will be obtained if T5 is substituted for the 4X format code. Note that a T or X format code tells the computer to skip to the next *field,* but a slash tells it to skip to the next *record.* The slash permits the programmer to describe more than one record in one FØRMAT statement.

If the problem does not require that the identification number be stored, it may be ignored on both cards by the following statements:

⌐12345⌐6⌐7
```
 40   FØRMAT(4X,F8.2/T5,F6.2)
      READ(1,40)YR2DAT,CURENT
```

Sometimes a programmer may elect to use T or X format codes to omit reading selected fields. Likewise, he may elect to omit reading one or more entire records which is a technique called *selective reading.* During a reading operation, each slash encountered causes a card to be fed. Thus, if two or more slashes appear in sequence, one or more cards will be fed without being read. The next two statements illustrate this selective reading technique.

⌐12345⌐6⌐7
```
 88   FØRMAT(//I2,I3///I4/)
      READ(1,88)I,J,K
```

As always, the READ statement causes one card to be fed into the reading station. But, before any reading takes place, the two slashes cause two more cards to be fed. This automatically ejects the first two cards, which are not read, and places the third card at the reading station. Next, the third card is read, and the integer data in the first five columns (I2,I3) are stored at I and J. Next, three more cards (one for each slash) are fed, and the first four columns (I4) from the last of these cards are read and stored as the current value of K. The list is now satisfied, but the final slash causes one more card to be fed. This final card is not available for reading even though another READ statement is executed later in the program because the READ statement, as always, ejects the card at the reading station and replaces it with another card. (Incidentally, if no more READ statements are executed during the program, this final card will automatically be ejected into the stacker when the program terminates.)

The effect of these statements can perhaps be more clearly illustrated if it is assumed that the input hopper contains the following data cards:

1⟌12345
   77777

2⟌12345
   65432

3⟌12345
   11222

4⟌12345
   44444

5⟌12345
   55555

6⟌12345
   12345

7⟌12345
   78901

8⟌12345
   24680

The execution of the READ statement will cause the first seven cards to be *fed,* but only data from cards 3 and 6 will be *read.* Following execution of the READ statement, card 8 will remain in the input hopper, card 7 will be located at the reading station, and the first six cards will be in the stacker. The following data will be stored:

Variable Name	Data Stored
I	11
J	222
K	1234

Note that when slashes appear at the beginning or end of a FØRMAT statement, the number of records (cards in this case) skipped equals the number of slashes; if slashes are embedded, the number of records skipped is one less than the number of slashes appearing in sequence.

OUTPUT

Output statements are used to transmit data from internal storage to a record in an external output device. Many types of output devices may be used including magnetic tape drives, magnetic disk drives, cathode ray tubes, card punches, and printers. The type of output selected by the programmer will depend upon the requirements of the problem to be solved. Generally, as a matter of convenience, the final solution will be printed. If the output will later be required as input to the same or a different program, it will probably be in some form which is machine readable. Programs are often designed to generate more than one kind of output.

No attempt will be made in this book to enter into a full discussion of all the various devices which are available for output; such a discussion is reserved for a course in computer hardware or systems design. However, the output from two important devices, the card punch and the high-speed printer, will be discussed in detail. Card output will be discussed first, followed by printed output.

Data Card Output

Output data cards, like input data cards, have no restrictions as to format. The number, sequence, and length of the fields must be designed to fit the requirements of the problem. Because the format is optional with the programmer rather than implied by the rules of FORTRAN, it must be explicitly described to the computer via a nonexecutable FØRMAT statement.

The FØRMAT Statement. The general form of a FØRMAT statement that is referenced by a WRITE statement is identical to that of a FØRMAT statement referenced by a READ statement which was illustrated previously in this chapter. If desired, one FØRMAT statement may be referenced by one or more READ and/or WRITE statements.

Format Codes. The general form of the format codes used to describe input and output data are also identical, but a few differences in restrictions and uses will be discussed next.

It is permissible to omit decimal points in floating point fields on input data cards. But, on output data cards, a decimal point is always automatically punched in the position indicated by an F, E, or D format code specification.

The X format code, when used to describe input cards, indicates the field is not to be read. When used to describe output cards, it indicates the field is not to be punched, or stated another way, the field is to be left blank.

On input data cards, the T format code may be used to indicate where to begin reading. On output data cards, it may be used to indicate where to begin writing. Any columns skipped over will, of course, be blank.

The WRITE Statement. Two statements are required to transmit data from internal storage into an output data card. One is the FØRMAT statement previously covered, the other is the WRITE statement which is discussed in this section. The WRITE statement is an executable I/O statement which can direct the computer to write one or more data cards via the card punch. The WRITE statement can also be used for other types of output records, but this section is concerned with only punched cards as output media.

General Form and Function.   The WRITE statement tells the computer what to write, specifies the output device where the record is located, and references a FØRMAT statement which describes the record. The general form is similar to the READ statement, but particular attention should be directed to the difference in the device code specification:

```
|12345|6|7
```

nnnnn   WRITE(dc,fn)vn$_1$,vn$_2$, . . . vn$_m$

Legend:

nnnnn	Any unique one- to five-digit integer which specifies the statement *number*. It is required only if the statement is referenced by another statement in the program.
WRITE	A key word specifying the operation to be performed.
dc	An integer number, or an integer variable name, which specifies the *device code*. The standard FORTRAN IV device code number is 2 for the card punch and 3 for the printer. These codes are used throughout this book, but the reader is again cautioned to determine the device code numbers used at the installation where his programs will be processed.
fn	An integer *FØRMAT statement number* which references the statement that describes the output record. Note that "dc" and "fn" must be separated by a comma enclosed in parentheses and appear in the order indicated.
vn$_1$, . . . vn$_m$	Represents one or more optional *variable names* separated by delimiters. All variable names listed must agree both in mode and sequence with the format codes specified in the referenced FØRMAT statement.

To illustrate the WRITE statement, and at the same time to review the FØRMAT and READ statements, consider the following input data card:

```
|12|34|5678|9
 11|22|7.77|3.33
```

and the following series of statements:

```
|12345|6|7
    77   FØRMAT(2I2,T9,F4.2)
         READ(1,77)I,N,A
         WRITE(2,77)I,N,A
    88   WRITE(2,77)N,I,A
```

which will cause the following two output data cards to be punched:

```
|12|34|5678|9
 11|22|    |3.33
```

```
|12|34|5678|9
 22|11|    |3.33
```

The first output card is an exact duplicate of the input card except that the third field is blank; but the second output card, resulting from the execution of statement number 88, has the first two data fields reversed because N precedes I in the list of variable names.

All three I/O statements reference the same FØRMAT statement in the preceding illustration. This technique is a convenience to both the programmer and the keypunch operator but can be used in relatively few applications. It can be used only if the variable names and the corresponding format codes are in the same mode (integer or floating point) and if the field lengths are sufficient to accommodate the data. To illustrate:

```
┌123│45│67│89
 111│22│33│.4
```

Assume that the problem requires that the above card be read in and that an output card be punched with the same data but with the fields in a different sequence. The WRITE statement in the following series of statements will cause some problems:

```
┌12345│6│7
   99   FØRMAT(I3,I2,I2,F2.1)
        READ(1,99)K,L,M,X
        WRITE(2,99)L,K,X,M
```

After the READ statement is executed, the variable names will have the following current values:

Variable Name	Current Value
K	111
L	22
M	33
X	.4

The WRITE statement will cause the computer to write the two-digit current value of L in the first three-column integer field in the output card because the data fits the field and the modes agree. At this point, the problems begin. The second integer field is only two columns in length so it cannot accommodate the three-digit current value of K. The transportation of X and M results in a conflict in mode even though the field lengths are compatible. All these problems could be solved by adding the following statement to the partial program:

```
┌12345│6│7
   77   FØRMAT(I2,I3,F2.1,I2)
```

Of course, the format number specified in the WRITE statement must be changed from 99 to 77 so it would reference this additional statement.

Scaling. It is the programmer's responsibility to specify an output field of sufficient size to accommodate the output data. The process of determining the required field size is called *scaling*. This process can perhaps best be described by an illustration.

Suppose an input data card has two five-column fields, each containing data punched in ordinary decimal form. The solution to the problem requires that the data in the first field be multiplied times the data in the second field. The output card is to contain only the product of the multiplication. The programmer has prepared the following statements:

```
|12345|6|7
   66   FØRMAT(F5.2,F5.2)
        READ(1,66)H,R
        ANSWER=H*R
        WRITE(2,44)ANSWER
   44   FØRMAT(
```

Before he can complete FØRMAT statement number 44, the programmer must go through the process of scaling. Assume that both input fields contain unsigned data (if unsigned, it is assumed to be positive). The maximum value of ANSWER requires a format code of F9.4 (99.99 times 99.99 equals 9998.0001).

The programmer must always specify a field of sufficient length to accommodate all whole numbers in his output (that is, the numbers preceding the decimal point). But, he may increase or decrease the length of the fraction (that is, the number of decimal point positions) according to the required precision. Thus, if he specifies F12.7, the maximum value of ANSWER will be punched as 9998.0001000 in the output card field. If this is a commercial application, only two decimal positions (to indicate dollars and cents) might be required. The output field will contain the value 9998.00 if the format code F7.2 is specified.

But suppose the problem is to determine the rental charge in dollars and cents for a certain machine. H represents the hours the machine was used during one day, and R represents the rate per hour which does not exceed $3.00. Because there are only 24 hours in a day, the maximum value of ANSWER is 72.00 which can be punched in an F5.2 field.

The foregoing illustration indicates that the programmer must be thoroughly familiar with all the facts of the problem to be solved before attempting the scaling process.

It is always the programmer's responsibility to specify a field of sufficient length to accommodate the maximum possible output value. If the value 72.00 is to be punched in an output card, the format code must specify a field length of five or more columns. If a field length of four or less is specified, the computer will *not* truncate one or more digits. Instead, it will tell the programmer that his field length specification is in error by punching an asterisk in each column in the output field. If an attempt is made to punch the value 72.00 using the following FØRMAT statement:

```
|12345|6|7
    55   FØRMAT(F4.2)
```

the resulting output will be:

```
|12345|6|7
****
```

Other programmer errors can also result in an asterisk in each column of the specified output field. If a variable name in a WRITE statement does not agree in mode to the corresponding format code or if a variable name in a WRITE statement is misspelled, the programmer can expect to see "stars" in his output.

Particular caution is required in scaling exponential form output data. As illustrated previously, the programmer is allowed considerable flexibility with *input* data in exponential form. The exponent may vary from two to four columns in length. One position is required for the letter E or D. If the exponent is negative, one position is required for the sign; but if it is positive, the position may be signed, left blank, or omitted. The actual numeric exponent may occupy either one or two positions. For example, E1, E+1, E 1, E 01, or E 1 are all valid methods of expressing input exponents. But, if exponential form *output* is specified, the exponent *always* occupies four positions. One position is required for the letter E or D, one position for the sign which is blank if positive, and two positions for the numeric exponent. If the numeric exponent is only one digit in length, it is automatically preceded by a zero.

There is one more factor to be considered in the scaling process. If there is a possibility that an output field will contain a negative value, one column must be allowed for the minus sign. It will automatically be punched in the column preceding the first significant digit in the field unless no space is allowed in which case *it will be truncated and the value will appear to be positive!* Many programmers follow the practice of always allowing an extra field position for the minus sign even though the solution to the problem logically calls for a positive answer. The reason for this practice will be explained by use of another illustration.

A program has been written to compute the number of hats on hand at year-end for a clothing store. Essentially, the program is designed to add the units in the beginning inventory to the units purchased and to subtract from this sum the units sold to arrive at the solution. Obviously, the store cannot have a quantity of less than zero hats on hand at year-end, so the program logically appears to call for a positive answer. But there are two basic reasons why the computer may produce a negative result. First, there may be an error in input, such as incorrect, duplicate, or omitted data. Second, the programmer may have committed one or more logic errors when writing his program such as adding instead of subtracting, using incorrect format codes, etc.

It should be obvious that the scaling process required for complex mathematical problems can be quite complicated and time consuming, but no complex scaling is required for the solution to any problems in this book. A good rule to follow, if there are no restrictions as to the output format, is to always allow one or more extra columns in the output field.

Selective Writing. Selective reading, described earlier in this chapter, causes certain input data cards to be ignored because they are fed without being read. On the other hand, selective writing, discussed in this section, causes certain output data cards to be ignored because they are ejected without being written (punched).

If the program calls for data card output, the computer operator is responsible for having blank (unpunched) cards in the card punch hopper and one card located at the "writing station." The writing station is designed to punch holes in the various punching positions as directed by the WRITE statement. Only one card can be located at this station at any one time. The execution of the WRITE statement always causes one or more cards to be ejected into the stacker. Before a WRITE statement is executed, there must always be a card at the writing station to initialize the operation. Each time a card is ejected a new card is automatically fed from the hopper into the writing station. Figure 5–2 illustrates these series of steps.

FIGURE 5–2
Schematic of the Card Path through a Card Punch Device

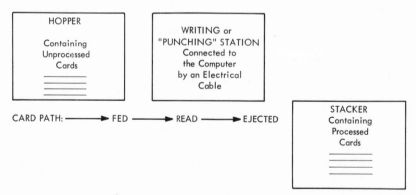

The schematic illustrations (Figures 5–1 and 5–2) are nearly identical for a card reader and a card punch. The only difference is that the former device has a "reading station," the latter a "writing station." But the sequence of operations in reading and writing are quite different. The READ statement always causes one or more input cards to be fed; a card must be fed before it can be read. The WRITE statement always causes one or more output cards to be ejected, but any writing must be done before it is ejected.

Writing, like reading, always continues until the list is satisfied. If the number of variable names in the WRITE list is less than or equal to the number of available format codes, the card is ejected when the list is satisfied. If the WRITE list contains more variable names than the number of available format codes, a card is ejected each time a close (rightmost) parenthesis is reached; writing then continues until the list is satisfied at which time the last card written is ejected.

Slashes in a FØRMAT statement also indicate the end of a record. As many slashes may be used as are required for the problem, and they may appear in any sequence. Each slash within the format code section causes a record to be ejected. The next field written is determined by the format code following the slash. The computer "looks ahead" at the format codes before ejecting a card when the list is satisfied. If the last format code used to satisfy the list is followed by one or more slashes instead of another format code, the computer will eject one card for each slash; it will then eject one more card, as always, because the list is satisfied.

To illustrate selective writing, assume that the following values are stored in the computer:

Variable Name	Value Stored
I	11
J	222
K	1234

Further assume that the program includes the following statements:

```
|12345|6|7
   88   FØRMAT(//I2,I3///I4/ )
        WRITE(2,88)I,J,K
```

As always, a card must be located at the writing station before the WRITE statement is executed. But, before any writing takes place, the two slashes cause two cards to be ejected. The third card is now located at the writing station. The first five columns of this card (I2,I3) are written (punched) with the integer data stored at I and J. The next three slashes cause three more cards to be rejected. The first of these three is the card containing I and J, the next two are blank. Next, the first four columns (I4) are punched with the data stored at K. The last slash ejects the card containing K. Finally, because the list is now satisfied, one more blank card is ejected.

The output cards will appear as follows:

1⌐123456‾

2⌐123456‾

3⌐123456‾
  11|222

4⌐123456‾

5⌐123456‾

6⌐123456‾
  1234

7⌐123456‾

Note again that if slashes appear at the beginning or end of a FØRMAT statement, the number of records skipped is equal to the number of slashes; but if slashes are embedded, the number of records skipped is one less than the number of slashes appearing in sequence.

It is suggested that this illustration of the effects of slashes in a FØRMAT statement which is referenced by a WRITE statement be compared to the effects when referenced by a READ statement illustrated previously in this chapter. To facilitate comparison, the FØRMAT statements, data, and variable name lists are identical in both illustrations. (See pages 73–74.)

Printed Output

The discussion, thus far, in this chapter has been limited to card input and output. The previous section described the operation of the card punch. Each output card is considered to be a "record" when the card punch is used as the output device. A card is ejected when a slash or a close (rightmost) parenthesis is reached or when the list is satisfied. FØRMAT statements may describe cards (records) as less than but never more than 80 columns in length. Each line of printing is considered to be a "record" when the printer is used as the output device. The record is ejected (that is, the paper advances one line) if the close (rightmost) parenthesis is reached *before* the WRITE list is satisfied.

Several models of printers are available with System/360 and/370. Models vary as to speed, number of print positions (length of the line in "columns"), and size of the character set (number of different digits, letters, and special characters). Even though a printer may have 120 or 132 print positions, the record described should obviously never exceed the width of the paper stock used for output. For purposes of illustration, it will be assumed in this book that the printer has 120 character positions and the paper width is of corresponding size. It will also be assumed that the character set includes all valid FORTRAN numbers, letters, and special characters and also the following special characters (which can also be read as input data):

$$\&\ ''\ :\ >\ ?\ \#\ \%\ @\ <\ ;$$

The Output Image.   Before data is transmitted from internal storage to an output device, it goes through an *editing* process. This process, among other things, right-justifies the data in the field specified by the format code. It replaces high-order (leftmost) zeros with blanks. It also eliminates plus signs because unsigned data is assumed to be positive. The data actually transferred from internal storage to the output device is sometimes called the *output image.* Thus, if the value of N is +37, and the format code is specified as I4, the output image will contain blanks in the first two field positions followed by a 3 and 7 respectively in the last two positions.

If the output device is a card punch, the output record (a punched card) will exactly correspond to the output image. But, if the output device is a printer, the output record (one line of printing) will not exactly correspond to the output image. The output image for a printed record must always be constructed so that it contains one more character than the actual desired output. The extra character required must always be located in the first (leftmost) position of the output image. The character contained in this first position never appears in the output; that is, it is not printed. It is called the *carriage control character* and is used by the printer to control line spacing.

Line Spacing Control.   There are two types of spacing on printed output, vertical and horizontal; and both are controlled by the FØRMAT statement. *Vertical* spacing can be controlled by slashes and by the carriage control character discussed in this section. *Horizontal* spacing can be controlled by the T and X format codes, by including spaces in a Hollerith message or a literal within parentheses, and by overformatting.

When a record is printed, the output image is automatically shifted one position to the left so that the actual output does not contain the first character. The second character in the output image becomes the first character printed in the actual output; the third character in the output image is printed in the second position; the fourth character in the third position, etc. Thus, to print 120 characters on one line of printed output, the FØRMAT statement must be constructed to create an output image 121 positions in length. The first character in the output image, which is used for carriage control, is interpreted by the printing device as follows:

First Character in Output Image	Paper Advance before Printing
+	No advance
Blank	One line
0 (zero)	Two lines
1	First line of next page

There are several methods which can be used to cause the output image to contain the desired first character which controls *vertical* line spacing. These will be discussed in the following sections.

X Format Code. This code causes blanks in output. If used as the *first* code in the FØRMAT statement, it causes the output image to contain a blank in the first position. When the output image is shifted left, the blank becomes the carriage control character. As a result, when a WRITE statement is executed, the paper will advance one line before printing. For example, if A has a value of 12.45, the following statements:

$\overline{\lceil 12345 \vert 6 \vert 7}$

    17   FØRMAT(1X,F5.2)
          WRITE(3,17)A

will cause the value of A to be printed in the first five printing positions. Device number 3, indicated parenthetically in the WRITE statement, is the standard FORTRAN code for a printer.

T Format Code. This code can also be used to cause a blank in the carriage control position of the output image. The following statements will have the same effect as the preceding two statements:

$\overline{\lceil 12345 \vert 6 \vert 7}$

    18   FØRMAT(T2,F5.2)
          WRITE(3,18)A

The T2 format code specifies that the first (and only) available field begins in position 2, so the first position of the output image is blank. But, when the output image is shifted left one position, the blank becomes the carriage control character which causes the paper to advance one line before the record is printed.

Overformatting. Another technique that can be used to cause the paper to advance one line before printing is to *overformat* the first field; that is, specify the field longer in length than required for the output data. For example, if the first output field is determined via the scaling process to contain a positive value with a maximum length of five positions, the programmer might specify the format code as F6.2 instead of F5.2. This will cause the first position in the output image to contain a blank because high-order zeros and plus signs are edited out.

The overformatting technique, as well as the X and T format codes, can also be used to insert blanks between output data fields thus providing *horizontal* spacing. This is usually desirable on printed output because it facilitates reading. For example, if I, J, and K have current values of 111, 222, and 333 respectively, the following statements will cause I to be printed in the first three positions and will force three blanks between each data field:

|1̄2345|6|7
3   FØRMAT(I4,I6,I6)
     WRITE(3,3)I,J,K

The resulting printed output will be:

|1̄23|456789|
111| 222| 333

The three techniques discussed thus far have obvious limitations. They cannot be used to suppress vertical line spacing. They can provide only "single spacing." The two methods described next can provide any desired character in the carriage control position of the output image and thus provide any possible vertical spacing.

H Format Code. The H or "Hollerith" format code allows the programmer to write any message he desires within the FØRMAT statement. When the FØRMAT statement containing a "Hollerith message" is referenced by a WRITE statement, the message is automatically placed in the output image. The general form of the H format code is:

$$1Hm$$

Legend:

l   An integer number which specifies the *length* of the message field in columns or print positions.

H   Specifies the field contains a "Hollerith message."

m   Represents the *message* which must contain the exact number of characters specified by the field length. The message may be composed of any valid data characters.

The following incomplete statements provide all possible carriage control characters in the first position of the output image:

|1̄2345|6|7
     FØRMAT(1H+,...)
     FØRMAT(1H ,...)
     FØRMAT(1H0 ,...)
     FØRMAT(1H1 ,...)

H format codes may appear in any sequence in the FØRMAT statement. A Hollerith message is not restricted to the 48 valid FORTRAN characters; it may include any valid *data* character. Although it may be used for carriage control, its main purpose is to make the output more easily understood by the reader. For example, assume that the stored values of NUMEMP and PAY are 27 and 16.20 respectively. The following statements:

|1̄2345|6|7
16   FØRMAT(12H EMPLØYEE # ,I2,11H WAS PAID $,F5.2)
      WRITE(3,16)NUMEMP,PAY

will result in the following printed output:

|12345|6|7

EMPLOYEE # 27 WAS PAID $16.20

Note that the first Hollerith message contains three blanks. The first blank is used for carriage control so does not appear in the printed output. The second blank provides a space between EMPLØYEE and # in the printed output. The last blank results in a space preceding the value of NUMEMP. Contrast this with the second message which does not provide a space following the dollar sign. All characters, *including blanks,* are counted to determine the message length. Note also that no variable name in the WRITE list corresponds to the data in the Hollerith message. The output message is automatically generated as a result of the H format code.

The programmer can think of the Hollerith message as being stored in the FØRMAT statement; each time this statement is referenced by a WRITE statement, the message is automatically written.

A Hollerith message is often called a *literal* because the message is literally written character for character as it appears in the FØRMAT statement. The H format code was the only way literals could be written in older versions of FORTRAN. A new and usually more convenient method is provided in FORTRAN IV which is described next.

Literals within Apostrophes. Literal data may be enclosed within apostrophes, in which case no field length is specified. Either of the following statements will produce the same results when referenced by a WRITE statement:

|12345|6|7

```
7    FØRMAT(5X,13H MY ANSWER IS,F7.2)
4    FØRMAT(5X,'MY ANSWER IS',F7.2)
```

The following incomplete statements provide all possible carriage control characters in the first position of the output image:

|12345|6|7

```
3    FØRMAT('+',...)
9    FØRMAT(' ',...)
5    FØRMAT('0',...)
6    FØRMAT('1',...)
```

This type of literal provides an easy method of writing headings over data columns. For example, these two statements:

|12345|6|7

```
37    FØRMAT(T3,'CØL-1',T9,'CØL-2')
      WRITE(3,37)
```

will produce the following printed output:

```
123456789
```
COL–1 COL–2

The T format code specifies that the first literal begins in column 3; but when the output image is shifted one position to the left, the literal is printed starting in column 2. The apostrophes are *not* printed, only the literal contained within the apostrophes. It is possible to have an apostrophe within a literal if it is indicated by two consecutive apostrophes. For example, the literal 'JØE DØE"S' will be printed as JOE DOE'S. Note that the WRITE statement does not contain a list of variable names because the FØRMAT statement does not contain any format codes which specify data fields.

Unlike variable names, literals may be composed of more than six numbers and/or letters and may include any valid data character. The two literals in the preceding illustration can be treated as one literal at the programmer's option. For example, the following two statements:

```
12345|6|7
```
    38 FØRMAT(T3,'CØL–1 CØL–2')
        WRITE(3,38)

will also produce this output:

```
123456789
```
COL–1 COL–2

Another variation, which will produce the same output, would be to include two blanks preceding CØL–1 in the literal:

```
12345|6|7
```
    39 FØRMAT('   CØL–1 CØL–2')

To illustrate further, the following statements can be used to print a multiple-line heading:

```
12345|6|7
```
    22 FØRMAT(T2,'MARCH')
    66 FØRMAT(1X,'TØTAL')
        WRITE(3,22)
        WRITE(3,66)

The above statements will produce the following printed output:

```
1 2 3 4 5 | 6 | 7
```
MARCH
TOTAL

A more convenient method of producing the same output would be to include a slash in the FØRMAT statement to control the vertical line spacing:

```
|12345|6|7
    44   FØRMAT(T2,'MARCH'/1X,'TØTAL')
         WRITE(3,44)
```

TERMINATING A PROGRAM

All programs have a *logical* as well as a *physical* end. The logical end is that point in the program where all statements have been executed the desired number of times and the program has completed the task for which it was designed. The statements which signal the logical and physical ends of a program are *not* I/O statements. They are included here to finish the presentation of all statements necessary to write complete elementary programs.

The STØP Statement   *CALL EXIT*

The *logical,* not the *physical,* end of a program is indicated by a STØP statement. Its purpose is to tell the computer to terminate execution of the program. It may appear at any point in the program provided it will not be executed until the program is finished. Some programs, illustrated later in this book, have several logical ends so require several STØP statements; but all programs should include at least one. Its general form is:

```
|12345|6|7
    nnnnn   STØP  CALL EXIT
```

Legend:

nnnnn   Any unique one- to five-digit integer which specifies the statement *number.* It is required only if the statement is referenced by another statement in the program.

STØP   A key word which specifies the operation to be performed.

The END Statement

The *physical* end of a program is indicated by an END statement. It tells the computer that any cards which might follow this statement are not a part of the source deck so they are to be ignored in the translation process. Stated another way, the END statement tells the computer that it now has the entire source program so it can begin translating.

The general form of an END statement is:

```
|12345|6|7
         END
```

END is a key word which identifies the statement. It should be noted that this statement is *not* numbered. A number is not required because it is not permissible to reference this statement by another statement in the program. Some compilers permit this statement to be numbered, but others assume an error so this practice is not recommended.

It is important to distinguish between the logical and physical ends of a program. It is possible to have several logical ends but only one physical end. Thus, a program may have no more than one END statement. If it is omitted, the program may not compile.

This completes the presentation of all essential information required to write programs which will solve elementary problems such as those at the end of this chapter. Beginning programmers will soon discover that the art of preparing statements is very exacting. If even one comma is omitted or incorrectly positioned, the program will either fail to compile or it will produce invalid output. Even experienced programmers expect a few "bugs" and consider themselves lucky if a program properly compiles and executes the first time it is processed. Fortunately, much can be learned by searching out and correcting various types of programming errors. Debugging techniques which will be useful to beginning programmers are illustrated and explained in Appendix A.

PROBLEMS

All source program decks processed on IBM System/360 or/370 must be accompanied by system control cards. They are used to direct the computer and are not related to the FORTRAN language. The reader should refer to Appendix D if control cards are not furnished by the instructor.

1. Write a program to compute the gross pay (in dollars and cents) for one employee. No input data card is to be used. Instead, enter the following values into the program as constants:

$$\text{Time} = 40.25 \text{ hours}$$
$$\text{Rate} = \$4.03 \text{ per hour}$$

Required output is one printed line containing a gross pay, time, and rate.

2. Write a program to determine the interest and maturity value of a promissory note (in dollars and cents) where:

$$\text{Interest} = PRT/365$$
$$\text{Maturity Value} = \text{Principal} + \text{Interest}$$

Instead of using an input card, enter all required values into the program as constants.

$$\text{Principal} = \$450.00$$
$$\text{Rate} = 7\%$$
$$\text{Time} = 73 \text{ days}$$

Required output is one printed line containing principal, rate, time, interest, and maturity value.

3. Write a program to compute the capacity in gallons of a cylinder where:

$$\text{Gallons} = \frac{\pi R^2 H}{231}$$

Do not use an input card; enter all required values into the program as constants.

Pi $= 3.1416$
Radius $= 2$ inches
Height $= 25$ inches

Required output is one printed line containing pi, radius, height, and gallons. Each output field is to be separated by two or more blank spaces.

4. Write the program described in Problem 3, but change the output so that it is "single spaced" with the value of: (*a*) pi printed on the first line, (*b*) radius and height on the second line, and (*c*) gallons on the third line.

Use only one WRITE statement.

5. Write a program to convert Fahrenheit temperature to centigrade temperature. The conversion formula is:

$$C = \frac{5}{9}(F{-}32)$$

The Fahrenheit temperature is to be read from the first five columns of an input card which contains a decimal point and any positive temperature (such as 212.0°) in the following format (X's represent digits):

$\overline{|123456}$
XXX.X

The following printed output is to appear on one line and should begin in the first printing position (X's represent digits):

XXX.X DEGREES FAHRENHEIT EQUALS XXX.X DEGREES CENTI-GRADE.

Note that there is a period following the word "CENTIGRADE." The first literal is to be written within apostrophes and the second as a Hollerith message. *Don't forget that an input data card is required for this program.*

6. Write a program to compute the total charge for one customer where net charge equals units times unit price and total charge equals net charge plus freight charge.

The first two cards in the source deck must be comment cards. The first comment should be TØTAL CHARGE PRØGRAM and the second a "blank comment" to provide a blank line in the program listing.

Input consists of two cards. The first input card is in the following format:

Field Name	Card Column	Required Field Contents
Customer Number	1–4	1234
Number of Units	5–7	125
Unit Price	8–12	01.10

The format of the second input card is as follows:

Field Name	Card Column	Required Field Contents
Customer Number	1–4	1234
Freight Charges	5–9	06.25

Use only one READ statement to read the two input cards.

Use two WRITE statements to obtain the output which is to consist of two printed lines separated by one blank line. The first output line is to contain the following "headings" in the position indicated:

Print Positions or "Columns"	Required Field Contents
1–8	CUSTØMER
11–15	UNITS
18–27	UNIT-PRICE
30–36	FREIGHT
39–43	TØTAL

The first two "headings" (CUSTØMER and UNITS) are to be written as one Hollerith message; the others are to be written within apostrophes.

The second output line should be blank, and the third should contain numeric data in the following format:

Field Name	Print Positions or "Columns"	Required Field Contents
Customer Number	3–6	1234
Number of Units	12–14	125
Unit Price	20–24	1.10
Freight Charges	32–35	6.25
Total Charge	39–44	143.75

Don't forget that two input data cards are required for this program.

CHAPTER
6

CONTROL STATEMENTS

THE first five chapters of this book were designed to provide the reader with the technical vocabulary as well as the information required to write elementary but complete programs. Many illustrations were used to explain the uses of statements and to impress the reader with the fact that programming is an art rather than an exact science. The rules of FORTRAN are strict, but there are many optional methods of achieving the same results. Various options may be chosen to save programming time as well as compilation and/or execution time.

Before considering the advanced programming techniques covered in this chapter, it may be advisable to briefly review the general FORTRAN programming routine covered thus far.

BRIEF PROGRAMMING REVIEW

The computer is a robot. It must be told when to start, what to do, and when to stop. The computer operator and certain control cards, described in Appendix D, tell the computer when to start. After the computer is started, the program statements tell the computer what data to use, what steps to take, what to do with the results, and when to stop.

Data is stored internally at symbolic addresses represented by variable names composed by the programmer. The first letter of a variable name implies the mode in which data will be stored as covered in Chapter 3.

All data required for solution of the problem to be solved must be provided to the computer. Such data may be provided directly in the program and/or from an external source. Chapter 4 discussed how constants and arithmetic statements can be used to provide data directly in the program. Chapter 5 described two methods of writing literal data directly into program statements. Chapter 5 also illustrated how the READ statement, referenced to a FØRMAT statement, can be used to obtain data from an external source.

Arithmetic statements, covered in Chapter 4, can be used to tell the computer what to do with the data and how and where to store the results. The arithmetic expression to the right of the equal sign may contain various combinations of variable names and/or constants separated by one or more delimiters. The manner in which such an expression is written determines the type and sequence of calculations to be performed as well as the mode of the result. The variable name to the left of the equal sign implies the mode and specifies the symbolic location where the result of the arithmetic expression is to be stored. If the mode of the result of an arithmetic expression is not consistent with the mode in which the result is to be stored, the computer automatically converts the mode of the result before storing it.

The computer automatically executes statements in the order in which they appear in the program. The location of FØRMAT statements is optional because they are nonexecutable. But, it is the programmer's responsibility to arrange all executable statements in the proper order if he is to obtain the desired results. The computer is told to terminate the program by a STØP statement described in Chapter 2 and illustrated again in Chapter 5. The last statement in every FORTRAN program must always be an END statement.

The STØP statement is the only control statement which has been covered thus far in this book. It has always been the last executable statement because all programs presented have been the "straight-line" type. A straight-line program is designed to execute each statement only once and then terminate. But most problems require a considerable number of "decisions" to be made by the computer. The results of these "decisions" may cause certain statements to be executed more than once, not executed at all, or executed in a different sequence than the order in which they appear in the program. This and the following chapter cover the several control statements which give the programmer the options of "branching" and "looping."

BRANCHING AND LOOPING

Normally the computer executes statements in the order in which they appear in the program. Several control statements are available to enable the programmer to change this normal order of execution. If a control statement is to tell the computer to execute a statement which is *not* the next in sequence, there must obviously be some way to reference the specific statement within the program to which control is to pass. This referencing is done by use of statement numbers (sometimes called "labels").

The preceding chapter illustrated how READ and WRITE statements are referenced to nonexecutable FØRMAT statements by use of statement numbers. Control statements which can change the normal order of execution also reference statements by number, but there is one important distinction—such control statements must always reference an *executable* statement. They cannot reference a nonexecutable statement or a statement number which does not exist in the program.

It is often desirable to cause the computer to go back and repeat the execution of a segment of the program or even the entire program a number of times using different data each time. Some programs require different statements to be executed under different circumstances. Such "decision making" requires a control statement which allows referencing to two or more alternative statement numbers.

The process of causing the computer to skip to an executable statement either preceding or following a control statement is called *branching*. A series of instructions which are repeated during the execution of the program are referred to as a "loop." The process of repeating a series of instructions is called *looping*.

GØ TØ STATEMENTS

Basic FORTRAN IV provides two types of GØ TØ statements. One type is an *unconditional* control statement. It is called "unconditional" because it allows only one statement to be referenced; when executed, it always branches to the same statement.

The other type is a *conditional* control statement. It allows two or more statement numbers to be referenced. It is "conditional" in that it causes branching to one of two or more statements based on a decision made by the computer.

Each type will be discussed and illustrated in the following sections.

Unconditional GØ TØ

This is the less complicated of the two types of GØ TØ statements. The general form is:

| 12345 | 6 | 7 |

nnnnn   GØ TØ sn

Legend:

nnnnn   Any unique one- to five-digit integer which specifies the statement *number*. It is required only if the statement is referenced elsewhere in the program.

GØ TØ   A key word specifying the operation to be performed. The key word is GØTØ (without an embedded blank), but this is one of those rare cases where an embedded blank (which is always permitted in key words) is usually used to improve readability.

sn   An integer number which references an executable statement appearing elsewhere in the program.

It should be noted that no delimiter is used to separate the key word from the statement number. Although unnecessary, programmers often provide a blank following the key word to improve readability.

The unconditional GØ TØ is an executable statement which directs the computer to branch to the statement referenced. It may reference any preceding or following executable statement but should never reference itself. It should be especially noted that *any statement immediately following an unconditional GØ TØ must always be numbered* because unless it can be referenced, it can never be executed.

The unconditional GØ TØ statement should not ordinarily be used in any program which does not also contain one or more conditional control statements. It is not considered good technique if statements appear in a program which can never be executed because it wastes the programmer's time, the compiler's time, and requires more memory area to store the extra instructions. Neither is it considered good programming technique to construct programs in such a manner that the computer is unable to execute a STØP statement and thus terminate execution.

The three complete programs which follow illustrate the effect of an unconditional GØ TØ statement. Each program is particularly designed to demonstrate how this statement when used without one or more conditional control statements can result in poor programming technique. The second and third programs emphasize some of the problems which can result from the use of an unconditional GØ TØ statement.

The following program illustrates the effect of an unconditional GØ TØ statement which directs the computer to skip ahead instead of executing the statements in order.

```
┌12345│6│7
    66   FØRMAT(I6)
         READ(1,66)N
         GØ TØ 22
         N=N−3
    22   WRITE(2,66)N
         STØP
         END
```

The GØ TØ 22 statement causes the computer to branch directly to the WRITE statement and thus ignore the arithmetic statement. This program is constructed to permit the computer to execute the STØP statement and terminate the program, but it demonstrates poor programming technique because the program contains an instruction which can never be executed. In fact, if the unconditional GØ TØ statement and the arithmetic statement were both removed from the source program, it would produce the same results.

This second example uses an unconditional GØ TØ statement which directs the computer to skip back instead of ahead in the program:

```
|12345|6|7
    22    FØRMAT(I4,I5)
    33    FØRMAT(I6)
    70    READ(1,22)I,J
   700    K=I+J
          WRITE(2,33)K
          GØ TØ 70
          STØP
          END
```

The statements in this illustration will be executed in order until the GØ TØ 70 statement is encountered. Each time this unconditional GØ TØ statement is executed it causes the computer to branch back to the READ statement and repeat the program. The sequence in which the statements appear makes it impossible for the program to execute the STØP statement. The program contains an uncontrolled or *perpetual loop* from which there is no possible exit.

Does this mean the computer will run forever? No, there are several types of "interruptions" which will cause the computer to terminate execution of the program. It should be emphasized that these "interruptions" are provided by the computer system, not by the FORTRAN compiler. For example, a program will always terminate during the execution of a READ or WRITE statement which references an I/O device that contains no records. A program will also terminate if an input record is read which contains an invalid character according to the format code specifications. This illustrative program will probably not terminate until either the input or output device runs out of cards or until the READ statement causes the computer to read a system control card containing invalid characters according to the input format codes (I4, I5).

This final example is identical to the preceding one except that the unconditional GØ TØ statement is located in a different sequence and the program contains two keypunching errors occasionally encountered by programmers as a result of improper coding.

```
|12345|6|7
   22   FØRMAT(I4,I5)
   33   FØRMAT(I6)
  7 0 READ(1,22)I,J
  70 0 K=I+J
        GØ TØ 70
        WRITE(2,33)K
        STØP
        END
```

First, note the two keypunching errors. The last digit (zero) of statement numbers 70 and 700 appear in column 6 instead of column 5. A zero in column 6 has the same effect as a blank so the computer assumes that the READ statement is numbered 7 and the arithmetic statement is numbered 70.

Because the unconditional GØ TØ precedes the WRITE statement, the computer will read only one card, execute the arithmetic statement, and then get into a perpetual loop. And what a perpetual loop—it will continually compute and store the sum of I and J! This program is unlikely to be terminated by an I/O device running out of cards or by the reading of invalid input data because only one card is read, and the WRITE statement can never be executed. This program will probably be terminated by the computer operator or possibly by an automatic timing device.

The three preceding illustrations demonstrated the function of the unconditional GØ TØ, how it should *not* be used, and some of the problems it can cause. After conditional control statements have been covered in the following sections, it will be demonstrated how the unconditional GØ TØ can be used effectively.

Computed GØ TØ

The computed GØ TØ can also be used to skip ahead or back in the program. It is a conditional control statement because it causes branching to one of two or more statements based on a decision made by the computer. The decision is based on the current value of a specified integer variable name. The general form is:

```
|12345|6|7
nnnnn   GØ TØ(sn_1,sn_2,...sn_m),ivn
```

Legend:

nnnnn	Any unique one- to five-digit integer which specifies the statement *number*. It is required only if the statement is referenced elsewhere in the program.
GØ TØ	A key word specifying the operation to be performed.

$(sn_1, \ldots sn_m)$ A series of two or more *statement numbers* enclosed in parentheses. Each must be separated by a comma. The statement numbers are used to reference executable statements appearing elsewhere in the program.

,ivn   A comma followed by an *integer variable name* which is required to have a current value established by some previously executed statement in the program. The current value of the integer variable name in a computed GØ TØ statement is often called the "index value."

It should be noted that the open (leftmost) parenthesis is a required delimiter following the key word GØ TØ. The last statement number in the series must be followed by two delimiters: a close (rightmost) parenthesis, and a comma.

The computed GØ TØ tells the computer to branch to the statement whose *position* in the list of statement numbers corresponds to the current value of the integer variable name. Thus, if the current value is 1, it will branch to the statement whose number appears first in the list, if 2 to the second in the list, etc. For example, the statement:

|1 2 3 4 5|6|7
GØ TØ(4,3,3,9),K

will cause a branch to statement number 4 if the current value of K is 1, to statement number 3 if the current value is either 2 or 3, and to statement number 9 if the current value is 4. Note that the computer associates the current value of K with the *position* of the statement number in the list, not with the actual number of the statement. For example, if the current value of K is 4, it does not go to statement number 4. Instead, it goes to the fourth statement number in the list, which in this case is statement number 9.

Because the current value of the integer variable name is used as a sort of pointer or indicator to tell the computer which statement number on the list is to be executed next, it is often called an *index value*. To facilitate discussion, this term will be used throughout the remainder of this book.

The programmer may include as many statement numbers in the list as he desires. The statement numbers may appear in any sequence, and the same number may appear more than once in the list as illustrated in the example.

But, what if the index value in the preceding example had been other than 1, 2, 3, or 4? Then it would be considered an *invalid* index value which will be covered in later sections of this chapter. Before covering various complexities, the use of the computed GØ TØ using valid and convenient index values will be explained via an illustrative program.

Valid and Convenient Index Values. To illustrate the use of the computed GØ TØ statement, consider the following problem. (Examine the problem carefully because several illustrations based on this problem will be used throughout this chapter.)

Lucky Company management has decided to pay a special bonus to all employees. The bonus is to be based upon a percentage of the current weekly payroll. The bonus percentage varies according to the number of years the employee has worked for the company. The weekly payroll cards have been punched with a code to indicate the type of bonus each employee is to receive. The bonus plan may be summarized as follows:

Years of Employment	Percentage of Weekly Pay	Bonus Code
More than 5	200%	01
1 to 5	100	02
Less than 1	50	03

The weekly payroll cards are in the following format:

Field Name	Card Columns	Illustrative Field Contents
Employee Number	1–4	1234
Department Number	5–6	09
Hours Worked	7–11	38.50
Rate per Hour	8–16	11.25
Date of Birth	17–22	120934
Bonus Code	23–24	01

A program is to be written which will read only one input card, compute the designated bonus, then write only one output card. The required format of the output card is as follows:

Field Name	Card Columns
Employee Number	1–4
Regular Pay	5–11
Bonus	12–19
Total Pay	20–27
Bonus Code	79–80

The flowchart in Figure 6–1 illustrates one method of solving the Lucky Company problem. The diamond-shaped "decision symbol" in the flowchart indicates a three-way branch. This will be represented by a computed GØ TØ statement in the illustrative program which follows. After branching to one of the three different bonus computations, the program will flow "straight line" until it is terminated by a STØP statement.

Because the problem does not require the data contained in either the

FIGURE 6-1
Flowchart for the Lucky Company Problem
Illustrating Three Terminal Points

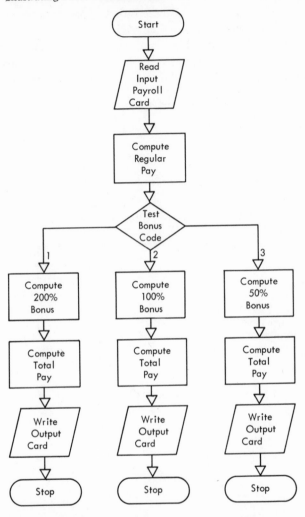

department number or date of birth fields, it will be ignored in the FØRMAT and READ statements. This will save programming time and will reduce the amount of computer memory required to store the object program. The variable name in the computed GØ TØ statement will be called KØDE instead of CØDE because it must be in integer mode. The flowchart in Figure 6-1 calls for three STØP statements, but there can be only one END statement. As always, the END statement must appear last in the program. The following program is one method of solving the Lucky Company problem:

```
|12345|6|7
   77   FØRMAT(I4,2X,2F5.2,T23,I2)
   88   FØRMAT(I4,F7.2,2F8.2,T79,I2)
        READ(1,77)NUMEMP,HØURS,RATE,KØDE
        REGPAY=HØURS*RATE
        GØ TØ(55,65,75),KØDE
   55   BØNUS=REGPAY*2.00
        TØTPAY=REGPAY+BØNUS
        WRITE(2,88)NUMEMP,REGPAY,BØNUS,TØTPAY,KØDE
    1   STØP
   65   BØNUS=REGPAY
        TØTPAY=REGPAY+BØNUS
        WRITE(2,88)NUMEMP,REGPAY,BØNUS,TØTPAY,KØDE
    2   STØP
   75   BØNUS=REGPAY/2.00
        TØTPAY=BØNUS+REGPAY
        WRITE(2,88)NUMEMP,REGPAY,BØNUS,TØTPAY,KØDE
    3   STØP
        END
```

The preceding program follows the flowchart in Figure 6–1. It contains three STØP statements and one conditional control statement. The index value of the computed GØ TØ statement causes a branch to one of three statements which is the beginning of a complete routine. Except for the BØNUS computation, all three routines are identical.

Figure 6–2 is a simplified flowchart of the Lucky Company problem which indicates only one STØP statement. This flowchart will be used to illustrate a shorter program which will produce the same results. The following program is designed to demonstrate how the unconditional GØ TØ statement, previously covered, can be effectively used in combination with a computed GØ TØ statement.

```
|12345|6|7
   77   FØRMAT(I4,2X,2F5.2,T23,I2)
   88   FØRMAT(I4,F7.2,2F8.2,T79,I2)
        READ(1,77)NUMEMP,HØURS,RATE,KØDE
        REGPAY=HØURS*RATE
        GØ TØ(55,65,75),KØDE
   55   BØNUS=REGPAY*2.00
        GØ TØ 33
   65   BØNUS=REGPAY
        GØ TØ 33
   75   BØNUS=REGPAY/2.00
   33   TØTPAY=REGPAY+BØNUS
        WRITE(2,88)NUMEMP,REGPAY,BØNUS,TØTPAY,KØDE
    3   STØP
        END
```

FIGURE 6–2
Flowchart for the Lucky Company Problem
Illustrating One Terminal Point

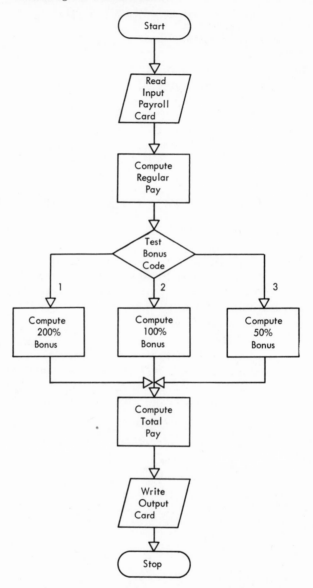

If the index value of the computed GØ TØ statement is 1 or 2, the computer will branch to statement numbers 55 or 65 respectively. The unconditional GØ TØ following these statements causes the computer to jump directly to statement 33. The combinations of the computed GØ TØ and unconditional GØ TØ statements thus cause the computer to omit statements which should not be executed. If the index value is 3, the computer will skip ahead to statement number 75. It is unnecessary that this statement be followed by a GØ TØ 33 statement because the computer will automatically go to statement 33 since it is next in sequence.

Establishing Convenient Index Values. The bonus code punched in the input cards of the Lucky Company was either 1, 2, or 3 which was convenient for the programmer. But what if instead of a 1, 2, or 3, the cards have been punched with either a 6, 8, or 12 respectively? Then the programmer has several alternatives.

He could, for example, change his computed GØ TØ statement as follows:

```
12345 6 7
         GØ  TØ(3,3,3,3,3,55,3,65,3,3,3,75),KØDE
```

Now, if the index value is 6, the computer would branch to the sixth statement number in the series which is 55. Likewise, if the index value is 8 or 12, the computer would branch to statement numbers 65 or 75 respectively. Because statement number 55 must appear in the sixth position in the list, it is necessary to have five preceding statement numbers. The programmer is not permitted to pick any number at random as a sort of "filler" for these five positions in the list. The numbers used must reference an executable statement which appears in the program. In this case, 3 references a STØP statement in each of the two preceding program illustrations. Thus, the program will terminate if, as the result of an error, the index value is 1, 2, 3, 4, 5, 7, 9, 10, or 11.

It should be apparent that if the bonus code had been 97, 98, or 99 instead of 1, 2, or 3 respectively, the length of the computed GØ TØ statement would require several continuation cards.

The programmer can often avoid extremely long computed GØ TØ statements by converting the bonus code punched in the card to a more convenient value. To illustrate this technique without using large values, assume again that the bonus codes are 6, 8, or 12 instead of 1, 2, or 3 respectively. The programmer could replace the one computed GØ TØ statement in the Lucky Company program illustrations with the following two statements:

```
12345 6 7
         KKØDE=KØDE/2-2
         GØ  TØ(55,65,3,75),KKØDE
```

The above arithmetic statement will cause the following values to be stored at KKØDE:

KØDE	KKØDE
6	1
8	2
12	4

Note that the variable name in the computed GØ TØ statement must be KKØDE instead of KØDE in this illustration.

It is not necessary to use a different variable name to change the index value. For example, the programmer could use the following two statements:

```
|12345|6|7
        KØDE=KØDE/2−2
        GØ TØ(55,65,3,75),KØDE
```

The above arithmetic statement will change the values of KØDE from 6, 8, or 12 to 1, 2, or 4. This is not a good technique in the case of the Lucky Company problem because KØDE is required in the output; it will be necessary to convert the value of KØDE back to 6, 8, or 12 before the WRITE statement is executed.

A "tricky way" to accomplish the desired result would be to use the following two statements:

```
|12345|6|7
        KKØDE=KØDE/4
        GØ TØ(55,65,75),KKØDE
```

Because the result of integer mode arithmetic is always integer, the above arithmetic statement will store the following values at KKØDE:

KØDE	KKØDE
6	1
8	2
12	3

The above technique is illustrated to review the effect of integer arithmetic and to demonstrate that just as there may be several ways to "skin a cat," likewise there may be several ways to write a statement. But, programmers are cautioned that cute programming such as this may sometimes cause unforeseen problems elsewhere in the program.

Establishing Valid Index Values. There are only first, second, third, fourth, etc., positions in the list of statement numbers in a computed GØ TØ statement. Thus, a zero or a negative index value is invalid. If the Lucky Company had used the bonus codes 0, 1, or 2 instead of 1, 2, or 3, an arithmetic statement could be used to validate the invalid code:

```
|12345|6|7
        KKØDE=KØDE+1
```

It was emphasized earlier in this chapter that the variable name in a computed GØ TØ statement must be in integer mode. If, for some reason, a value to be used as an index is in floating point mode, it must be converted to integer mode to make it valid.

Effect of Invalid Index Values. A valid index value cannot be less than one nor greater than the number of choices provided in the computed GØ TØ list. For example, the following statement contains a list of six statement numbers and thus provides six choices depending upon the value of N:

$$\overline{|12345|6|7}$$
GØ TØ(1,2,5,2,7,4),N

If, in this example, the value of N is less than one or more than six, it is invalid. The reason it is invalid is because if the index value is not within the range of one through six the computer has not been instructed where to go.

If an index value falls outside the allowable range, it may be the result of a keypunching error. It could also be caused by the programmer not providing for all possibilities or committing a logic error in his program.

The effect of an invalid index depends upon the compiler used. In most versions of FORTRAN, the program will fail. Basic FORTRAN IV provides that if the index value is outside the allowable range, the computer will automatically "drop through" and execute the next statement. This can be used to advantage; but unless the program is carefully designed, it might still fail or give incorrect results. In the case of the Lucky Company programs, illustrated previously in this chapter, an invalid index value would always result in the employee receiving a 200 percent bonus.[1]

IF STATEMENT

Only one type of IF statement (technically termed the "arithmetic IF") is provided in Basic FORTRAN IV. The IF is similar to the computed GØ TØ in that both are conditional control statements which cause the computer to skip ahead or back to some other executable statement in the program. However, they differ not only as to format but also in the number of branches which can be provided and in the way in which they operate.

The computed GØ TØ references two or more executable statements, but the IF must always reference three. The computed GØ TØ contains an integer index value, established by a previously executed statement in the program, which is used to determine where to branch. But the IF statement contains an arithmetic expression which may be in either integer or floating point mode. When the IF statement is executed, the result of this

---

[1] At this point it is suggested that Problems 1 through 5 be done before proceeding with the rest of the text.

expression or "argument" is computed. Instead of this result being stored at a symbolic address, as is caused by an arithmetic statement, it is automatically compared to zero. The computer then branches to one of the three referenced statements depending upon whether the result is evaluated as less than, equal to, or greater than zero. Stated another way, the branch is dependent upon whether the result of the arithmetic expression is negative, zero, or positive.

General Form

The general form of an IF statement is:

¯¯¯¯¯¯¯¯¯¯
|12345|6|7

nnnnn   IF (ae) sn_1,sn_2,sn_3

Legend:

nnnnn	Any unique one- to five-digit integer which specifies the statement *number*. It is required only if the statement is referenced elsewhere in the program.
IF	A key word specifying the type of operation to be performed.
(ae)	Any valid *arithmetic expression* enclosed in parentheses which is evaluated to determine whether the current value of the result is less than, equal to, or more than zero.
sn_1	An integer which references the statement which will be executed next when the evaluation of (ae) is negative.
sn_2	An integer which references the statement which will be executed next when the evaluation of (ae) is equal to zero.
sn_3	An integer which references the statement which will be executed next when the evaluation of (ae) is positive.

The following example of an IF statement will be used to illustrate its form and function:

¯¯¯¯¯¯¯¯¯¯
|12345|6|7

IF (KØDE−2) 55,65,75

In this illustration if KØDE has a current value of 1, the evaluation will be less than zero which will cause a branch to statement number 55; if KØDE is 2, the zero evaluation will cause control to pass to statement number 65; if KØDE is 3, the next statement executed will be number 75. This IF statement could be substituted for the computed GØ TØ statement in the Lucky Company programs presented earlier in this chapter because if the KØDE is always 1, 2, or 3 it has the same effect as:

¯¯¯¯¯¯¯¯¯¯
|12345|6|7

GØ TØ (55,65,75),KØDE

If the bonus codes in the Lucky Company problem were always 97, 98, or 99 instead of 1, 2, or 3 respectively, the following statement:

‾1‾2‾3‾4‾5‾|6|7

    IF (KØDE—98) 55,65,75

could be substituted for the following two statements:

‾1‾2‾3‾4‾5‾|6|7

    KKØDE=KØDE—96
    GØ TØ (55,65,75),KKØDE

The evaluation of the arithmetic expression in an IF statement is always less than, equal to, or more than zero; so it is impossible to "drop through" to the next statement. Therefore, *any statement immediately following an IF statement must always be numbered* because unless it can be referenced, it can never be executed. When one of the statement numbers in the IF statement references the immediately following statement, a more efficient object program is compiled.

IF statements are sometimes used in combination with a computed GØ TØ for the purpose of eliminating invalid index values which may result from keypunching errors. To illustrate, assume that the Lucky Company problem used 6, 7, or 8 instead of 1, 2, or 3 for the bonus codes. The following series of statements will cause the computer to branch to statement number 3 (a STØP statement) if the bonus code is any integer other than 6, 7, or 8:

‾1‾2‾3‾4‾5‾|6|7

        IF (KØDE—6) 3,98,98
  98   IF (KØDE—8) 99,99,3
  99   KKØDE=KØDE—5
        GØ TØ (55,65,75),KKØDE

The first IF statement above will cause the computer to branch to statement number 3 (STØP) if KODE is less than 6. If KØDE is equal to or more than 6, control will pass to the next IF statement which will cause a branch to the STØP statement if KØDE exceeds 8. Thus, control will pass to statement 99 and on to the computed GØ TØ only if the current value of KØDE is 6, 7, or 8.

The preceding examples illustrated the form and general function of IF statements. The following problem will demonstrate a more complex application.

Joe's Store is open for business seven days a week. At the end of each day a data card is prepared which indicates the amount of sales for each department. The problem is to prepare a program to compute the total sales for each day, and also the total sales for the month. The input data deck contains 31 cards (already sequenced by date) in the following format:

Field Name	Card Columns	Illustrative Field Contents
Department 1	1–6	100.00
Department 2	7–12	200.00
Department 3	13–18	300.00
Department 4	19–24	400.25

Output for each day is to be single spaced on a printer in the following format:

Field Name	Print Positions or "Columns"
Department 1	1–6
Department 2	9–14
Department 3	17–22
Department 4	25–30
Daily Total	51–57

The monthly total is to be printed in "columns" 50–57. It is to be separated from the last daily total by one blank line and preceded by this literal message:

MONTHLY TOTAL $

The solution to the Joe's Store problem requires a program which will:

1. Compute and write the total sales for each day.
2. Accumulate a running sum of the total sales for the month as each card is processed.
3. Write the total sales for the month after exactly 31 input cards have been processed.

The routine for computing and writing the total sales for each day can be repeated 31 times, but it is more efficient to use only one routine and a looping technique. The unconditional GØ TØ cannot be used to cause looping in this case because it will result in a perpetual loop as illustrated earlier in this chapter. This problem requires an exit from the loop after 31 input cards have been processed, so the monthly total will be printed before the program terminates.

The total sales for the month can be accumulated by beginning the program with an arithmetic statement which initializes the current value of a floating point variable name such as TØTMTH to zero. After the total sales for each day is computed, the amount can be added to TØTMTH (a process called *incrementing*).

To avoid an uncontrolled or perpetual loop, an integer variable name, such as KØUNT, can be initialized to zero and incremented by 1 on each pass through the loop. An IF statement can be used to provide an exit from the loop after 31 input cards have been processed.

A solution to this problem is illustrated by the flowchart in Figure 6–3 and the complete program which follows.

FIGURE 6–3
Flowchart for Joe's Store Problem Illustrating a Controlled Loop

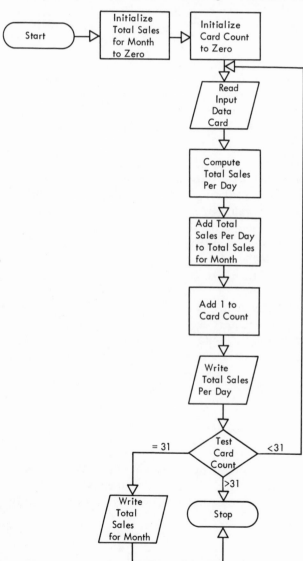

The following program follows the flowchart in Figure 6–3 and solves the Joe's Store problem:

```
|12345|6|7
        TØTMTH=0.00
        KØUNT=0
   7    READ(1,100)DEPT1,DEPT2,DEPT3,DEPT4
        TØTDAY=DEPT1+DEPT2+DEPT3+DEPT4
        TØTMTH=TØTMTH+TØTDAY
        KØUNT=KØUNT+1
        WRITE(3,200)DEPT1,DEPT2,DEPT3,DEPT4,TØTDAY
        IF(KØUNT−31)7,6,3
   6    WRITE(3,300)TØTMTH
   3    STØP
 100    FØRMAT(4F6.2)
 200    FØRMAT(1X,F6.2,3F8.2,T52,F7.2)
 300    FØRMAT(/T36,'MØNTHLY TØTAL $',T51,F8.2)
        END
```

After each of the first 30 input cards is processed, the IF statement will be evaluated as less than zero causing a branch to the READ statement and a recycle through the loop. After the 31st card is processed, the IF statement will be evaluated as equal to zero so the computer will exit from the loop, branch to the final WRITE statement, then automatically execute the next statement (STØP) in order. The program logic makes it impossible for KØUNT to exceed 31, so the IF statement can never be evaluated as more than zero. Thus, the third statement number in the IF list appears unnecessary in this case. But, it cannot be omitted because the rules of FORTRAN require that an IF statement must always reference three executable statements.

The following three statements in the Joe's Store program control the number of times (or "iterations") the computer cycles through the loop:

```
|12345|6|7
        KØUNT=0
        KØUNT=KØUNT+1
        IF(KØUNT−31)7,6,3
```

Many variations of these three statements could be used to produce the same results. For example, the IF statement could be changed to provide an exit from the loop when KØUNT exceeds 30 instead of when it equals 31:

```
|12345|6|7
        IF(KØUNT−30)7,7,6
```

It would also be possible to initialize KØUNT to some value other than zero and/or to increment KØUNT by some value other than one. Of course, any change in the initialization and/or incremental values would also require a change in the IF statement to accomplish the desired results.

The following statement in the Joe's Store problem reviews three methods of obtaining blanks in the output image:

⌐1̅2̅3̅4̅5̅|̅6̅|̅7̅
200   FØRMAT(1X,F6.2,3F8.2,T52,F7.2)

Legend:

1X   Causes a blank in the first position of the output image which, when shifted left, causes single spacing.

3F8.2   Causes two blanks to precede these three six-position data fields as a result of overformatting.

T52   Causes a string of 20 blanks to precede the last data field.

To illustrate a technique often useful in programming, the Joe's Store program is designed so each line indicating the total sales for the day can be sequentially numbered from 1 through 31. For example, FØRMAT statement number 200 could be changed to include one additional format code at the end of the list:

⌐1̅2̅3̅4̅5̅|̅6̅|̅7̅
200   FØRMAT(1X,F6.2,3F8.2,T52,F7.2,I4)

and the first WRITE statement could be changed to include one more variable name at the end of the list:

⌐1̅2̅3̅4̅5̅|̅6̅|̅7̅
          WRITE(3,200)DEPT1,DEPT2,DEPT3,DEPT4,TØTDAY,KØUNT

It should be noted that if KØUNT is incremented immediately *following* instead of preceding the execution of the above WRITE statement, the lines will be numbered sequentially from zero through 30 instead of 1 through 31.

The Joe's Store program contains only one loop. The statements comprising the loop (called the "loop range") will be executed 31 times. Each time the computer passes through the loop range it will use different input data because read-in is destructive. That is, each time the READ statement is executed, the current values of each variable name are initialized to the value of the data contained in the input card.

Many programs require more than one loop and may also require some or all of the data from each of selected input cards to be saved for later use in the program. More complex applications will be covered in later chapters but the following illustration will demonstrate the general principle of multiple loops and of saving data for later use in the program.

Signa Phi Nothing Fraternity has recently completed a charitable fund drive on their campus which extended over a period of several weeks. Some students gave nothing, some contributed once, others two or more times. Each time a contribution was received, a punched card was prepared in the following format:

Field Name	Card Columns	Illustrative Field Contents
Student Number	1–4	1001
Amount Received	5–9	12.50

The total number of cards prepared is unknown, but it is known that 1,000 students made one or more contributions during the fund drive. The problem is to prepare a program that will compute the total amount received from each student and the total amount collected during the fund drive.

The cards have been arranged in ascending sequence by student number. Each student has a unique number. Thus, all cards for each student are together rather than randomly scattered throughout the input deck. The required output for each student is one printed line indicating the student number and the total amount contributed in the following format:

Field Name	Print Positions or "Columns"	Illustrative Field Contents
Student Number	1–4	1001
Total Donations	8–13	125.50

The final output line, indicating the total amount of contributions received during the fund drive, is to be in the following format:

Field Name	Print Positions or "Columns"
Fund Drive Total	6–13

All output is to be "double-spaced" on a printer.

The Signa Phi Nothing Fraternity problem can be solved by a program which will compare each card read in, other than the first, to the preceding card to determine whether the student number has changed. A solution to this problem is illustrated by the flowchart in Figure 6–4 and the complete program which follows.

FIGURE 6–4
Signa Phi Nothing Fraternity Problem Flowchart Illustrating
Multiple Loops and a Technique for Saving Data for
Later Use in Program

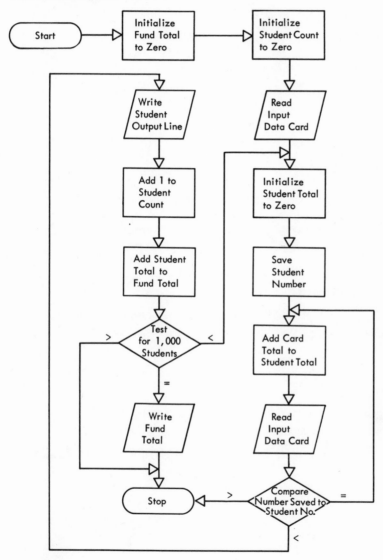

```
|12345|6|789
C ***SIGNA PHI NØTHING FRATERNITY PRØGRAM***
C
  100    FØRMAT(I4,F5.2)
  200    FØRMAT('0',I4,T9,F6.2)
```

```
300   FØRMAT('0',T7,F8.2)
      FUNTØT=0.00
      KØUNT=0
      READ(1,100)NUMSTU,CDTØT
  1   STUTØT=0.00
      NUMSAV=NUMSTU
  2   STUTØT=STUTØT+CDTØT
  3   READ(1,100)NUMSTU,CDTØT
      IF(NUMSAV−NUMSTU)4,2,6
  4   WRITE(3,200)NUMSAV,STUTØT
      KØUNT=KØUNT+1
      FUNTØT=FUNTØT+STUTØT
      IF(KØUNT−1000)1,5,6
  5   WRITE(3,300)FUNTØT
  6   STØP
      END
```

The two illustrative programs in this section have demonstrated how the IF statement can be used to provide an exit from a loop. The following section covers loops in general and three different methods of loop control using the IF statement.

LOOP CONTROL

Loops may be classified into two basic types: uncontrolled and controlled. Each type will be illustrated via partial programs in the following sections.

Uncontrolled Loops

This is the perpetual or "closed" loop discussed previously in the unconditional GØ TØ section of this chapter. For example:

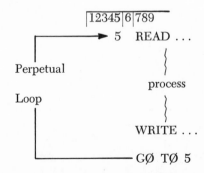

This type of loop provides no programmed exit and continues until it is interrupted by the computer system. It should be avoided.

Controlled Loops

Controlled loops require:

1. A point of entry into the loop.
2. One or more executable statements which are to be repeated.
3. A method of determining the number of iterations (how many times the loop is to be repeated).
4. An exit point from the loop.

Programmers should be particularly cautious to avoid omitting data or cycling through the loop an incorrect number of times. Usually the first and last passes through the loop cause the most problems.

Three methods of loop control will be illustrated, all using an IF statement as an exit point.

Loop Control Via Program.   The number of passes through the loop may be determined by the program rather than from an external source. The Joe's Store and Signa Phi Nothing Fraternity programs, previously presented, used this type of approach as illustrated below:

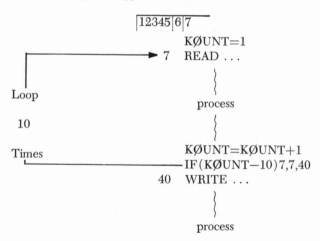

This program is designed to process 10 cards only before breaking out of the loop. To process an input deck containing more or less than 10 cards, the program must be changed and recompiled. This technique can be used only if the number of required passes through the loop is known.

Loop Control Via Header Card.   This method also requires that the number of required passes through the loop be known but will work for any number of input cards without changing the program. Instead of entering the number of required passes through the loop directly into the program as a constant, it is punched into a data card. This card is called a "header card" because it is the first card processed. Because it controls the

number of passes through the loop, it is sometimes called a "control card."
To illustrate:

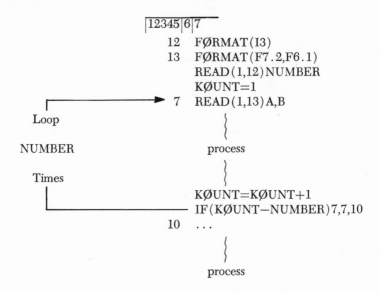

This program will always process the number of cards indicated by the header card before it exits from the loop.

Loop Control via Trailer Card. This method will also process any number of cards without changing the program. It has a further advantage in that it is unnecessary to know the number of cards in the input deck. The program is written to automatically break out of the loop when the last data card (which serves as a "control card") is read. The "trailer card" is always last in the input data deck. It is in the same format as all other input data cards but must contain a unique value in one of the fields.

For example, suppose each input data card contains the following data fields:

Field Name	Card Columns	Illustrative Field Contents
Customer Number	1–4	1234
Amount	5–10	526.32

The trailer card is in the same format but contains the unique number 9999 in the customer number field and zeros in the amount field. To illustrate:

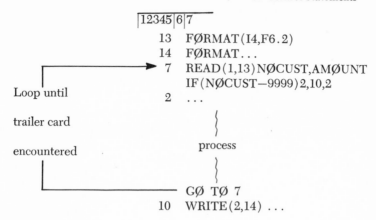

Arithmetic Expressions

Any valid arithmetic expression may be placed between the parentheses of an IF statement. It may be in integer or floating point mode. Great care must be taken with floating point expressions or undesired branching may result because exact values are rare in this mode.

Beginning programmers often find the truncation resulting from integer division to be rather distracting. Using floating point values alleviates this truncation problem, but it does not entirely eliminate it. Just as some fractional values cannot be represented exactly in decimal notation (such as ⅓ which is *about* .33333), likewise, some cannot be represented exactly in binary. To further complicate the situation, some fractional values which can be represented exactly in decimal notation (such as ¹⁄₁₀ which is .1) have no exact binary equivalents. Thus, when an innocent-looking decimal value is converted to binary for internal storage, it may be truncated to the allowable number of binary digits. As a consequence, a floating point expression which should obviously yield an exact decimal result may not do so within the computer. In most computations, this presents no difficulty because the computer maintains far more precision than is required for output. But, when testing for a zero condition in an IF statement with a floating point expression, difficulties usually arise because an exact zero will seldom be found. For this reason, it is recommended that beginning programmers avoid floating point expressions in IF statements whenever possible.

PROBLEMS

The following problems are designed to review the unconditional and computed GØ TØ statements. Each program should be written to provide for all possible branches even though only one specific data card is to be processed.

1. Nifty Corporation manufactures only one product. Sales orders are sent to the factory from salesmen in the field; no sales are made at the factory. All units sold are individually crated and shipped directly from the factory to the customer. Customers are charged $900.00 per unit plus the cost of shipping. Shipping charges vary according to the "freight zone" in which the customer resides:

Freight Zone	Per Unit Freight Charges
1	$12.50
2	26.75
3	36.25

Write a program to compute the total charge for one sale. Use a computed GØ TØ statement to test the freight zone. Input is one card in the following format:

Field Name	Card Columns	Required Field Contents
Customer Number	1–4	1234
Freight Zone	5	3
Units Sold	6–7	10

Required output is one printed line in the following format:

Field Name	Print Positions or "Columns"	Required Field Contents
Customer Number	1–4	1234
Freight Zone	7	3
Units Sold	10–11	10
Total Charge	14–21	9362.50

2. Write a program to calculate the amount of interest and the maturity value of a bank loan where:

$$I = PRT/365 \text{ and } MV = P + I$$

Input is one card in the following format:

Field Name	Card Columns	Required Field Contents
Note Number	1–6	012345
Principal	7–15	012345.70
Time in Days	16–19	0365
Rate Code	20–21	05

Four different rate codes are used to indicate the interest percentage as follows:

| | Interest Rate |
Rate Code	(Percent)
01	6.75
02	7.50
03	8.75
05	10.00

Use a computed GØ TØ statement to test the rate code.

Required output is one printed line containing the same data as the input card as well as interest and maturity value which should both be carried to two decimal places. The required format is:

Field Name	Print Positions or "Columns"
Note Number	1–5
Principal	6–14
Time in Days	15–18
Rate Code	19–20
Interest	25–31
Maturity Value	35–42

3. Write a program to compute the registration fee for a student where:

Registration fee = $22.50 per credit hour + Tuition

Input is one card in the following format:

Field Name	Card Columns	Required Field Contents
None	1	Blank
Student Number	2–6	12345
None	7–8	Blanks
Date of Birth	9–14	121253
Tuition Code	15	2
Credit Hours	16–19	12.5

Three codes are used to indicate the amount of tuition as follows:

	Tuition Code	Tuition Amount
In-State	1	$185.00
Out-of-State	2	415.00
Scholarship	4	None

Use a computed GØ TØ statement to test the tuition code.

Required output is one printed line in the following format:

Field Name	Print Positions or "Columns"
Student Number	1–5
Registration Fee	8–13

4. Write a program to compute the net price of a sales invoice where:

List Price = Units times Unit Price
Discount = List Price times Discount Percentage
Net Price = List Price less Discount

Input is one card in the following format:

Field Name	Card Columns	Required Field Contents
Customer Number	1–5	12345
Units	6–7	10
Unit Price	8–12	37.95
Discount Code	13–14	03

Four codes are used to identify the discount percentage:

Type of Customer	Discount Code	Discount Percentage
Wholesaler	3	60
Retailer	2	40
Cash Customer	1	10
Charge Customer	0	5

Use a computed GØ TØ statement to test the discount code.
Required output is one printed line in the following format:

Field Name	Print Positions or "Columns"
Customer Number	1–5
Net Price	7–13

5. Speedtrap City has a population of only 200 citizens. It is divided into two sections by a major highway which passes through the main business district. The posted speed limit is 70 m.p.h. for the highway but only 30 m.p.h. within the city limits. Electronic timing devices have been installed at each end of the city to detect speeders.

Anyone arrested for exceeding the speed limit has two choices. He may go directly to the police department traffic division and pay a fine of $5.00 for each mile per hour in excess of the posted speed limit (a speed of 30½ m.p.h. would result in a fine of $2.50). His second choice is to wait and appear in traffic court which convenes at 7 P.M. each evening. If he is found guilty, he is fined $3.00 for each mile per hour in excess of the posted limit. If the fine is not paid, he is given a jail sentence.

A punched card, in the following format, is prepared for each offender who exceeds the 30 m.p.h. speed limit:

Field Name	Card Columns	Required Data
Culprit Number	1–5	12345
Arresting Officer Number	6–7	02
Actual Speed in m.p.h.	8–13	055.50
Disposition Code	14–15	22

Four disposition codes are used:

Disposition	Code
Paid Fine Immediately	22
Found Guilty	24
Found Not Guilty	26
Jailed	28

Write a program to read one input card and compute the fine if the input card is coded 22 or 24 (compute nothing if card is coded 26 or 28). Use a computed GØ TØ statement to test for disposition code. If the card is coded 22 or 24, print one output line in the following format:

Field Name	Print Positions
Culprit Number	1–5
Amount of Fine	7–12
Disposition Code	14–15

6. Write the program described in Problem 1 in this chapter with the following change only: Use one IF statement, instead of a computed GØ TØ, to test the freight zone.

7. Write the program described in Problem 2 in this chapter with the following change only: Use two IF statements, instead of one computed GØ TØ, to test the rate codes.

8. Write the program described in Problem 3 in this chapter with the following change only: Use IF statements, prior to the computed GØ TØ, to test for any invalid tuition codes resulting from keypunching errors.

9. Write the program described in Problem 4 in this chapter with the following changes only: (1) assume that the input deck contains 10 data cards instead of 1 (use an IF statement for loop control), and (2) output is to be printed on 10 "single-spaced" lines, one for each input card.

Required input data:

Customer Number (Cols. 1–5)	Units (Cols. 6–7)	Unit Price (Cols. 8–12)	Discount Code (Cols. 13–14)
54321	10	37.95	03
2	10	37.95	02
3	10	37.95	01
4	10	37.95	00
5	10	37.95	01
6	10	37.95	02
7	10	37.95	03
8	10	37.95	03
9	10	37.95	00
10	10	37.95	01

10. Write the program described in Problem 5 in this chapter with the following changes only:

1. Assume that the input deck contains 10 data cards instead of 1 (use an IF statement for loop control). Required input data:

Culprit Number (Cols. 1–5)	Arresting Officer Number (Cols. 6–7)	Actual Speed in M.P.H. (Cols. 8–13)	Disposition Code (Cols. 14–15)
12345	01	055.50	22
6	2	31.00	22
7	3	31.00	24
8	4	31.50	24
9	5	32.00	26
50	6	32.00	28
1	7	40.00	24
2	8	40.00	22
3	9	80.00	28
4	10	31.50	26

2. Output (for each card coded 22 or 24) is to be "double-spaced" on a printer.

11. A man takes a job at a pencil factory for 31 days. The factory has a large inventory but is short of cash, so the man agrees to be paid in pencils. He is to receive one pencil the first day. Each succeeding day he is to receive twice as many pencils as the day before. Thus, he will receive two the second day, four the third, eight the fourth, etc.

Write a program to compute the number of pencils he will earn each day and a running total of his "earnings." No input card is to be used. Output is to be on a printer, indicating on 31 successive lines the line number, his pay for each day, and the accumulated amount of his "earnings" to date. Output is to be in FØRMAT(I3,2I14).

12. Write a program to select the largest of three different positive integers which are punched in one input data card in the following format:

Field Name	Card Columns	Required Field Contents
None	1	0 (zero)
NUMBR1	2–6	Any integer data
None	7–8	Blanks
NUMBR2	9–13	Any integer data
None	14–15	Blanks
NUMBR3	16–20	Any integer data
None	21–25	00000 (zeros)
None	26–29	Blanks
Identification	30–44	CARD NUMBER 1
None	45–80	Blanks

Ignore the fields from columns 21 through 80 on input.

Output is to be on a printer. One line is to contain the three integers in the following format:

Field Name	Printing Positions or "Columns"
NUMBR1	1–5
NUMBR2	8–12
NUMBR3	15–19

Following the above output line, two lines are to be left blank followed by one output line containing the largest of the three integers in the first five printing positions or "columns." Use selective writing technique which requires only one WRITE statement referenced to a FØRMAT statement containing slashes to control the output line spacing.

13. Prepare a program to compute the social security deduction and net pay of each employee and to compute the total social security deduction and total net pay for all employees. "Time-and-a-half" is paid for all hours in excess of 40. Assume that the social security rate is 4.8 percent and that all employees are subject to this deduction.

The input data deck contains one card for each of the 10 employees in the following format:

Employee Number (Cols. 1–4)	Date of Birth (5–10)	Hours Worked (11–15)	Rate per Hour (16–19)	Dept. Number (20)	Employee Name (61–80)
1001	100948	39.00	1.50	1	PATRICIA B. ANDERSON
1002	111249	35.00	2.80	2	WASHINGTON H. BROWN
1003	111249	39.25	2.65	3	JANE ANN COOPER
1004	111249	41.75	4.00	4	RAYMOND D. DOOLITTLE
1005	111249	60.00	1.00	5	SAMUEL R. ENGERS
1006	111249	38.50	4.20	6	PATRICIA FITZGERALD
1007	111249	80.00	2.00	7	MARTIN S. GERSZEWSKI
1008	111249	45.00	3.00	8	CARL J. HILL
1009	111249	18.00	6.42	9	RAYMOND P. INOMOTO
1010	111249	50.00	9.00	1	MARK A. JOHNSON

Use an IF statement for loop control. Read only the input data fields required to solve the problem.

Required output for each employee is one printed line containing the following data fields from left to right:

Field Name
Employee Number
Rate per Hour
Hours Worked
Social Security Deduction
Net Pay

The first 22 printing positions or "columns" of each output line *must* contain blanks. "Dress-up" output with reasonable spacings between fields and with a heading indicating the contents of each field. (For example, the net pay field may be headed up with the words "NET PAY.")

Required output for the final line (total social security and net pay for all employees) should be positioned so it appears directly below the fields totaled with the decimal points aligned.

14. Write a program to compute the end-of-month balance for each pilot member of a local flying club. The number of cards to be processed is unknown. The last card in the data deck is a "trailer card" which contains the unique value 999 in the Pilot Number field. Use an IF statement for loop control based on this trailer card. Use the following input data cards:

Pilot Number (Cols. 1–3)	Amount (6–12)	Code (15–16)
101	−107.50	01
102	−107.50	01
102	6.50	02
102	1.00	02
103	−107.50	01
103	7.50	02
103	10.00	03
103	10.00	03
104	15.50	01
104	25.00	02
104	15.50	03
999	(trailer card)	

Three code numbers are used to identify the type of input card as follows:

1. Code 1 identified a *Balance Forward* card. Each pilot has one such card which may contain:
   A. A *positive* balance (if he owes the club money from last month).
   B. A *negative* balance (if he has overpaid and has a "credit balance").
   C. A *zero* balance.
2. Code 2 identifies a *Flight Charge* card. There is one such card for each flight made during the month. All amounts are *positive*.

3. Code 3 identifies a *Payments on Account* card. There is one such card for each payment made by the pilot. All amounts are *positive*.

Input data cards are in ascending numerical sequence by pilot number. All input cards must be processed; none can be omitted. Required output is one or more descriptive "header" lines followed by one line only for each pilot which contains his number and end-of-month balance with reasonable spacing between the fields. It is also required that one output card, in the same format as the input cards, be punched for each pilot. This output card is to contain the pilot number, end-of-month balance, and the integer 1 in the code field. It can be used as the Balance Forward input card when the same program is processed next month.

15. Write a program to compute the total *hours* of computer time used by each student in computer programming class number 66 and the total *hours* of computer time used by all students in this class.

The input deck contains one card for each time a student in *any* computer programming class processes a "job" (program). The cards have been sorted by student number, thus all cards for each student are together rather than scattered randomly throughout the input deck. Each student has a unique number, but the numbers are not related to the class. That is, student number 01 may be in class 66, number 02 in class 33, number 03 in class 66, etc.

The number of cards for each student is unknown. The number of students is also unknown so a trailer card will be used to determine the end of the input deck. The trailer card contains the unique value 99 punched in the Class Number field.

No student is enrolled in more than one class. All cards for classes other than class number 66 are to be ignored.

Input Data Cards

Student Number (Cols. 1–4)	Class Number (5–6)	Minutes for Job (7–12)
1111	66	1.25
1111	66	28.75
1112	66	120.00
1113	67	240.00
1114	66	59.50
1114	66	15.50
1115	65	240.00
1115	65	240.00
1116	98	360.00
1117	14	8.00
1118	66	48.60
1118	66	11.40
1118	66	60.23
1119	66	33.00
1119	66	33.23
1120	66	48.23
1120	66	12.00
0000	99	000000 (trailer card)

All output is to be single-spaced on a printer. The total time on the final output line is to be followed by one blank and the literal message: HOURS

Required Output for Each Student in Class Number 66

Field Name	Print Positions or "Columns"	Illustrative Field Data
Student Number	1–4	1111
Class Number	7–8	66
Hours of Time	10–16	0.50

Required Final Output

Field Name	Print Positions or "Columns"	Illustrative Field Data
Total Time	1–8	22.74

16. Write a program to compute the total cost and the average cost of processing programs written by members of your class. Processing cost is $82.50 per hour.

The input deck contains one card for each time a student processes a job (program). The cards have been sorted *alphabetically* by student name, thus all cards for each student are together rather than scattered randomly throughout the input deck. The number of cards for each student is unknown.

Each student has a unique number, but the numbers have *not* been assigned in alphabetic sequence. All students in your class have been assigned numbers within the range of 1001 through 1050, but the input deck contains cards for students other than those enrolled in your class. Students enrolled in other courses have been assigned numbers outside this range, but no student is assigned the unique number 9999 which is reserved for the "trailer card."

Input Data Cards

Student Number (Cols. 7–10)	Student Name (21–40)	Hours for Job (66–71)
1017	ADAMS, JOHN	1.000
1050	BAKER, JOHN	.384
1050	BAKER, JOHN	.116
1026	CARLSON, JOE	.200
1050	CARLSON, SAM	10.000
1011	DOBBS, JOE	3.000
0999	ELLIS, JOE	1.234
2000	ELLIS, JOHN	5.678
1033	ELLIS, SAM	3.000
1001	FEATHERINGHAM, JAMES	4.000
1049	GATES, JOE	.008
1049	GATES, JOE	.002
1022	HALL, JANE	2.000
1002	IVERS, MARY	5.000
3412	JAMES, ALICE	5.000
5555	JAMES, CARL, JR.	5.333
1044	JAMES, DIANE	60.975
1044	JAMES, DIANE	60.025
9998	KELLY, SAM	12.345
9999	***TRAILER CARD***	000000

Disregard the alphabetic data field on input.

Output

Required output for each student in your class is one line only which contains the student's number and the total cost of processing his jobs. The final output line is to contain the total cost of processing all jobs in your class and the average processing cost per student. All output is to be double-spaced using a high-speed printer. Each output field should be scaled to determine its proper size.

CHAPTER
7

ADDITIONAL CONTROL STATEMENTS AND ALPHAMERIC INPUT/OUTPUT TECHNIQUES

P REVIOUS chapters included a description of various procedures which can be used for loop control and for processing a limited amount of alphameric input and output. This chapter expands upon these procedures by introducing new "short-cuts" and more convenient programming techniques.

THE DØ STATEMENT

The DØ statement is one of the most powerful in the FORTRAN language. Its purpose is to provide in one statement the four operations required for loop control:

1. Establish a counter or "index" by initializing a variable name to a specific current value.
2. Increment that value by a specific amount on each cycle through the loop.
3. Test that value each cycle and provide an exit from the loop after the required number of cycles or "iterations."
4. Designate the statements within the loop which are to be repeated.

Stated another way, indicate or define the extent of the loop which is called the "loop range."

For example, suppose it is necessary to execute this operation 20 times and then exit from the loop and continue further processing:

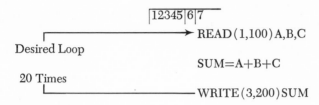

As illustrated in Chapter 6, loop control can be provided as follows:

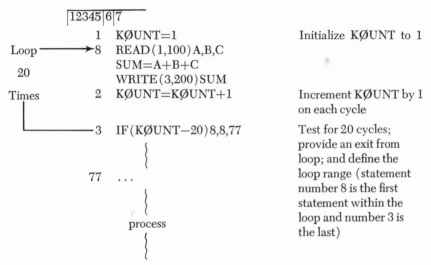

The three statements (numbered 1, 2, and 3) providing loop control in the above illustration can be replaced by one DØ statement thus saving the programmer time and probably requiring less compilation and execution time. The following partial program will provide the same results as the preceding illustration:

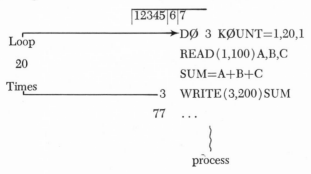

The DØ statement in the preceding partial program directs the computer to execute in sequence the statements through statement number 3, 20 times; or, stated another way, "DØ through 3, 20 times." "DØ 3" directs the computer to execute all statements through statement number 3, then return to the DØ statement. "KØUNT=1,20,1" tells the computer to initialize KØUNT to the current value of 1; each time it returns to the DØ statement from the last statement in the loop, KØUNT is to be incremented by 1; after 20 iterations or passes through the loop, it is to exit and execute the first statement following the last statement in the loop range or "DØ range."

This is more fully explained in the legend following the illustration of the general form of a DØ statement.

General Form

The general form of a DØ statement is as follows:

```
|12345|6|7
nnnnn    DØ sn ivn=ov,tv,iv
```

Legend:

nnnnn	Any unique one- to five-digit integer which specifies the statement *number*. It is required only if the statement is referenced elsewhere in the program.
DØ	A key word specifying the type of statement.
sn	An integer specifying the last *statement number* in the loop range or DØ range.
ivn	An *integer variable name* whose current value is initialized and incremented by the DØ statement. It serves as a counter for the number of iterations through the loop. It is sometimes called an "index."
=	A required delimiter or separator following the integer variable name.
ov	An unsigned integer constant or integer variable name whose current value is used to initialize or establish the *original value* of "ivn" when the DØ loop is first entered. This original value must be 1 or more.
,tv	An unsigned integer constant or integer variable name, preceded by a comma, whose current value is used as a *test value*. After executing the last statement (sn) in the DØ range, control returns to the DØ statement. If the current value of the index or counter (ivn) exceeds this test value, the computer exits from the loop by automatically "dropping through" to the statement following the last statement (sn) in the DØ range; otherwise it automatically cycles through the DØ range again.
,iv	An optional unsigned integer constant or integer variable name, preceded by a comma, whose current value must be 1 or more. It is used as an *increment value*. Each time control returns to the DØ statement from the last statement (sn) in the DØ range, this increment value is automatically added to the counter or index (ivn). This addition is made before the counter or index (ivn) is compared to the test value (tv). Stated another way: first it increments, then it tests. If this increment value is omitted, the computer automatically assumes an increment value of 1. If omitted, the preceding comma must also be omitted.

Illustrative Examples

The general form of the DØ statement may be summarized as follows:

	Last Statement Number in the DØ Range	Integer Variable Name Used as an Iteration Counter or Index	Initialized or Original Value of Iteration Counter or Index	Test Value	Increment Value
DØ	sn	ivn	$=$ ov	,tv	,iv

The last statement in the DØ range must obviously be numbered (labeled) or it cannot be referenced. Any integer variable name which will satisfy the requirements of the program may be selected by the programmer. Any integer number greater than zero may be used as the initial, incremental, or test value. If the incremental value is omitted, it is assumed to be 1.

To illustrate, each of the following statements will cause 20 iterations:

```
|12345|6|7
        DØ  6  INDEX=1,20
        DØ  6  INDEX=1,20,1
        DØ  6  INDEX=2,21,1
        DØ  6  INDEX=3,22,1
        DØ  6  INDEX=101,120
        DØ  6  INDEX=1,39,2
        DØ  6  INDEX=1,40,2
```

The last two DØ statements above will cause the following operations: INDEX will be initialized to 1 the first time the DØ statement is encountered in the program. Processing will then continue through the last statement in the DØ range (statement number 6) at which time control will automatically return to the DØ statement. INDEX will be incremented by 2, changing its current value from 1 to 3. It will then be compared to 39 or 40 to determine if it exceeds the test value. After the first cycle it does not exceed the test value, so it will recycle through the loop. On each successive pass through the loop, INDEX will be incremented by 2 changing its current value to 5, 9, 11, 13, 15, etc. After 20 passes through the loop, the current value of INDEX will be 41. This will cause an exit from the loop because it exceeds the test values of 39 or 40. If the test value had been 38, the loop would have been iterated only 19 times, whereas a 41 test value would have caused 21 iterations.

The first two partial program illustrations in this section demonstrated how one DØ statement can replace three statements which provide loop control. Depending upon the program logic and the complexity of the problem to be solved, one DØ statement can replace many statements in a program. For example, the following partial program uses four statements to provide loop control:

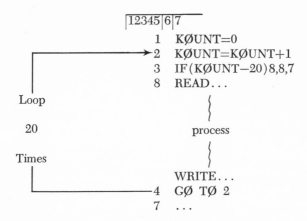

|12345|6|7
1   KØUNT=0
2   KØUNT=KØUNT+1
3   IF(KØUNT−20)8,8,7
8   READ...

Loop

20   process

Times
               WRITE...
4   GØ TØ 2
7   ...

The four statements (numbered 1, 2, 3, and 4) in the above illustration provide the loop control. They could be replaced by one DØ statement as illustrated below:

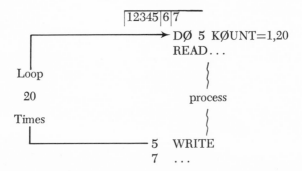

|12345|6|7
DØ 5 KØUNT=1,20
READ...

Loop

20   process

Times
5   WRITE
7   ...

It should be noted that if both the initial and incremental values are 1, the test value will always indicate the exact number of passes which will be made through the loop. This "one-one combination" is easy for the program mer to use and is quite popular. But it should be noted that in many case s the program logic may make it desirable or mandatory to initialize and/or increment by some value other than 1.

There are also many cases where it is desirable or required that an integer variable name, instead of an integer constant, be used for the initialization, incremental or test values. For example, to control a loop via "header card" technique, covered in the previous chapter, a variable name would be required as the test value:

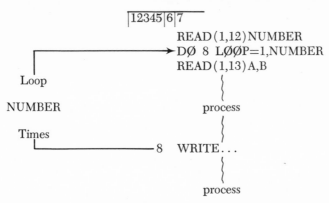

If integer variable names are used for the initialization, test and incremental values, the DØ statement can be extremely powerful because the current values of any or all of these variable names can be changed according to a multitude of conditions. Thus, one DØ may replace hundreds of statements, depending upon the complexity of the problem to be solved.

Multiple DØ Statements.   As many DØ statements as the problem requires and the computer system capacity permits may be used in a program. It may contain more than one independent DØ loop and/or it may contain "nested" DØ loops. An example of each type of multiple DØ loop will be illustrated next.

Independent DØ Statements.   The following partial program illustrates two independent DØ loops:

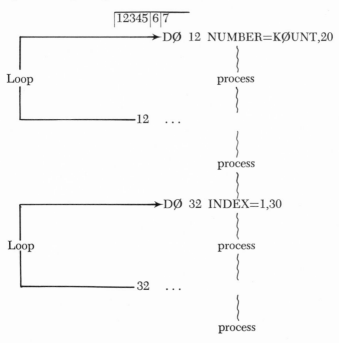

Nested DØ Statements. When one DØ loop is contained within the range of another DØ loop, the inner loop is said to be *nested*. The following partial program illustrates a nested DØ loop:

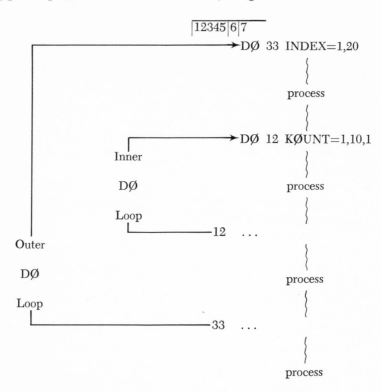

The preceding illustration will cause the computer to cycle through the outer loop 20 times and inner loop 200 times (the nested loop will be cycled 10 times on each cycle through the outer loop). The programmer may nest as many DØ loops as is required. For example, one or more additional DØ loops could have been nested within the inner loop in the preceding illustration.

Programming Considerations

The DØ statement is very powerful and can be effectively used to the programmer's advantage if he is thoroughly familiar with the function of the statement and certain restrictions.

1. The DØ range may be defined as all statements in a DØ loop from the first (which must be a DØ statement) through the last. Any statement between the first and last statements are referred to as statements

within the DØ range. All DØ loops must be originally entered via the first statement in the DØ range.

2. When control passes to a DØ statement from any statement other than the last statement in the DØ range, the current value of the index is automatically initialized; when control passes to a DØ statement from the last statement in the DØ range, the current value of the index is automatically incremented.

3. The current values of the variable name which serves as an index and of the integer variable names which are used for initializing, testing, and incrementing should not be changed by statements *within* the DØ range.

4. Any statement may be used *within* the DØ range, but there are some restrictions and general rules as to what is allowed as the last statement in the DØ range.

    A. One general rule is that the last statement cannot be a nonexecutable statement. Basic FORTRAN IV allows one exception to this general rule; a FØRMAT statement is permitted to be the last statement in the DØ range. Because some FORTRAN compilers do not allow this exception, programmers often follow the general rule and disregard the exception to keep their program "device independent."

    B. Another general rule is that the last statement cannot be a control statement. Because the DØ statement is designed to automatically transfer control from the last statement in the DØ range back to the DØ statement, any statement conflicting with this automatic transfer is not permitted. Thus, an unconditional GØ TØ, computed GØ TØ, IF, STØP, PAUSE, RETURN, or another DØ is not allowed as the last statement in the DØ range.

5. There are two ways to exit from a DØ loop:

    A. The normal method of exit is automatic; control drops through to the first executable statement following the DØ range when the current value of the index exceeds the test value. It should be noted that after control is transferred out of a DØ loop in this normal manner, the index becomes undefined and no assumption can be made as to its current value. It should also be noted that if exit is made by this normal method, the DØ loop can be reentered only via the first statement in the DØ range.

    B. Another method of exit may be provided by the programmer; it is always permissible to transfer control out of any DØ loop (independent or nested), by a statement *within* the DØ range. It should be noted that after exit is made via this method, the current value of the index is retained and is available for later use in the program. It should also be noted that if exit is made by this method, the DØ loop can be reentered either via the first statement in the

DØ range or via a statement *within* the DØ range. Reentry *within* the DØ range is permitted only under restrictive conditions when DØ loops are nested.

6. When nested DØ loops are used in a program, the following rules apply:
   A. A different variable name must be used for the index value of each DØ loop in a nest.
   B. All statements in the range of the inner (nested) DØ loop must be included in the range of the outer DØ loop. (The same statement may be used as the last in the range of both the inner and outer DØ loops.)
   C. As previously indicated, all DØ loops must be originally entered via the first statement in the DØ range. In the case of nested DØ loops, the nest must be originally entered via the first statement in the outermost DØ range.
   D. Reentry *within* a DØ loop is permitted only to the innermost loop of a nest. The following restrictions apply:
      1. An exit must have been made from the innermost loop of the nest as the result of a statement *within* this loop.
      2. The statements executed between the time of exit from and reentry to this innermost loop are called the "extended DØ range." Reentry to the innermost loop can only be made from a statement within this extended DØ range.
      3. The extended DØ range must not include a DØ statement.
      4. The index, initial, test, or increment values may not be changed in the extended DØ range.

The preceding explanation of how a DØ statement functions indicates there are several restrictions to its use. Fortunately, it is possible to avoid some of these restrictions by special programming techniques.

For example, it was noted that after a normal exit from a DØ loop (when the index exceeds the test value), the index becomes undefined; and no assumption can be made as to its current value. But some programs may require the current value of the index for later processing, after a normal exit from a DØ loop. It is possible to save this current value by storing it at another variable name, in either integer or floating point mode, before exit from the loop. To illustrate this programming technique, assume the following problem:

Beginning in January, a man deposits $100 per month for 12 consecutive months in a savings institution and makes no withdrawals. All deposits are made on or before the 10th day of each month because deposits made during this time earn interest for a full month. Interest is not compounded; the savings institution pays interest annually on December 31 at the rate of 5 percent per year based on the number of months during the year that the investor's money is on deposit. Thus, the $100 January deposit would earn interest for 12 months, the February deposit for 11 months, the March deposit for 10 months, etc.

The solution to the problem requires a program which will (1) compute and print on 12 consecutive lines sequentially numbered from 1 through 12, the amount of interest earned on each monthly deposit, and (2) compute and print on the following line the total interest earned during the year and the average interest earned per month.

Figure 7–1 illustrates a program and the resulting output which solves this problem; some brief comments on each statement follow Figure 7–1.

FIGURE 7–1
Program illustrating use of the DØ index within a DØ loop and a technique for saving the current index value, for later use in the program, after a normal exit from the DØ range. Resulting output immediately follows the program listing.

```
1 TOTINT=0.00
2 RATE=.05
3 PRIN=100.00
4 YRINT=PRIN*RATE
C
5 DO 9 MONTHS=1,12,1
6 SAVEMO=MONTHS
7 ZINTMO=YRINT*((12.-(SAVEMO-1.))/12.)
8 WRITE(3,12)MONTHS,ZINTMO
9 TOTINT=TOTINT+ZINTMO
C
10 AVEINT=TOTINT/SAVEMO
11 WRITE(3,13)TOTINT,AVEINT
12 FORMAT(1X,I2,T6,F5.2)
13 FORMAT(T6,F5.2,'    AVERAGE = $',F4.2)
14 STOP
  END
```

```
 1    5.00
 2    4.58
 3    4.17
 4    3.75
 5    3.33
 6    2.92
 7    2.50
 8    2.08
 9    1.67
10    1.25
11    0.83
12    0.42
     32.50    AVERAGE = $2.71
```

Following are some brief comments on each statement in the program illustrated in Figure 7–1:

Statement Number	Comments
1	Initializes total interest for the year to zero.
2	Initializes rate of interest to 5 percent.
3	Initializes the principal (amount of monthly deposit) to $100.00.
4	Computes the amount of interest for one year ($5.00). Values for arithmetic expressions that remain constant within a DØ loop should be computed before entry to avoid calculating the same expression each time the DØ loop is executed.
5	Establishes the loop control.
6	Saves the index MØNTHS at the floating point variable name SAVEMØ. Each time through the loop SAVEMØ will be incremented by 1; after exit from the loop, MØNTHS will become undefined but SAVEMØ will retain the current value of 12. The index was saved in floating point mode so it could be used in the arithmetic expressions in statements 7 and 10 thus keeping these expressions consistent in mode.
7	Computes the interest earned on each monthly deposit: January = $5.00 * 12./12. February = $5.00 * 11./12. March = $5.00 * 10./12. etc.
8	Index MØNTHS is used to sequentially number the output lines. If SAVEMØ had been used with F2.0 format code, a decimal point (or period) would have followed the line number.
9	Increments the total interest for the year by the amount of interest earned on the monthly deposit.
10	Computes the average interest. The constant (12.) could have been used instead of SAVEMØ for the divisor in this case. If the test value had been an integer variable name instead of an integer constant, this technique of saving the index value may be a great convenience to the programmer.
11	Writes total interest for the year and average interest per month.
12	Describes output lines for each month.
13	Describes final output line. Note how the use of the T format code in statements 12 and 13 ease the task of aligning the total interest for the year directly below the interest per month.
14	Terminates the program.
None	The END statement may be numbered but should not be referenced by another statement. It must always appear last in the source program.

Figure 7–1 illustrated how the index can be used to sequentially number the output lines, but there are many other ways in which the index can be used in a DØ loop. The only restriction to the use of variable names used for the index, initial, test, and increment values is that they cannot be changed by a statement in the DØ range. Figure 7–1 was particularly

designed to illustrate how to avoid the problem of losing the current value of the index after a normal exit from a DØ loop. The following section illustrates a method of avoiding the problem of ending a DØ range with a forbidden statement.

THE CØNTINUE STATEMENT

The CØNTINUE statement is a "dummy statement" that can be placed anywhere in the source program prior to the END statement (which must always be the last statement in any FORTRAN program). The CØN-TINUE statement does not affect the sequence of execution; when this statement is encountered by the computer, it is ignored, and the computer continues on to whatever it would ordinarily do next. This dummy statement is sometimes referred to as a "do nothing" statement, but it has a very important purpose and is often required as the last statement in a DØ range.

Purpose of the CØNTINUE Statement

The main purpose of a CØNTINUE statement is to provide the programmer with a statement that can be used to end a DØ range that would otherwise end with a forbidden statement.

A CØNTINUE statement might also be required as the last in a DØ range even if the last statement is not forbidden. For example, a control statement may be required *within* the DØ range to test for a special condition; if this special condition is encountered, it may be required that control return to the DØ statement and the index incremented without executing any additional statements in the DØ range. The control statement *within* the DØ range cannot reference the DØ statement because the index is incremented only when control automatically returns from the last statement in the DØ range. But the control statement *within* the DØ range can reference a CØNTINUE statement located last in the DØ range; control will then automatically pass back to the DØ statement, and the index will be incremented without executing any additional statements in the DØ range.

Many programmers follow the practice of always using a CØNTINUE statement as the last in any DØ range. This practice relieves the programmer of concern with the rules and restrictions regarding the last statement in a DØ range.

General Form

The general form of a CØNTINUE statement is:

```
|12345|6|7
nnnnn   CØNTINUE
```

Legend:

nnnnn   Any unique one- to five-digit integer which specifies the statement number. It is usually required because this statement is usually referenced by a DØ statement or by a control statement *within* a DØ range.

CØNTINUE   A key word specifying the type of statement.

Illustrative Example

Assume that a problem requires that an input deck of 100 cards be read and processed. The input deck contains three data fields: A, B, and KØDE. All input cards containing the value 7 in the KØDE field are to be ignored; the data in the A and B fields of all other cards are to be added and the resulting SUM written on a printer; the SUM of each card processed is to be accumulated for further processing.

The following partial program illustrates an example of a situation where a CØNTINUE statement is required because of a control statement *within* the DØ range.

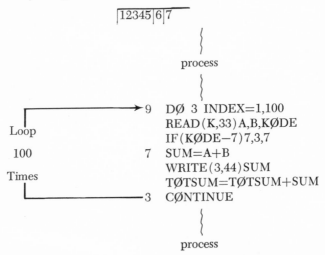

Note that the IF causes a branch to the CØNTINUE when a KØDE value of 7 is encountered. From the CØNTINUE, control automatically passes back to the DØ; and the INDEX is incremented by 1. If a KØDE value of 7 caused a branch back to the DØ directly, the index would have been initialized rather than incremented. As a consequence, there could not be a normal exit from the loop after processing 100 cards.

More advanced applications using DØ and CØNTINUE statements will be presented in the following chapters.

ALPHAMERIC INPUT AND OUTPUT DATA

The only type of input data covered thus far in this book has been numeric; the only type of output data covered has been numeric with the exception of two types of literals permitted in output FØRMAT statements, (1) the Hollerith message (H format code) and (2) literals enclosed in apostrophes. This section covers two methods of reading alphameric input data and one additional method of writing alphameric output data. Alphameric (sometimes called "alphanumeric") data may consist of any letter, number, or special character acceptable to the computer system; alphameric data is not restricted to the FORTRAN character set.

Alphameric Input Data Using FØRMAT Literals

Before discussing input, alphameric output via FØRMAT statement literals enclosed in apostrophes will be briefly reviewed. Assume the following partial program:

```
12345|6|7
   6   FØRMAT('  MESSAGE NØ. 1')
   7   FØRMAT(T22,'FINAL ANSWER',F7.2)
   8   WRITE(3,6)
   9   WRITE(3,7)DATA
```

When statement number 8 in the preceding illustration is executed, the computer will automatically write MESSAGE NØ. 1 in the first 13 printing positions or columns of the printer. Note that the literal contains 14 characters, but the blank preceding the word MESSAGE is used for line spacing control and will not be printed. Statement number 9 will cause the printer to write FINAL ANSWER in printing positions or columns 21 through 32 and the current value of DATA in the following 7–column field.

Alphameric literal data can also be read into a FØRMAT statement literal via an input device. To illustrate, assume the following partial program:

```
12345|6|7
   6   FØRMAT('  MESSAGE NØ. 1')
   7   FØRMAT(T22,'FINAL ANSWER',F7.2)
   4   READ(1,6)
   5   READ(1,7)DATA
         . . .
```

When READ statement number 4 is executed, the computer will replace the 14–position literal in FØRMAT statement number 6 with the data contained in the first 14 columns of the input card. Remember, read-in is destructive so each time statement number 4 is executed, the literal will be replaced by the input data. Likewise, each time READ statement number 5 is executed, any data contained in columns 22 through 31 on the input card will replace the literal in FØRMAT statement number 7; the floating point data in the following 7–column floating point field will initialize, or replace, the current value of DATA.

In effect, input data read into a FØRMAT statement literal is stored in the FØRMAT statement rather than at a symbolic address represented by a variable name. The number of alphameric characters read in is always equal to the number of positions between the apostrophes. If this same FØRMAT statement is referenced by a WRITE statement, the literal will always appear in the output image.

This method of alphameric input has some obvious disadvantages. The only way to get the literal data out of the computer is to reference the same FØRMAT statement by a WRITE statement, but there is no way to change the location of the literal in the FØRMAT statement. If a card punch is used as the output device, the output card will always contain the literal in the same columns as the previously read input card. If a printer is used as the output device, this method could cause some problems. For example, if the literal was located in the first 14 positions of the FØRMAT statement and the WRITE statement referenced a printer, the first position of the literal would not be printed. Furthermore, because the first position in the output image determines the line spacing on a printer, unless the first position of the literal is known and controlled, line spacing will be unpredictable. It should be noted that integer or floating point data as well as alphabetic letters and special characters may appear in an alphameric literal. But numeric data read into a FØRMAT statement literal is not available for use in any statement in a program except a WRITE statement. Literal data cannot be manipulated or used in the same manner as data located at a symbolic address represented by a variable name; it can be changed only by execution of another READ statement.

Now that the disadvantages of this method have been covered, an effective use will be illustrated. The following program will reproduce an exact copy of each of 100 cards in an input deck:

```
|12345|6|7
    8   FØRMAT('1234567890123456789
    1 0123456789012345678901234 56
    2 789012345678901234567890123
    3 4567890')
        DØ 7 LØØP=1,100
        READ(1,8)
    7   WRITE(2,8)
        STØP
        END
```

Note that any valid alphameric characters could have been used to compose the 80–position literal between the apostrophes; sequential numbers were used to make the illustration easier to follow.

One final point should be made concluding the discussion on FØRMAT statement literals. Although all illustrations in this section used literals enclosed in apostrophes, the other type of literal, the Hollerith message, can be used in a similar manner.

Alphameric Input Data Using the A Format Code

The A or "alphameric" format code provides a method of reading alphameric data into a symbolic address represented by a variable name similar to the technique used with I and F format codes. If alphameric data can be addressed by a variable name, it can be omitted from the output image or included in any desired location. Thus, most of the restrictions associated with alphameric literals stored in a FØRMAT statement can be avoided.

The general form of the A format code is:

$$rA1$$

Legend:

r   An integer which specifies the number of times the format code is to be *repeated*. It is optional with the programmer and omitted if the code is used only once.

A   Specifies that the field contains *alphameric* data.

1   An integer which specifies the *length* of the field.

Before discussing the A format code, the I and F format codes will be briefly reviewed. The first character of integer and floating point variable names implies the mode of the input data; the variable names must begin with an alphabetic letter and cannot exceed six letters and/or numbers in length; an integer variable name must begin with one of the letters I through N, whereas a floating point variable name must start with a letter other than I through N. If I format code is specified, the computer automatically tests the data in the input field to assure that it contains no characters other than numbers, a high-order sign, and blanks. If F format code is specified, the computer allows only numbers, a high-order sign, blanks, and a decimal point in the input field.

When A format code is specified, the computer does not test the input field to assure it contains only valid integer or floating point data; it accepts any alphameric character compatible to the computer system. The first character of an alphameric variable name does not imply the mode, so it may be any of the 27 alphabetic letters. But the restriction that the variable name must begin with an alphabetic letter and must not exceed six letters and/or numbers in length still applies. These rules for the composition and length of a variable name do not apply to the *data* stored at a variable name.

Each alphabetic letter, special character, and number read into the computer in A format code is individually stored in a unique internal code;

because alphameric data is stored digit by digit rather than converted into normal integer or floating point internal representation, it is not available for arithmetic operations.

FORTRAN is designed to handle long strings of integer and floating point numbers. No problems in this book, and few in actual practice, exceed this numeric capacity, so the maximum size of numeric input fields has not been emphasized. But FORTRAN has rather severe restrictions on the maximum length of an alphameric field which should be emphasized—it may not exceed four columns in length. (There is one exception to this rule. If the program contains an "explicit statement" specifying the variable name associated with the field to be double precision, the field may be eight columns in length. Explicit statements are covered later in this book, and this exception will be ignored in this chapter.)

To illustrate the use of the A format code, assume that an input data card is in the following format:

Field Name	Card Columns	Illustrative Field Contents
Employee Number	1–4	1234
Employee Name	5–24	JOE DOAKS, JR.
Hours Worked	25–29	40.50

The following statements can be used to describe and read the above data card:

```
|12345|6|7
    8   FØRMAT(I4,5A4,F5.2)
        READ(1,8)NUMEMP,N,A,M,E,S,HØURS
```

A unique variable name must always be assigned to each input data field corresponding to the format codes describing the data. Because the format code specifies five contiguous A4 fields, five variable names (N, A, M, E, and S) are assigned to the five alphameric fields.

Alphameric Output Using the A Format Code

If alphameric data is read into the computer using A format code, it can be written out only if A format code is specified for the output.

The following program will read an alphameric field located in the last 24 columns of one input card; output will be written on one line in the 24 printing positions of columns 31 through 54:

```
|12345|6|7
   88   FØRMAT(T57,6A4)
    9   FØRMAT(T32,6A4)
```

READ(1,88)A1,A2,A3,A4,A5,A6
WRITE(3,9)A1,A2,A3,A4,A5,A6
STØP
END

PROBLEMS

1. Write the program described in Problem 11 in the preceding chapter with the following change only: Use a DØ statement, instead of an IF, for loop control.

2. Write the program described in Problem 12 in the preceding chapter with the following changes only:

1. The input data deck contains the following 10 cards instead of only 1 (use a DØ statement for loop control):

First Value (Cols. 2–6)	Second Value (9–13)	Third Value (16–20)	Card Identification (30–43)
1	2	3	CARD NUMBER 1
1	3	2	CARD NUMBER 2
2	1	3	CARD NUMBER 3
2	3	1	CARD NUMBER 4
3	1	2	CARD NUMBER 5
3	2	1	CARD NUMBER 6
1	1	2	CARD NUMBER 7
1	2	1	CARD NUMBER 8
2	1	1	CARD NUMBER 9
3	3	3	CARD NUMBER 10

2. Read the alphameric identification data into a FØRMAT statement literal;

3. Write the literal by using the same FØRMAT statement for output and input; and

4. Output is to be one printed line for each input card," "single-spaced" in the following format:

Field Name	Printing Positions or "Columns"
First Value	1–5
Second Value	8–12
Third Value	15–19
Largest Integer	22–26
Card Identification	29–42

3. Write the program described in Problem 13 in the preceding chapter with the following changes only: (1) use a DØ statement, instead of an IF, for loop control; (2) read in the employee names using A format code; and (3) write employee names, using A format code, in the first 20 printing positions or columns.

4. Write a program to compute and write an Interplanetary Weight Chart indicating how much a man would weigh on various planets based on the following facts:

Planet	Percentage of Earth Weight
Moon	16
Mars	38
Venus	85
Jupiter	264

No input data cards are to be used. Use a DØ statement to control the computation and writing of earth weights from 90 through 220 pounds in increments of 5 pounds. Corresponding weights for the other planets are also to be computed and written under control of the DØ statement.

Use a printer for output. The first header line should contain the word INTERPLANETARY and the second the words WEIGHT CHART. The third line should be blank, and the fourth should contain the names of the planets in the following sequence from left to right:

EARTH MOON MARS VENUS JUPITER

Use only one WRITE statement to write the header lines. The output data should be single-spaced following the header lines. Weights are to be carried to one decimal place.

5. Write a program to compute for each employee: (1) current social security deduction for the week; (2) current net pay for the week (gross pay less social security deduction); (3) new year-to-date cumulative earnings; and (4) new year-to-date cumulative social security deductions.

Input data deck contains the weekly payroll cards for 10 employees in the following format:

Old Year-to-Date Earnings (Cols. 2–9)	Old Year-to-Date Soc. Sec. Ded'ns (10–15)	Rate per Hour (16–20)	Hours for Current Week (21–25)	Employee Name (26–45)	Employee Number (46–50)
12345.78	374.40	10.20	40.50	JOHN P. DOE	12345
4000.00	192.00	5.00	40.00	JON DOACKSON	12346
8888.88	374.40	8.00	40.00	JOHN DOACKSON	12347
7800.00	374.40	6.00	32.00	CAROL DOACKSON	12348
7400.00	355.20	10.00	40.00	JON P. DOACKSON	12349
6000.00	288.00	10.00	40.00	JOHN P. DOACKSON	12350
7400.00	355.20	10.00	20.00	JANET P. DOACKSON	12351
7400.00	355.20	10.00	50.00	MARY JANE DOACKSON	12352
7799.99	374.39	10.00	40.00	MARY DOAKS DOACKSON	12353
1000.00	48.00	10.00	10.00	OMEGA DOAKS DOACKSON	12354

Use a DØ statement for loop control. Do not compute "overtime" in this program.

Assume that the social security deduction rate is 4.8 percent of the first $7,800.00 of earnings during the year. Thus, some employees may have no social security deduction for the week, some may have a deduction on only a portion of their current weekly earnings, and others on all of their weekly earnings.

Output is to be single spaced on a printer with one line for each employee in the following sequence from left to right:

> *Field Name*
> Employee name
> Old year-to-date earnings
> Current pay for the week
> New year-to-date earnings
> Old-year-to-date soc. sec. ded'ns.
> Current social security ded'ns.
> New year-to-date soc. sec. ded'ns.

Allow reasonable spacing between each output field. Dress up the output with descriptive headings.

6. Write the program described in Problem 5 in this chapter with the following changes:

1. In addition to the printed output, punch one output data card for each employee in the same format as the input data card (to be used as input data the next payroll period) but:
   A. "Old year-to-date earnings" is to be changed to the computed "new year-to-date earnings."
   B. "Old year-to-date social security deductions" is to be changed to the computed "new year-to-date social security deductions."
   C. "Rate per hour," "hours for current week," and "employee name" fields are to be left blank.
2. Assume that employee number 12347 is the son of the owner. Because he is celebrating his 21st birthday during the current week, he is to receive double his regular pay. Assume that the exact location of his card in the input data deck is unknown, so test all input cards for this particular employee number within the DØ loop. When the card is encountered, exit from the DØ range, compute his pay, and return to complete the processing. His "birthday bonus" is subject to social security deductions if he has not already earned $7,800 or more during the year.

7. Immediately following his graduation, Joe Doe is employed at his first full-time job. Once each year company management determines monthly salaries of each employee for the following calendar year. Joe's take-home pay was increased to $600.00 per month, so he decides to start a regular savings plan.

Beginning in January he will invest 5 percent of his take-home pay at the beginning of each month. His investment will earn 6 percent interest per year based on the number of months his investment is on deposit. (For example, his January deposit will earn $^{12}/_{12}$ of 6 percent, his February deposit $^{11}/_{12}$ of 6 percent, etc.)

He decides to continue this plan for 10 years and make no withdrawals. He expects the interest rate to continue at 6 percent per year. Interest will be compounded annually; at the end of each year his interest will be left on deposit to be added to his total investment. Thus, each year he will earn interest on his monthly deposits plus 6 percent of his beginning-of-the-year balance.

Joe believes the company will continue its policy of determining monthly salaries only once each year, effective at the beginning of each calendar year. He expects his monthly take-home pay to be 10 percent more each year than the preceding year.

Write a program to compute the amount of Joe's investment account at the end of 10 years. Output is to be on 10 single-spaced printed lines. Each output line is to contain the following data fields from left to right:

Line number
Beginning-of-the-year balance (before any investment)
Total investment during the year
Total interest earned during the year
End-of-the-year balance

Allow reasonable spacing between the output data fields. Dress up the output with descriptive headings.

8. Write a program to compute and print the speed chart illustrated below. It indicates the time required to travel one mile for all speeds from 10 m.p.h. through 250 m.p.h. which are evenly divisible by 10. No input data cards may be used—this must be a "self-operational program." A DØ loop is required.

Speed	Time to Travel One Mile		
10	6 MINS	0.0	SECS
20	3 MINS	0.0	SECS
30	2 MINS	0.0	SECS
40	1 MINS	30.0	SECS
50	1 MINS	12.0	SECS
60	1 MINS	0.0	SECS
70	0 MINS	51.4	SECS
80	0 MINS	45.0	SECS
90	0 MINS	40.0	SECS

Etc. through:

250	0 MINS	14.4	SECS

CHAPTER
8

ONE-DIMENSIONAL ARRAYS AND SPECIFICATION STATEMENTS

$\int$ OME programs must be designed to store large quantities of related data. Each data item must always be assigned a unique variable name because it is impossible to store two or more different data items in the same place at the same time. In previous chapters in this book, the programmer has been responsible for assigning all variable names. This chapter covers various methods of directing the compiler to assign a unique variable name to each item in a related group. The programmer is required to assign a variable name to the group, but the compiler will assign a different subscript to this name for each item within the group. The subscript, which makes the variable name unique, also identifies the position of the item within the group. Data stored in this manner is called an *array*. It is difficult to appreciate the real power of a computer until the use of arrays has been mastered.

When a program includes an array, the compiler must always be given descriptive information regarding the array size and type. The non-executable statement which furnishes this information is called a *specification statement*. There are several different types of specification statements, some of which are used to describe the nature of nonarray data. Five types are covered in this chapter.

ONE-DIMENSIONAL ARRAYS

An array is a list, or table, of related data items stored internally in a reserved area. Each item in an array is called an *array element*. All elements in a given array must be in the same mode. A *one-dimensional array* is simply a list of either integer, floating point, or alphameric data values. To illustrate a one-dimensional array, assume that a list of integers consists of the following values in the order indicated:

$$7, 6, 4, 3, \text{ and } 2$$

The programmer might assign the variable name LIST for convenience in referring to this integer array. The mode of the variable name assigned to the array must agree with the mode of the data values; if the above array consisted of floating point instead of integer values, a floating point variable name would be required.

A customary way of referring to individual items within a list is by *subscript*. "LIST sub one" refers to the first item in a list, "LIST sub two" refers to the second item, etc. Thus, in ordinary mathematical notation, the elements in the preceding integer array called LIST would be:

$$\text{LIST}_1 \text{ is } 7$$
$$\text{LIST}_2 \text{ is } 6$$
$$\text{LIST}_3 \text{ is } 4$$
$$\text{LIST}_4 \text{ is } 3$$
$$\text{LIST}_5 \text{ is } 2$$

Subscript Indication

Previous chapters have indicated that FORTRAN does not permit the use of *superscripts* in the usual method, because input and output media have no provision for such indication. For example, instead of indicating "R raised to the power of two" as R^2, the superscript is indicated by two preceding asterisks (R**2). Likewise, *subscripts* cannot be indicated in the usual method. In FORTRAN, subscripts are enclosed in parentheses which follow the variable name. To illustrate, the individual elements in the previous LIST array example, subscripted as required in FORTRAN, would be

$$\text{LIST}(1) \text{ is } 7$$
$$\text{LIST}(2) \text{ is } 6$$
$$\text{LIST}(3) \text{ is } 4$$
$$\text{LIST}(4) \text{ is } 3$$
$$\text{LIST}(5) \text{ is } 2$$

Subscripts are not permitted on independent variable names which are not associated with an array. But subscripted variable names are required if the source program contains an array and must be used to symbolically address an element within an array. The variable name for each array element is always the array variable name followed by a unique subscript. Rules for independent variable names, previously covered, also apply to array variable names. It should be noted that the length and composition of the subscript is not considered when composing the array variable name. In effect, it is something "extra" which is added to the end of a valid variable name. The rules for the composition of subscripts, which must be enclosed in parentheses, will be covered next.

Numeric Subscripts.   As previously indicated, the variable name assigned to the array must be consistent in mode with the type of data to be stored. An array may contain either integer, floating point, or alphameric data; but in Basic FORTRAN IV a numeric subscript must always be an unsigned *integer constant*. A subscript identifies the position of an element within an array. Its current value must be more than zero because there is no zero or minus position in the array list.

Variable Name Subscripts.   A variable name may also be used as a subscript, but there are three restrictions in Basic FORTRAN IV:

1. Only an *integer* mode variable name is permitted.
2. If the subscript consists of only an integer variable name, its current value must be greater than zero because there is no zero or minus position in the array list.
3. The integer variable name, used as a subscript, cannot be subscripted. Stated another way, a subscript within a subscript is not permitted.

Arithmetic Expression Subscripts.   A numeric or a variable name subscript is actually an arithmetic expression enclosed in parentheses. An arithmetic expression, as defined previously in this book, may consist of one constant, one variable name, or a combination of variable names and/or constants separated by delimiters; it may be in integer, floating point, or mixed mode. But the mode, form, and content of arithmetic expressions permitted as subscripts have severe restrictions.

The rules for subscripts containing one constant or one variable name were covered in the two preceding sections. When an arithmetic expression used as a subscript in Basic FORTRAN IV contains other than one variable name or one constant, several rules apply. Each variable name and/or constant must be in *integer* mode; a variable name subscript cannot be subscripted; the evaluated result of the arithmetic expression must be greater than zero; and only certain combinations of variable names, constants, and arithmetic operators are permitted. The valid combinations are illustrated in the following section.

Valid Subscript Forms.   Only seven forms of arithmetic expressions are allowed as subscripts in Basic FORTRAN IV; *absolutely no other forms are permitted*. The valid forms are as indicated following:

c

vn

vn+c

vn—c

c*vn

c*vn+c

c*vn—c

Legend:

vn   A nonsubscripted integer *variable name*.

c   An unsigned integer *constant*.

It cannot be overemphasized that absolutely no form of arithmetic expression, other than those previously indicated, is permitted as a subscript in Basic FORTRAN IV. Beginning programmers often have difficulties because of failure to recognize the severe restrictions of the subscript form. To emphasize these restrictions, the following invalid subscripted variable names are illustrated:

Subscripted Variable Name	*Reason Invalid*
A(0)	Current value of subscript must be more than zero.
B(+3)	Subscript cannot be signed.
C(2.)	Subscript must be in integer mode.
D(N(3))	Subscript cannot be subscripted.
E(2+N)	Variable name must precede constant when either a plus or minus sign is used in subscript.
F(N*2)	Constant must precede variable name when multiplication sign is used in subscript.
G(I+N)	Subscript cannot contain more than one variable name.
H(3+2)	Subscript cannot contain more than one constant unless it also contains a variable name.
I(2/N/3)	Subscript cannot contain two identical arithmetic operators; the only permitted operators are +, —, and *.

Use of Arrays

A program may contain as many arrays as is required for the problem to be solved and is permitted by the capacity of the computer. To demonstrate the use and convenience of arrays in general, and one-dimensional arrays in particular, various alternative methods of solution of the following illustrative problem will be presented throughout a major portion of this chapter.

Illustrative Problem. An input deck consists of three data cards, in identical format, each containing one unsigned positive floating point data field. All input data are to be totaled and divided by three to compute the average; the difference between the value contained in each input data field and the average of all input values is to be computed. Output is to consist of three cards in identical format, each containing two floating point data fields; one data field is to contain the input value, the other the difference between the input value and the average of all input values. It should be noted that all input data values must be stored in different internal locations so they will be available for computing the average, the difference between each input value and the average, and also so they will be available for output after all computations are finished.

The input cards contain the following data:

	Card Columns	Actual Data
Card 1	1–4	1.15
Card 2	1–4	1.75
Card 3	1–4	1.60

One method of solving this problem would be to use only one variable name, such as DATA, in the READ statement. But each time a card is read in, the current value of DATA would change. Because each input value is required for further processing after the average of all input values has been computed, the program would have to be designed to save each input value at three unique variable names such as SAVE1, SAVE2, and SAVE3. One way to do this would be to use three identical READ statements, each followed by an arithmetic statement; the first arithmetic statement could store the current value of DATA at SAVE1, the next at SAVE2, and the last at SAVE3. This would be an inconvenient method of solving the problem.

Another method of solution would be to prepare two identical sets of input cards. The first set of three cards would be individually read, the total accumulated, and the average computed. Next, each card in the second set of cards would be read, the difference between the average and the input value would be computed, and then the input value and difference would be written. This would also be an inconvenient method of solving the problem.

The most convenient method of solving this problem would be to assign a unique variable name to each input value when the READ statement is executed. This unique variable name may be assigned by the programmer or by the compiler. Variations of each method will be discussed next.

As covered in preceding chapters, the following partial program could be used to read the input data:

```
|12345|6|7
    81    FØRMAT(F4.2)
          READ(1,81)A1
          READ(1,81)A2
          READ(1,81)A3
```

This partial program would assign a unique unsubscripted variable name to each input value; these stored values would thus be available for further processing.

When the READ list exceeds the number of format codes, the FØRMAT statement is automatically reused until the list is satisfied. Thus, the programmer could also use the following partial program to read the input data:

```
12345 6 7
   82   FØRMAT(F4.2)
        READ(1,82)A1,A2,A3
```

The problem only requires three input cards, but what if it contained 500? The programmer would then be required to either prepare 500 READ statements or one READ statement with 500 unique variable names if he used either of the preceding two techniques. In this case, it would be more convenient to use an array, as illustrated next.

Array Input via DØ and READ Statements.   If the programmer uses a DØ statement to read in an array, his partial program might appear as follows:

```
12345 6 7
   83   FØRMAT(F4.2)
        DØ 8 LØØP=1,3
    8   READ(1,83)A(LØØP)
            {
            {
        process
```

The DØ index (LØØP) will have a current value of one on the first pass through the DØ range, two on the second, and three on the third. The above partial program will thus cause the computer to automatically assign the subscripted variable names A(1) to the value from the first card, A(2) to the second, and A(3) to the third.

It should be noted that the preceding partial program will direct the computer to read 500 values into the array if the DØ statement test value is simply changed from 3 to 500. Consider the difficulty of writing a program to store 500 different data items if an array, combined with the powerful DØ statement, was not used. Instead of a relatively short program, a long repetitious one would be required. This should clearly indicate one convenience of an array.

Array Input via a READ Statement with an "Implied DØ."   FORTRAN provides an even more efficient method of reading data into an array than illustrated in the previous section. Whenever possible, the programmer should use a READ statement with an "implied DØ" to read an array instead of using a DØ statement and a READ statement. This method reduces execution time as well as programming time. An "implied DØ" can only be used with READ and WRITE statements. (An "implied DØ" in a WRITE statement is illustrated later in this chapter.)

When an "implied DØ" is used, it appears in the READ list and includes all information of a regular DØ statement except the first two elements: "DØ sn." The key word DØ is omitted to distinguish it from a regular DØ statement; a statement number is not referenced because unlike a regular DØ which can be used to repeat a series of statements, an "implied DØ" repeats only the statement in which it appears. For this reason, this type of READ statement is sometimes called "self-indexing."

To distinguish it from variable names which normally appear in a READ list, an "implied DØ" specification must be enclosed in parentheses. Within the parentheses are one or more subscripted variable names separated by commas and followed by the "implied DØ" which must be preceded by a comma. If the increment value is omitted, one is assumed as in a regular DØ statement.

The following partial program uses a READ statement with an "implied DØ" to read in the entire array in the illustrative problem:

```
|12345|6|7
    84    FØRMAT(F4.2)
          READ(1,84)(A(LØØP),LØØP=1,3)
              {
              {
              {
          process
```

In the illustrative problem, it is known that the input deck contained three cards so a test value of three is used. If header card technique was used, the test value would have been a variable name with a current value indicating the number of cards to be read.

But, it should be noted that when an input deck contains an unknown number of cards and an IF statement is used to test for a trailer card, the "self-indexing" READ statement cannot be used because there is no way to change the test value during execution of the READ statement. Of course, if it was known that the input deck did not exceed 100 cards, for example, a regular DØ with a test value of 100 and a READ statement could be used to read in the array with an IF statement *within* the DØ range to provide an exit when the trailer card is encountered.

One final point should be made before concluding the discussion on various methods of array input: The READ list may include as many different arrays as is required by the problem and is permitted by the capacity of the computer.

Addressing Elements in an Array. Each element, or data value, within an array must have a unique subscripted variable name; if a variable name is not associated with an array, it cannot be subscripted. If an element in an array is required in a source program statement, it must be "called for" or addressed by its unique subscripted variable name. For example, execution of the first of the following two arithmetic statements will double the current value of the third element in an array called "X" and store the product at the symbolic address DØUBLE; execution of the second statement will double the first element and store the product at the second element in the same array.

```
|12345|6|7
   85   DØUBLE=X(3)*2.
        X(2)=X(1)*2.
```

Of course, following execution of the two preceding statements, the current values of X(3) and X(1) will remain unchanged, but the current value of the second element in the X array will be double the current value of the first element.

Going back to the illustrative problem, if the input data had been read in as an array, as indicated, it would be stored as follows:

Subscripted Variable Name	Stored Data
A(1)	1.15
A(2)	1.75
A(3)	1.60

The next step in the solution to the problem is to compute the total and average of the three values stored in the array. There are several ways this can be done. For example, the average can be computed by one statement:

```
|12345|6|7
   86   AVE=(A(1)+A(2)+A(3))/3.00
```

It can also be computed by two statements:

```
|12345|6|7
   87   SUM=A(1)+A(2)+A(3)
        AVE=SUM/3.00
```

It can also be computed by four statements:

```
|12345|6|7
   88   SUM=0.00
        DØ 7 N=1,3
    7   SUM=SUM+A(N)
        AVE=SUM/3.00
```

Because the illustrative problem has only three elements in the array, the first of the three preceding illustrations would be the most convenient for computing the total and average. But, if the array had 500 elements instead of only 3, the first two methods would require the programmer to list 500 subscripted variable names separated by plus signs. The last of the three preceding illustrations would obviously be the most convenient in this case because only the test value of the DØ statement would have to be changed from 3 to 500. It should be pointed out that if the data had not been read in as an array, the programmer could not use the third method illustrated; the compiler can make a variable name unique only by assignment of different subscripts, and only elements in an array may have subscripted variable names. This should illustrate another convenience of an array.

Creating Arrays via DØ and Arithmetic Statements. As previously covered in this chapter, a DØ and a READ statement or a READ statement with an "implied DØ" can be used to create an array at input time. Arrays can also be created via a DØ statement and an arithmetic statement. (An "implied DØ" is never allowed in an arithmetic statement; it is only allowed in READ and WRITE statements.)

Suppose it is decided to create another one-dimensional array in the illustrative problem. The following statements will establish an array with each element containing the difference between the average and each element of the A array:

```
|12345|6|7
   89   DØ 5 L=1,3
    5   DIFF(L)=A(L)−AVE
            {
            {
         process
```

The three values in the A array are 1.15, 1.75, and 1.60, so 1.50 is the average. The DIFF array would thus be as follows:

Subscripted Variable Name	Stored Data
DIFF(1)	−0.35
DIFF(2)	0.25
DIFF(3)	0.10

Array Output via DØ and WRITE Statements. If the DIFF array in the preceding section is *not* created, the following partial program can be used to write the output for the illustrative problem:

```
|12345|6|7
  810   FØRMAT(F4.2,2X,F5.2)
        DØ 9 K=1,3
        DIFF=A(K)−AVE
    9   WRITE(2,810)A(K),DIFF
```

If the DIFF array is created, it will not be necessary to recompute DIFF; so the following partial program can be used to write the output:

```
|12345|6|7
  811   FØRMAT(F4.2,2X,F5.2)
        DØ 9 K=1,3
    9   WRITE(2,811)A(K),DIFF(K)
```

Array Output via a WRITE Statement with an "Implied DØ." An "implied DØ" can be used in a WRITE statement in the same manner as in a READ statement. If the DIFF array is created, the following partial program can be used to write the output for the illustrative problem:

```
|12345|6|7
  812   FØRMAT(F4.2,2X,F5.2)
        WRITE(2,812)(A(K),DIFF(K),K=1,3)
```

A WRITE statement with an "implied DØ" should always be used whenever possible because it reduces execution time as well as programming time. It should be noted again that a READ or WRITE statement with an "implied DØ" simply repeats itself; unlike a DØ statement, it cannot execute a series of statements. As previously indicated, this type of statement is sometimes called a "self-indexing" READ or WRITE statement. It should also be noted that a "self-indexing" WRITE statement cannot be used in the illustrative problem if the DIFF array is not created. The reason, of course, is because there is no way to compute DIFF in a WRITE statement; DIFF must be computed by an arithmetic statement.

A "self-indexing" WRITE statement may include both independent and array variable names. To illustrate, assume that the output for the illustrative problem was to include, in order, the following fields: Average, Card Number, Input Value, and Difference. The following partial program could be used to write the output:

```
|12345|6|7
  813   FØRMAT(F4.2,I1,F4.2,F5.2)
        WRITE(2,813)AVE,(K,A(K),DIFF(K),K=1,3)
```

Note how the "implied DØ" is enclosed in parentheses to distinguish it from the independent variable name AVE appearing in the WRITE list. Also note that K (card number) must be within the parentheses containing the "implied DØ" or it will be undefined.

Reading and Writing Arrays without Subscripts. Before concluding the discussion on one-dimensional arrays, one more programming "shortcut" will be covered. It should be noted that this technique cannot be used when it is necessary to READ or WRITE only selected elements in an array; it can only be used to READ or WRITE an entire array.

When an array is used in a program, the general rule is that the variable name of the array cannot appear in any statement unless it is subscripted. There is one exception to this rule: an unsubscripted array name may be used in I/O statements, that is, READ and WRITE statements. This method is preferred but can be used only if an entire array is to be read or written and if a specification statement indicates the exact number of elements in the array. (Specification statements are covered later in this chapter; the illustrations in this section, as in previous sections, assume that all arrays are properly described in the program.)

Reading Arrays without Subscripts. The following statements will read in the entire A array in the illustrative problem:

```
|12345|6|7
   814   FØRMAT(F4.2)
         READ(1,814)A
```

The above statements will produce the same results as the DØ and READ or the "self-indexing" READ, previously illustrated. The compiler will automatically assign the unique subscripted variable name A(1) to the first element read in, A(2) to the second, and A(3) to the third.

In the illustrative problem, each array element was punched in a separate input card. If all three elements had been punched in the first 12 columns of one card, the following statements could be used to read in the array:

```
|12345|6|7
   815   FØRMAT(3F4.2)
         READ(1,815)A
```

A(1) would be read from the first four columns, followed by A(2) and A(3).

There is an advantage in having more than one array element in a card. A card reader is a mechanical device and extremely slow in comparison to the electronic speed of a computer. Thus, if a large array is to be read from a card reader, it requires less input time, and is therefore more efficient, if each card contains as many array elements as possible. For example, if a 4,000–element integer array is punched one element per card in I2 format code, 4,000 cards will have to be read from the card reader; but only 100 cards can contain the entire array if each card contains 40 elements in 40I2 format code.

A READ statement may include any combination of unsubscripted array variable names, subscripted array variable names, and independent (nonarray) variable names; but the programmer must be extremely cautious when using such combinations. A thorough knowledge of the operation of the READ statement is required, and the input data deck must be properly formatted and sequenced to obtain the desired results.

The FØRMAT statement specifies the type, location, and length of data fields in an input record. But the order of the variable names in a READ list (from left to right) specifies the order in which data will be read into internal storage. When an unsubscripted array variable name is encountered in the list, the entire array is always read before continuing on to the next variable name. To illustrate the effect of a combination of different types of variable names in a READ list, consider the following statement:

$\overline{|12345|6|7}$
816   READ(1,8)A,B,C(1),D

Assume that A is an independent variable name, B and D are unsubscripted array variable names, and C(1) is the first element of the C array. The above statement will store in order: A, the entire B array, C(1), and finally the entire D array.

Writing Arrays without Subscripts. The following statements will write out the A array only in the illustrative problem:

$\overline{|12345|6|7}$
817   FØRMAT(F4.2)
          WRITE(2,817)A

The above statements will cause A(1) to be punched in the first card, A(2) in the second, and the final element in the array, A(3), in the third. If the format code is changed to 3F4.2, the A array will be punched in the first 12 columns of one card in the following sequence: A(1), A(2), and A(3).

The preceding statements illustrate the use of an unsubscripted variable name in a WRITE list, but they do not solve the illustrative problem; the output required is A(1) and DIFF(1) in the first card, A(2) and DIFF(2) in the second, and A(3) and DIFF(3) in the third.

The current values of the variable names in a WRITE statement are always written in the sequence in which they appear in the list, from left to right. Whenever an unsubscripted array variable name is encountered in the list, the entire array is written, as indicated in the preceding illustration. Thus, this "shortcut" technique cannot be used to solve the illustrative problem as developed up to this point in the discussion. To illustrate, the following statements would cause the entire A array to be written, followed by the entire DIFF array:

$\overline{|12345|6|7}$
818   FØRMAT(F4.2,2X,F5.2)
          WRITE(2,818)A,DIFF

The current values of the elements in the two arrays are:

Array Element	Current Value
A(1)	1.15
A(2)	1.75
A(3)	1.60
DIFF(1)	−0.35
DIFF(2)	0.25
DIFF(3)	0.10

Thus, the preceding statements will result in the following output:

```
 123456789
```

Card 1	1.15	1.75
Card 2	1.60	−0.35
Card 3	0.25	0.10

The above output, of course, does not meet the requirements of the illustrative problem and demonstrates that the programmer cannot always take advantage of all "shortcuts" available in FORTRAN.

It would be possible to use this "shortcut" technique to solve the problem if another array, called AMERGE for example, was created. The AMERGE array should contain the combined or "merged" elements of the A and DIFF arrays in the following sequence:

AMERGE Elements	A and DIFF Elements
(1)	A(1)
(2)	DIFF(1)
(3)	A(2)
(4)	DIFF(2)
(5)	A(3)
(6)	DIFF(3)

The required output could then be obtained by the following statements:

```
 12345 6 7
  819   FØRMAT(F4.2,2X,F5.2)
        WRITE(2,819)AMERGE
```

Various routines for manipulating arrays, including a method of creating the AMERGE array, are covered in the final section of this chapter.

Solution to Illustrative Problem. The illustrative problem used throughout the preceding sections of this chapter has been discussed and illustrated step by step. Now a complete program providing a solution to the problem will be illustrated, but the program contains two minor changes. To provide a more complete illustration of output possibilities, six input cards are used instead of three; to provide printed instead of punched output, a printer is specified as the output device. The statement numbers used in the listed program correspond to those used in the text to provide a reference to the description of each program step. This program and the resulting printed output is illustrated in Figure 8–1.

FIGURE 8–1

A program providing a solution to the illustration program used throughout the preceding sections of this chapter with two minor changes: Six input cards are used instead of three and output is printed instead of punched. Resulting output follows the program listing.

```
C      *** ILLUSTRATIVE PROBLEM, CHAPTER 8 ***
C
       DIMENSION A(6),DIFF(6)
   814 FORMAT(F4.2)
       READ(1,814)A
C
    88 SUM=0.00
       DO 7 N=1,6
     7 SUM=SUM+A(N)
       AVE=SUM/6.00
C
       DO 5 L=1,6
     5 DIFF(L)=A(L)-AVE
C
   813 FORMAT(' INPUT CARD',I2,2X,F4.2,2X,F5.2)
       WRITE(3,813)(K,A(K),DIFF(K),K=1,6)
C
       STOP
       END
```

```
INPUT CARD 1    1.15    -0.35
INPUT CARD 2    1.75     0.25
INPUT CARD 3    1.60     0.10
INPUT CARD 4    1.50     0.00
INPUT CARD 5    0.01    -1.49
INPUT CARD 6    2.99     1.49
```

SPECIFICATION STATEMENTS

FØRMAT statements, previously described, are nonexecutable and are used to furnish the compiler with information required to execute READ and WRITE statements. The specification statements covered in this chapter are also nonexecutable and are used to furnish information required to execute other statements, but they are not used to describe input/output records. Instead, they are used to describe the nature of data used in the source program and to supply information required to allocate or reserve storage locations for this data. Five different specification statements are covered in this chapter.

The DIMENSIØN Statement

No array can appear in a source program unless it is described by a specification statement. A DIMENSIØN statement is one type of specification statement which can be used to direct the compiler to assign reserved sequential fields for storing an array. A DIMENSIØN statement specifies the array variable name, the type of data, and the number of elements in an array. One DIMENSIØN statement may be used to specify any number of arrays. Unlike FØRMAT statements, which may appear anywhere in the source program prior to the END statement, a DIMENSIØN statement must always precede any other statement which references the array.

An array may be "overdimensioned," but it should not be "underdimensioned." If a DIMENSIØN statement specifies that an array contains 100 elements, the compiler will reserve storage accordingly; any number of elements up to a maximum of 100 can be stored in this array but not more. When an array is "overdimensioned," it not only wastes storage but can also increase execution time. Whenever possible, an array should be dimensioned exactly; but if the size of an array is unknown, it must be "scaled" to allow for the maximum number of elements which may be produced by the program.

General Form. The general form of a DIMENSIØN statement used to describe a one-dimensionl array is:

```
12345|6|7
nnnnn    DIMENSIØN vn(ne)₁,vn(ne)₂,...vn(ne)ₘ
```

Legend:

nnnnn	Any unique one- to five-digit integer which specifies the statement *number*. It may be used at the programmer's option but is never required because this statement should not be referenced by another statement in the source program.
DIMENSIØN	A key word specifying the type of statement.
vn	A *variable name* assigned to an array which must be followed by (ne) and be consistent in mode to the type of data contained in the array.
(ne)	An unsigned integer, greater than zero, which specifies the *number of elements* in the array identified by the immediately preceding variable name. This information is used by the compiler to reserve storage area for the described array.
vn(ne)₁,...vn(ne)ₘ	A list of one or more array specifications which must be separated by commas.

Illustrative Examples.   Suppose that a program contains three different one-dimensional arrays. The first two arrays have been assigned the variable names A and DIFF which each contain a maximum of six elements; the third array, ITEMS, contains a maximum of 100 elements. Any one of the following statements can be used to describe these arrays:

```
12345|6|7
820   DIMENSIØN A(6),DIFF(6),ITEMS(100)
```

DIMENSIØN DIFF(6),A(6),ITEMS(100)
DIMENSIØN ITEMS(100),A(6),DIFF(6)

As illustrated in the above statements, the array specifications may appear in any sequence or be in any mode. As previously indicated, a separate DIMENSIØN statement can be used for each array; but it is usually less convenient.

The form of an array specification raises several interesting questions which will be covered next.

How does the compiler know when it encounters A(6) in a statement, for example, if it specifies an array containing a maximum of six elements or if it refers to the sixth element in an array called A? The compiler makes this decision based on the type of statement in which A(6) appears. A DIMENSIØN statement does not contain subscripted variable names; READ, WRITE, and arithmetic statements are not used to describe arrays.

If A(6) appears in a DIMENSIØN statement, how does the compiler know if it describes a numeric or an alphameric array? This decision is based on other statements in the source program. For example, if the A array is created by an arithmetic statement, it is obviously numeric; if created by a READ statement, the referenced format code specifies if the array is numeric or alphameric.

If A(6) describes a numeric field, what determines if the elements are in integer or floating point mode? The first letter of the variable name implies the mode. (It is possible to override this "implicit definition of mode" by an "explicit definition of mode" described in the following section of this chapter.) The mode of an array name must always agree with the mode of the data contained in the array. If the array is created by a READ statement, the mode of the variable name must agree with the format code specification. If an array is created by an arithmetic statement, the programmer must be cautious in assigning an array name because the rules of hierarchy, previously discussed, determine the mode of evaluation of an arithmetic expression; if the expression contains only integer data, the evaluation will be in integer mode; but if a mixed-mode expression is used, the evaluation will be in floating point mode.

When data is in floating point mode, what determines if it is single precision or double precision? If an array established by a READ statement is referenced to a D format code field, the data is in double-precision exponential form; if referenced to an E format code field, it is single-precision exponential form unless an explicit definition is used to override the implicit definition of mode. An array established by a READ statement referenced to an F format code field is single precision unless an explicit definition overrides the implied mode or unless the input field contains 8 through 16 digits instead of 7 or less. If an array is established by an arithmetic statement, the rules of hierarchy apply; an arithmetic expression including one or more double-precision floating point constants or variable names will always be evaluated as double precision. Even though an arithmetic expression is evaluated in single-precision mode, it may be stored in double precision if the variable name to the left of the equal sign is explicitly defined as a double-precision variable name.

The following section covers explicit definition of mode.

Explicit Specification Statements

Numeric data fields are implied to contain integer or floating point data according to the first letter of the assigned variable name. Floating point variable names are implied to be single precision unless specified as double precision by use of a D format code or unless initialized as double precision as the result of the evaluation of an arithmetic expression. Alphameric data fields are always implied to be single precision which limits the maximum field length to four characters. These are conventions of FORTRAN called "implicit definition of mode."

The purpose of explicit specification statements is to allow the programmer the option to override the implied mode of data fields. The three types of explicit specification statements provided in Basic FORTRAN IV are described and illustrated in the following sections.

Explicit specification statements should be located near the beginning of the program before any executable statements.

The INTEGER Statement. This statement allows the programmer the option of starting an integer variable name with a letter other than I through N because it overrides the implicit definition of mode. One INTEGER statement may be used to specify the mode of one or more variable names.

The general form of this statement is:

| 12345 | 6 | 7 |

nnnnn   INTEGER vn$_1$,vn$_2$,...vn$_m$

Legend:

nnnnn	Any unique one- to five-digit integer which specifies the statement number. It is never required because this statement should not be referenced by another statement in the program. It may be used at the programmer's option.
INTEGER	A key word specifying the type of statement.
vn$_1$,...vn$_m$	One or more independent or array floating point variable names, separated by commas, which are specified by this statement as integer mode. The variable names may appear in any sequence. If only one variable name is included in the statement, it should not be followed by a comma.

To illustrate, the following statement specifies APPLES, GRAPES, PEARS, and PLUMS as integer mode variable names:

$\overline{|12345|6|7}$

821   INTEGER APPLES,GRAPES,PEARS,PLUMS

This statement can be convenient to the programmer because it permits him to use more descriptive variable names in some cases. For example, assume that the program is designed to compute the number of units in an inventory and the input data cards have been punched in integer mode. The variable names in the preceding statement are more descriptive than NUMAPS, NUMGPS, NUMPRS, and NUMPLS.

This technique for changing floating point variable names to integer mode should be used with caution and only when it provides a convenience. It can increase the time required to write and debug a program. It is obviously more convenient to assign an integer code the variable name KØDE than to assign the variable name CØDE and then write a specification statement to convert it back to integer mode. It can also be confusing, particularly in a program containing many statements, if several floating point variable names are converted and others are not.

The REAL Statement. This statement can be used to convert one or more integer variable names which begin with one of the letters I through N to single-precision floating point ("real") mode.

The general form of this statement is:

$\overline{|12345|6|7}$

nnnnn   REAL $vn_1, vn_2, \ldots vn_m$

Legend:

nnnnn	Any unique unsigned integer which specifies the statement number. It is never required because this statement should not be referenced by another statement in the program. It may be used at the programmer's option.
REAL	A key word which specifies the type of statement.
$vn_1, \ldots vn_m$	One or more independent or array integer variable names, separated by commas, which this statement specifies as real mode. The variable names may appear in any sequence. If only one variable name is included in the statement, it should not be followed by a comma.

To illustrate, the following statement specifies NETPAY and MØNEY as single-precision floating point ("real") variable names:

$\overline{|12345|6|7}$

822   REAL NETPAY,MØNEY

This statement, like the INTEGER statement, can be convenient to the programmer because it also permits him to use more descriptive variable names in some cases. But this technique should also be used with caution and only when it actually provides a convenience. The variable name PAYNET, for example, is probably as descriptive at NETPAY used in the preceding statement illustration.

This statement, as well as the INTEGER statement, can often be of great convenience at debugging time. For example, suppose a programmer had consistently used the variable name NETPAY in several statements in a payroll problem. Because it is an integer variable name, it can only accommodate whole numbers and will drop the cents in the payroll computations. Rather than change every statement where the variable name NETPAY appears, it may be much more convenient to prepare one specification statement to convert NETPAY to real mode.

The DØUBLE PRECISIØN Statement. This statement can be used to convert one or more integer or real variable names to double-precision floating point mode. It can also be used to convert alphameric data fields, which are implied to be in single-precision mode, to double precision thus increasing the maximum field length from four to eight characters.

The general form is:

```
|12345|6|7
 nnnnn   DØUBLE PRECISIØN  vn₁,vn₂,...vnₘ
```

$\mathbf{\ast Extended \; Precision \; (use)}$

Legend:

nnnnn	Any unique one- to five-digit integer which specifies the statement number. It is never required because this statement should not be referenced by another statement in the program. It may be used at the programmer's option.
DØUBLE PRECISIØN	A key word specifying the type of statement.
vn₁, ... vnₘ	One or more independent or array variable names, separated by commas, which this statement specifies as double precision. If only one variable name is included in the statement, it should not be followed by a comma.

To illustrate, the following statement specifies NAME, DØUBLE, and ARRAY to be in double-precision mode:

```
|12345|6|7
  823   DØUBLE PRECISIØN  NAME,DØUBLE,ARRAY
```

Because single-precision floating point provides only a maximum of approximately 7 significant digits, this statement may be required by the problem to provide approximately 16 significant digits. For example, the sum of two or more single-precision floating point values may exceed seven significant digits; thus the sum field must be specified as double precision. This statement can be convenient for use with long alphameric fields because it increases the maximum field length from four to eight characters thus reducing the number of variable names which must be assigned to the field.

The EQUIVALENCE Statement

Ordinarily, the compiler assigns each variable name a unique storage location, and this location is not used for anything else. The EQUIVA-

LENCE statement tells the compiler to assign two or more specified variable names to the *same* location. It is a specification statement which, when used, must follow any DIMENSIØN or explicit specification statement but must precede all executable statements. The general form is:

$\overline{\lceil 12345 \vert 6 \vert 7}$

nnnnn   EQUIVALENCE$(vn_{a1}, vn_{a2}, \ldots vn_{am}), (vn_{b1}, vn_{b2}, \ldots vn_{bm})$

Legend:

nnnnn	Any unique one- to five-digit integer which specifies the statement number. It may be used at the programmer's option but is never required because this statement should not be referenced in the program.
EQUIVALENCE	A key word specifying the type of statement.
$vn_{a1}, \ldots vn_{am}$	Two or more variable names, enclosed in parentheses and separated by commas, which will share the same internal storage location. The variable names may be subscripted.
$vn_{b1}, \ldots vn_{bm}$	Two or more *optional* variable names, enclosed in parentheses and separated by commas which will share the same internal storage location. The variable names may be subscripted.

To illustrate, the following statement reserves only one storage location, and the variable names PEARS, DATES, PRUNES, and FIGS all refer to it:

$\overline{\lceil 12345 \vert 6 \vert 7}$

EQUIVALENCE(PEARS,DATES,PRUNES,FIGS)

The programmer must be particularly cautious that his uses of these variable names do not interfere with each other because they all share the same storage location so will always have the same current value; if the value of any one is changed, the values of all are changed.

To further illustrate, the following statement will cause PEARS and DATES to share one location and PRUNES and FIGS to share another:

$\overline{\lceil 12345 \vert 6 \vert 7}$

EQUIVALENCE(PEARS,DATES),(PRUNES,FIGS)

Some programs, particularly if they include arrays, are so long that they threaten to exceed the storage capacity of the computer. Since the EQUIVALENCE statement conserves storage space, it can be used to advantage in long programs which include relatively independent sections. For example, if A is used in one section and B in another in such a way that they do not interfere with each other, one storage location can be saved by making both share the same location.

A programmer might find the EQUIVALENCE statement particularly useful at debugging time if he has not been consistent in spelling one or more variable names. For example, suppose a variable name is indicated as PRINC in some statements and as PRIN in others. Rather than search through the program and change one of the variable names each time it appears, one EQUIVALENCE statement can be used to cause both to refer to the same thing. This statement can also be used to advantage when several programmers work on a program together and, by mistake, each uses a different variable name to refer to the same thing.

Statement Order

The order of executable statements is governed by the program logic, but the order of nonexecutable statements is governed by the rules of FORTRAN. Unlike the FØRMAT statement, which may be located anywhere before the END statement, the five specification statements covered in this chapter should precede all executable statements. As previously indicated, some specification statements must precede others. An acceptable order for the statements presented thus far in this book is as follows:

> DIMENSIØN
> Explicit (INTEGER, REAL, and DØUBLE PRECISIØN)
> EQUIVALENCE
> Input/Output, Arithmetic, Control, and FØRMAT
> END

ILLUSTRATIVE ARRAY ROUTINES

The number of routines and combinations of routines which can be used to create and manipulate array elements is almost infinite. This section illustrates and briefly describes some selected array routines. Each can be used as illustrated or modified and/or combined with other routines to solve many types of programming problems.

These routines are designed to demonstrate various techniques and to show the treatment of array elements as clearly as possible rather than to illustrate the optimum solution to the problem. Many of the illustrations are self-explanatory; complex routines are discussed in more detail. It is assumed that all arrays are properly "dimensioned."

Initializing All Array Elements to a Specific Current Value

It is sometimes required that all or selected elements in an array be initialized to the same current value. The following statements initialize all elements in an array containing N elements to zero:

```
|12345|6|7
 824   DØ 7 I=1,N
   7   ARRAY(I)=0.00
```

Creating Duplicate Arrays

Some programs must include two or more duplicate arrays. The original array may have to be retained for output, but various manipulations of the elements in the duplicate array(s) may be required. The following statements cause two duplicates of an existing array to be created:

```
⌐12345│6│7
   825   DØ 7 I=1,N
         DUP1ST(I)=ARRAY(I)
     7   DUP2ND(I)=ARRAY(I)
```

Duplicating an Array in Inverse Order

Sometimes it is necessary to reverse the order of elements in an array. For example, an array in ascending sequence may have to be changed to descending sequence. The following statements will not change the original array but will create a new array in reversed sequence (N is the number of elements in the array):

```
⌐12345│6│7
         K=N
         DØ 7 I=1,N
         CHANGE(I)=ARRAY(K)
     7   K=K−1
```

Creating an Array by Merging Existing Arrays

Some problems require creation of an array which contains all or selected elements from two or more existing arrays. The illustrated routine will result in creation of a new array called MERGE. It will contain elements of the two existing arrays combined or "merged" in the following sequence:

	New Array	
	MERGE(1)	J(1)
	MERGE(2)	K(1)
	MERGE(3)	J(2)
	MERGE(4)	K(2)
	MERGE(5)	J(3)
	Etc.	Etc.

Note than an increment value of two is used in the DØ statement in this routine:

```
|12345|6|7
        L=1
  826   DØ 7 I=1,N,2
        MERGE(I)=J(L)
        MERGE(I+1)=K(L)
    7   L=L+1
```

Selecting the Largest Value from an Array

The following statements select the largest value from an array and store the value at BIGNUM:

```
|12345|6|7
  827   BIGNUM=ARRAY(1)
        DØ 7 I=2,N
        IF(ARRAY(I)−BIGNUM)7,7,6
    6   BIGNUM=ARRAY(I)
    7   CØNTINUE
```

Note that a CØNTINUE statement must be the last statement in the DØ range and that the index is initialized at two to avoid comparing the value of the first element to itself. This routine initializes BIGNUM to the current value of the first element in the array. All other elements in the array are compared to the current value of BIGNUM; the current value of BIG-NUM is replaced by the current value of any array element which contains a higher current value. This routine does not change the current value of any array element.

Counting How Many Times a Specific Value Appears in an Array

The following statements will count the number of times the value 88 appears in an integer array called NARRAY:

```
|12345|6|7
  828   LØØK4=88
        KØUNT=0
    1   DØ 3 I=1,N
        IF(NARRAY(I)−LØØK4)3,2,3
    2   KØUNT=KØUNT+1
    3   CØNTINUE
```

Note that this routine requires the DØ range to end with a CØNTINUE statement. The variable name KØUNT is incremented by one each time the current value 88 is encountered in the array.

Searching an Array for a Specific Value

This illustrative routine demonstrates an exit from the DØ range before iteration is complete if the current value 88 is found in any array element. The DØ index is used to indicate, at the variable name LØCATN, the specific element in the array where the first 88 was encountered:

```
|1 2 3 4 5|6|7
    829   LØØK4=88
          DØ 2 I=1,N
          IF(NARRAY(I)−LØØK4)2,3,2
      2   CØNTINUE
          GØ TØ 4
      3   LØCATN=I
      4   . . .
```

Note that this routine requires a CØNTINUE statement as the last statement in the DØ range.

Searching Two Arrays for Matching Values

Some problems require that two arrays be searched for the first set of matching current values. The following statements solve this problem. LØCAT1 and LØCAT2 indicate the specific location in each array where the first set of matching values are encountered, and KURVAL indicates the current value of the first match.

```
|1 2 3 4 5|6|7
    830   DØ 2 I=1,N
          DØ 2 K=1,N
          IF(NARRAY(I)−KARRAY(K))2,3,2
      2   CØNTINUE
          GØ TØ 5
      3   LØCAT1=I
          LØCAT2=K
          KURVAL=NARRAY(I)
          GØ TO 7
      4   FØRMAT(' NØ MATCH FØUND')
      5   WRITE(3,4)
```

Note that this routine requires a CØNTINUE statement as the last statement in both DØ ranges. In this illustration, both the inner and outer DØ loops use the same CØNTINUE statement which is permitted with nested DØ loops. On each pass through the outer loop, the inner loop will cycle N times or until a match is found.

Computing Average of All Elements in an Input Array

Some problems require that data be read into the computer as an array, the elements totaled, and the average (arithmetic mean) computed. Obviously, to compute the average, all elements must first be read, then the exact number of input elements must be used as the divisor.

If the size of an input array is known, the divisor may be either a constant or a variable name with a current value equal to the number of elements. But, if the array size is unknown and a trailer card is used to determine the end of the input deck, the divisor must be equal to the number of elements read in *before* the trailer card was encountered.

The three routines for computing an average which follow assume that a DIMENSIØN statement specifies that the array contains 100 floating point elements. To demonstrate different input field lengths, seven columns are used for the first field in each input card, six for the second, and five for the third. It should be noted that a DØUBLE DIMENSIØN statement is required if the scaling process indicates the sum of all array element values exceeds seven significant digits.

Known Number of Array Elements. The following routine can be used to compute the average if (1) the input array contains exactly 100 elements as specified in the DIMENSIØN statement, (2) the first 33 cards contain three elements each, and (3) the final card contains the last element in the first seven columns:

```
|12345|6|7
  831   FØRMAT(F7.1,F6.2,F5.1)
        READ(1,831)ARRAY
        TØTAL=0.00
        DØ 7 I=1,100
    7   TØTAL=TØTAL+ARRAY(I)
        AVE=TØTAL/100.00
```

The relationship of the location of array elements in the input deck to the FØRMAT, READ, and DIMENSIØN statements cannot be over emphasized. The format codes indicate that each input card contains three sequential fields; the READ statement uses these codes in the specified sequence until the READ list is satisfied. The READ statement contains only one unsubscripted array variable name. When this "shortcut" method is used, the DIMENSIØN statement establishes the length of the READ list which, in this case, is actually ARRAY(1) through ARRAY(100). Thus, if the final element of the array is not punched in the first field of the last input card, it will be ignored in the illustrative routine because reading will terminate before the last element is encountered.

Of course, it is possible to write a program which will read array elements from any location in the input deck. For example, the following routine can be used to read 100 array elements if the final element is punched in columns 74 through 80 in the last input card:

```
|12345|6|7
  832   FØRMAT(F7.1,F6.2,F5.1)
        READ(1,832)(ARRAY(I),I=1,99)
    2   FØRMAT(T74,F7.1)
        READ(1,2)ARRAY(100)
```

Note that this illustration requires two READ statements. This illustration should make it obvious that it may be more convenient to prepare input data which agrees with a standard program routine than to prepare a program routine to agree with the input data.

The format codes F7.1, F6.2, and F5.1 were used in the two preceding illustrations to demonstrate how different field lengths can be used for array elements. Obviously, other format codes such as 3F8.2, 10F8.2, or F8.2 could also be used if the elements were punched accordingly in the input cards.

Sometimes it is necessary to store a large array which contains many elements with identical values, such as zero. A timesaving method which can be used in this case is to initialize all array elements to zero and then prepare an input deck containing only the nonzero elements. When this technique is used, both the value and an identification number of each element should be punched in the input cards so each element can be properly positioned in the array. This allows the input cards to be in any sequence, and fewer cards are required to "build" the array. The following routine can be used to read the nonzero elements into the array where N indicates the known number of input cards:

```
|12345|6|7
  833   FØRMAT(I3,F8.2)
        READ(1,833)(NUMELM,ARRAY(NUMELM),I=1,N)
```

The current value of NUMELM, read from the first three columns of the input card, is used as the subscript to properly position the element within the array. It should be noted that unless the entire array is initialized to zero prior to the execution of this routine, the elements not read in will contain "garbage."

Number of Array Elements Determined by Header Card. The following routine can be used to compute the average if the header card indicates the array contains 100 elements or less:

```
|12345|6|7
  833   FØRMAT(I3/(F7.1,F6.2,F5.1))
        READ(1,833)KØUNT,(ARRAY(I),I=1,KØUNT)
        TØTAL=0.00
```

```
      DØ 7 I=1,KØUNT
   7  TØTAL=TØTAL+ARRAY(I)
      CØUNT=KØUNT
      AVE=TØTAL/CØUNT
```

Note that the FØRMAT statement contains two sets of parentheses. The compiler will associate the variable name KØUNT with the first format code; the slash indicates the header card is to be ejected; and the entire array is then read according to the format code specifications within the innermost set of parentheses. When a close parenthesis is reached in a FØRMAT statement, the compiler automatically returns to the preceding open parentheses and reuses the same format codes until the READ list is satisfied. (In this case, the number of array elements to be read is determined by the current value of KØUNT.)

Note also that the same variable name (I) was used as an index in both the READ statement with the "implied DØ" and in the DØ statement. This is possible because after the READ statement is finished with the index it can be reinitialized and used again; only nested DØ loops require different variable names for each index.

KØUNT is converted to floating point mode to avoid a mixed mode expression in the final statement. In this particular case, a mixed mode expression would have produced the same results.

Finally, it should be noted that if the last input card contains only one element, it must be in the first field; if the final card contains two elements, they must be in the first two fields; and each card except the final one must contain three elements as indicated by the format codes. If the input data fields are not punched in this manner, one or more blank fields will be read with a corresponding number of input elements ignored. This is caused by the fact that the header card indicates, in effect, the number of sequential data fields to be read rather than the number of cards. Thus, each sequential data field must contain one array element.

Number of Array Elements Determined by Trailer Card. Assume that the input deck contains an unknown number of elements which does not exceed 100 as specified by the DIMENSIØN statement. The array elements are punched in sequential data fields as specified by the format codes. The last array element is the unique value 9.0 and is used as a "trailer element" to indicate the end of the array. It is not part of the array and must be excluded from the sum and divisor to compute the average.

The following routine provides an exit from the DØ loop if the "trailer element" is encountered; otherwise a message is written on the printer indicating 100 elements were read but the unique "trailer element" 9.0 was not encountered:

```
|12345|6|7
  834  FØRMAT(F7.1,F6.2,F5.1)
       SUM=0.00
```

```
        DØ 7 I=1,100
        READ(1,834)ARRAY(I)
        IF(ARRAY(I)−9.0)6,9,6
6       SUM=SUM+ARRAY(I)
7       CØNTINUE
8       FØRMAT(T2, 'NØ TRAILER')
        WRITE(3,8)
        STØP
9       CØUNT=I−1
        AVE=SUM/CØUNT
```

If the "trailer element" is encountered, the current value of the index is retained because a "special exit" rather than a "normal exit" is made from the DØ loop. But because the unique value 9.0 was read as an array element, 1 must be subtracted from the index to compute the divisor (CØUNT).

Sorting Values of Array Elements into Algebraic Order

Arranging data values in an ordered sequence is a process called *sorting*. A routine to sort array element values into algebraic sequence is more complex and not as self-explanatory as the other routines presented in this chapter.

To begin with an elementary example, assume that a *two-element array* is to be sorted into *ascending* numeric sequence. The following routine compares the values at the two storage locations and interchanges the contents if these values are *not* in ascending sequence:

```
|12345|6|7
835     IF(ARRAY(1)−ARRAY(2))10,10,7
7       SAVE=ARRAY(1)
8       ARRAY(1)=ARRAY(2)
9       ARRAY(2)=SAVE
10      CØNTINUE
```

Note that the IF statement compares the values of the two elements. If the value of the first is less than or equal to the second, the statements (7, 8, and 9) which interchange the contents of the two locations are ignored. But, if the value of the first element is more than the second, the statements which cause the interchange are executed. Note also that this interchange process requires a third storage location (SAVE) as shown in Figure 8–2.

Now, assume that a *four-element array* is to be sorted into *ascending* sequence. The following routine will compare the value of the first element to each of the other three in turn. The elements will be interchanged whenever the value of the first is greater than the value of the other element in a given comparison. After completion of the routine, the largest value will be located in the last (fourth) position in the array.

|12345|6|7

```
836   NESTED=3
      DØ 10 I=1,NESTED
      IF(ARRAY(I)−ARRAY(I+1))10,10,7
  7   SAVE=ARRAY(I)
      ARRAY(I)=ARRAY(I+1)
      ARRAY(I+1)=SAVE
 10   CØNTINUE
```

FIGURE 8-2
Interchanging the Location of Two Values

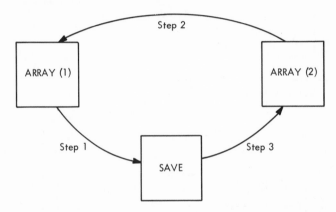

Note that the DØ statement will cause *three* passes through the loop. The effect of the preceding routine is illustrated with assumed values in Figure 8–3.

It should be particularly noted that the preceding routine is designed to sort only one array element; that is, the highest value is transferred to the last (fourth) position, but the sequence of the other array elements, as to each other, is not changed. To sort the next highest value it is necessary to repeat the same routine except that one less pass is required because the last element is already sorted so it is unnecessary to compare its value to that of any other element. To decrease the number of passes through the routine, it is necessary to change the test value (NESTED) of the DØ statement. Assuming that the test value is changed from 3 to 2, the effect of repeating the routine is shown in Figure 8–4.

Note that after the second execution of the sorting routine, the values of only two elements are properly ordered. The routine must be repeated again to properly order the remaining two elements; but, again, one less pass is required. Assuming that the test value (NESTED) of the DØ statement is changed to 1, the effect of executing the routine a third time is illustrated in Figure 8–5.

FIGURE 8–3
**Appearance of a Specific Array during Various Stages of
the Sorting Process**

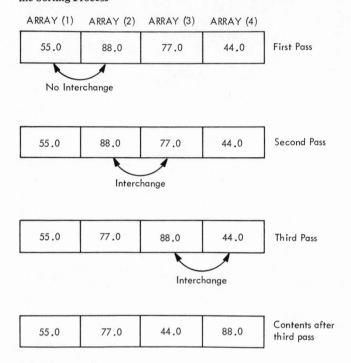

FIGURE 8–4
**Appearance of a Specific Array during Various Stages of
the Sorting Process**

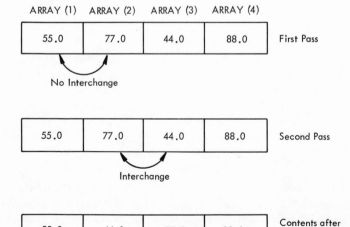

FIGURE 8–5
**Appearance of a Specific Array during Various Stages of
the Sorting Process**

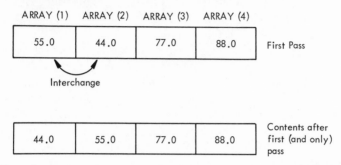

Following the third execution of the sort routine, all four array elements are properly ordered. Obviously, to sort a five-element array, the routine must be executed four times; and, likewise, to sort a 100–element array, it must be executed 99 times. But note again that each time the routine is repeated, the test value (NESTED) of the DØ statement can be decreased because there is one less value to sort on each succeeding pass through the loop.

As pointed out in Chapter 7, the rules of FORTRAN do not permit the test value of a DØ statement to be changed *within* the DØ range. Thus, it is required that it be changed after a normal exit from the DØ range and that the loop then be reentered at the DØ statement. One method of doing this is to nest the sorting routine within an outer DØ loop which is designed to control the index value of the nested DØ. This method is illustrated in the following routine which will sort an array containing N elements into *ascending* algebraic sequence:

```
|12345|6|7
  837   NESTED=N
    2   L=NESTED−1
    3   DØ 10 M=1,L
    4   NESTED=NESTED−1
    5   DØ 10 I=1,NESTED
    6   IF(ARRAY(I)−ARRAY(I+1))10,10,7
    7   SAVE=ARRAY(I)
    8   ARRAY(I)=ARRAY(I+1)
    9   ARRAY(I+1)=SAVE
   10   CØNTINUE
```

The routine illustrated above uses an outer DØ to control execution of a nested DØ which does the actual sorting. It demonstrates how an outer DØ can be used to initialize and change the test value of a nested DØ;

each time control passes to the nested DØ, it has a different test value. To illustrate the effect of this routine, assume the same array values as previously shown in Figure 8–3. After all values are compared and the first normal exit is made from the nested DØ, the second (largest) value is located at ARRAY(4); but all other values are moved up to the first three array positions and remain in the same sequence as to each other. Control then returns to the outer DØ which subtracts 1 from the test value of the nested DØ. The nested DØ is then executed a second time; but because the test value is changed, it compares only the first three unsorted values. This time it moves the next highest value to ARRAY(3). Control then returns to the outer DØ and back again to the nested DØ which reverses the locations of the remaining two values during its final execution.

Each routine illustrated in this section was designed to sort an array into ascending sequence. (If the array contains some identical values, technically the ordered array will not be in "ascending sequence" but will be "nondescending.") What would be the effect of changing the IF statement references from 10, 10, 7 to 7, 10, 10? With this minor modification, the previously illustrated routines will sort an array into descending (or "nonascending") sequence.

PROBLEMS

Long programs are often written in sections or "modules." After the first module is debugged and tested, other modules are added to the basic program, debugged and tested in turn until the entire program is completed. This modular method isolates errors and can reduce programming time. A program to determine grades for students enrolled in a computer programming class is used to demonstrate this method. The program requires:

A. Computation of the average (arithmetic mean) numeric grade of each student.
B. Computation of the average (arithmetic mean) numeric grade of the class.
C. Computation of the adjusted numeric grade of each student.
D. Assignment of letter grades based on the adjusted numeric grades of each student.
E. Sorting the adjusted average grades into algebraic sequence.
F. Reversing the order of the sorted array.

The input deck contains 20 cards in the following sequence and format:

Student Number (Cols. 1–2)	Student Name (Cols. 5–12)	Test Score (15–17)	Test Number (20)
1	A. DOAKS	87	1
2	B. DOAKS	79	1
3	C. DOAKS	70	1
4	D. DOAKS	70	1

Student Number (Cols. 1–2)	Student Name (Cols. 5–12)	Test Score (15–17)	Test Number (20)
5	E. DOAKS	79	1
6	F. DOAKS	74	1
7	G. DOAKS	93	1
8	H. DOAKS	70	1
9	I. DOAKS	68	1
10	J. DOAKS	100	1
1	A. DOAKS	89	2
2	B. DOAKS	95	2
3	C. DOAKS	66	2
4	D. DOAKS	62	2
5	E. DOAKS	77	2
6	F. DOAKS	86	2
7	G. DOAKS	83	2
8	H. DOAKS	64	2
9	I. DOAKS	48	2
10	J. DOAKS	100	2

Examine the input data carefully. Note that 10 students are enrolled in the class and have been assigned identification numbers 1 through 10. Each student has two cards in the input data deck, one for each test he has taken during the term. The first 10 cards in the input deck are sorted by student number, 1 through 10, and contain the test scores for the first test. The last 10 cards in the input deck are also sorted by student number, 1 through 10, and contain the test scores for the second test.

Output is to be printed and "dressed-up" with descriptive headings. Following the headings, there should be one output line for each student which contains the following fields in order from left to right:

Student Number
Student Name
First Test Score
Second Test Score
Average Test Score
Adjusted Test Score
Letter Grade

To simplify the programming logic, the student number may be ignored on input and the program designed to automatically indicate the student numbers from 1 through 10 in the output.

Output for the class average should be printed directly below the first, second, and average test score fields with the decimal points properly aligned.

Final output is to be the sorted adjusted averages which may be printed in any location below the previously described output.

Write a program in a series of modules, as indicated below, to solve this problem. The requirements for all modules should be carefully examined to reduce the number of changes required as each succeeding module is added to the program. The first module sets up the basic framework for the program.

Following modules are not to be run separately but added to the existing program.

Module 1
  A. Write all headings.
  B. Compute and print the following output for each student:
     1. Student number.
     2. First test score.
     3. Second test score.
     4. Average test score (arithmetic mean).

Module 2
  Compute and print the following output:
     1. Class average for first test.
     2. Class average for second test.
     3. Class average for all tests.

Module 3
  The instructor believes the average for all tests should be 80; if it is more, his tests were too easy; if less, his tests were too hard. Therefore, each student is to have his actual test average adjusted accordingly. For example, add five points to each student's actual average to determine his adjusted average if the class average is 75; deduct five if it is 85; and make no adjustment if it is 80.
  Compute and print the adjusted average for each student.

Module 4
  Include the students' names in the output.

Module 5
  Letter grades are assigned on the basis of the adjusted average of each student as follows:

Adjusted Average	Letter Grade
90 or more	A
70–89	C
Less than 70	F

  Compute and write the letter grade for each student.

Module 6
  Sort and write the adjusted average test scores in ascending algebraic order.

Module 7
  Reverse the order of the elements in the sorted array (or create another array in inverse order) and write the results.

CHAPTER
9

TWO-DIMENSIONAL AND THREE-DIMENSIONAL ARRAYS

A TWO-DIMENSIONAL array is simply a list of integer, floating point, or alphameric data elements arranged in rows and columns. It is also called a "matrix." A three-dimensional array is two or more related two-dimensional arrays. Specific elements in these types of arrays are referenced by a unique subscript; the rules for selecting array variable names and subscripts are the same as those described in the preceding chapter. But because the form is different, these types of arrays must be described and subscripted accordingly. The specification statement must indicate multiple dimensions, and the variable name of each element must include multiple subscripts.

TWO-DIMENSIONAL ARRAYS

A two-dimensional array consists of horizontal lists of elements called *rows* and vertical lists called *columns*. Following is an illustration of this type of array:

	Column 1	Column 2	Column 3	Column 4	Column 5	Column 6
Row 1	4.00	3.75	2.25	3.00	2.00	3.00
Row 2	3.25	2.25	0.50	0.25	2.00	3.75
Row 3	2.00	2.00	2.00	2.00	1.50	2.50
Row 4	2.25	1.75	1.00	1.25	1.75	1.00
Row 5	3.50	3.25	2.25	2.00	3.25	3.75

Assume that the illustrated array corresponds to the physical arrangement of a parking lot. The lot has 30 parking spaces arranged in five rows and six columns as indicated. The floating point data, contained in the array elements, represents the receipts for each parking space for one day. This data can be stored as one or more one-dimensional arrays. For example, it can be read as 1 array with 30 elements, as 5 arrays with 6 elements each, or as 6 arrays with 5 elements each. But suppose the problem requires computation of the average receipts for only the interior parking spaces in the lot. It is more convenient to solve this problem with a single two-dimensional array than with a series of one-dimensional arrays. To demonstrate how to manipulate data elements in a two-dimensional array, the illustrated parking lot array is assigned the variable name SPACES and is used as an example throughout this chapter.

Multiple Subscripting

Because a two-dimensional array is arranged in rows and columns, a single element is referred to by an array variable name followed by two subscripts. The subscripts are separated by commas and enclosed in one set of parentheses. The first subscript refers to the row, the second to the column.

For example, to refer to the element (with a current value of 1.00) located in row 4, column 3 in the SPACES array, the specification is:

SPACES(4,3)

If the independent variable names K and L have current values of 4 and 3 respectively, the same element can be referred to as:

SPACES(K,L)

The seven valid subscript forms previously covered in Chapter 8 also apply to each subscript when multiple subscripts are used. Thus, if K and L have current values of 4 and 3 respectively, the array element in row 5, column 2 can be referenced by either of the following unique subscripted variable names:

SPACES(5,2)
SPACES(K+1,L−1)

Multiple Dimensioning

The specification statement used to describe a two-dimensional array must specify the maximum number of rows and columns. The following statement specifies the exact dimensions of the SPACES array:

```
|12345|6|7
    91   DIMENSIØN  SPACES(5,6)
```

The dimensions are separated by a comma, and the number of rows precedes the number of columns as in the case of a subscript. One DI-MENSIØN statement may be used to describe as many one-dimensional and/or two-dimensional arrays as is required by the program and allowed by the capacity of the computer. It should be noted that 30 storage spaces are reserved for the two-dimensional array SPACES (5 times 6).

Reading and Writing Two-Dimensional Arrays

When a READ or WRITE statement contains an unsubscripted variable name, the entire array, as dimensioned in the specification statement, is always written. In the case of a 30–element one-dimensional array, the order in which the array is read or written is element number 1 through 30. If a 30–element two-dimensional array is specified, the order of transfer into or out of memory is more complex.

The value of the first subscript, representing the row, is increased more rapidly; the value of the last subscript, representing the column, is increased less rapidly. For example, assume that the following statements are used to describe, READ, and WRITE the parking lot array called SPACES:

```
|12345|6|7
    92   DIMENSIØN  SPACES(5,6)
     8   FØRMAT(F4.0)
         READ(1,8)SPACES
         WRITE(2,8)SPACES
```

The order in which the elements will be read, stored, and written will be:

1. SPACES(1,1)	7. SPACES(2,2)
2. SPACES(2,1)	8. SPACES(3,2)
3. SPACES(3,1)	9. SPACES(4,2)
4. SPACES(4,1)	10. SPACES(5,2)
5. SPACES(5,1)	11. SPACES(1,3)
6. SPACES(1,2)	Etc. through: SPACES(5,6)

Regardless of the method of input, two-dimensional array elements are always stored in the order indicated. Thus, the "shortcut" method of using an unsubscripted variable name in the READ statement requires extreme care in the preparation of the FØRMAT statement and in the arrangement of array elements in the input data deck. This "shortcut" method can be used for output only if the array elements are stored in corresponding sequence to the desired output format.

Assume that the elements of the SPACES array are punched in five input cards as follows:

```
     123456789
Card 1    4.00 3.75 2.25 3.00 2.00 3.00
Card 2    3.25 2.25 0.50 0.25 2.00 3.75
Card 3    2.00 2.00 2.00 2.00 1.50 2.50
Card 4    2.25 1.75 1.00 1.25 1.75 1.00
Card 5    3.50 3.25 2.25 2.00 3.25 3.75
```

The following partial program can be used to describe, read, and write the above data using a two-dimensional array:

```
12345 6 7
  93   DIMENSIØN SPACES(5,6)
   7   FØRMAT(6F5.2)
       DØ 8 NUMRØW=1,5
       READ(1,7)(SPACES(NUMRØW,NUMCØL),NUMCØL=1,6)
   8   CØNTINUE
       DØ 9 NUMRØW=1,5
       WRITE(3,7)(SPACES(NUMRØW,NUMCØL),NUMCØL=1,6)
   9   CØNTINUE
```

This partial program will write the output in identical format to the input, but all data will be shifted left one position because a printer is specified as the output device. Note that two DØ's are used for reading and writing in this partial program (one DØ statement and one "implied DØ").

Illustrative Routines

Each element in a two-dimensional array can be individually addressed; thus, any routine used for one-dimensional arrays can be applied if adjustment is made for the multiple subscripts. Only three routines are illustrated in this section; it is assumed that the SPACES array is dimensioned and read as indicated in the preceding section.

The following routine will compute the average of the six elements in row 3 only:

```
12345 6 7
  94   NUMRØW=3
       SUM=0.0
```

```
        DØ 7 NUMCØL=1,6
   7    SUM=SUM+SPACES(NUMRØW,NUMCØL)
        AVE=SUM/6.0
```

To compute the average of the five elements in column 6 only, the following routine can be used:

|12345|6|7

```
  95    NUMCØL=6
        SUM=0.0
        DØ 7 NUMCØL=1,5
   7    SUM=SUM+SPACES(NUMRØW,NUMCØL)
        AVE=SUM/5.0
```

The next routine illustrates a problem which is much easier to solve with a two-dimensional array than with a series of one-dimensional arrays. It will compute the average receipts from the 12 *interior* parking spaces only.

|12345|6|7

```
  96    SUM=0.0
        DØ 7 NUMRØW=2,4
        DØ 7 NUMCØL=2,5
   7    SUM=SUM+SPACES(NUMRØW,NUMCØL)
        AVE=SUM/12.0
```

Note how the initialization and test values cause columns 1 and 6 as well as rows 1 and 5 to be ignored; only the values of the interior elements are totaled and averaged. If the initialization and test values are changed to 1 and 5 in the outer DØ, and to 1 and 6 in the nested DØ, the sum of all elements in the array will be computed by statement number 7.

THREE-DIMENSIONAL ARRAYS

A one-dimensional array is simply a series of data elements of a defined length. A two-dimensional array is a series of data elements of defined length and width. A three-dimensional array is a series of related two-dimensional arrays; in addition to the surface dimensions of length and width, it also has depth. It consists of rows, columns, and *ranks*.

To illustrate a three-dimensional array, assume that there are two parking lots, instead of only one. For identification purposes, the lots are numbered 1 and 2. Each contains 30 parking spaces arranged in five rows and six columns as previously described.

Multiple Subscripting

Because a three-dimensional array is arranged in rows, columns, and ranks, a single element must be referenced by an array variable name followed by *three* subscripts. The subscripts are separated by commas and enclosed in one set of parentheses. The first subscript refers to the row, the second to the column, and the third to the rank. In the example, the rank identifies the parking lot number.

To illustrate, the element located in row 4, column 3, rank (lot number) 2 is specified as:

$$SPACES(4,3,2)$$

As previously indicated, the seven valid subscript forms may be used for any or all of the multiple subscripts.

Multiple Dimensioning

The specification statement used to describe a three-dimensional array must indicate, in order, the maximum number of rows, columns, and ranks. The following statement specifies the exact dimensions of the SPACES array for both parking lots:

```
|12345|6|7
  97    DIMENSIØN  SPACES(5,6,2)
```

This statement reserves 60 storage spaces for the SPACES array (5 times 6 times 2). One DIMENSIØN statement may be used to describe as many arrays as is required by the program and allowed by the capacity of the computer; the arrays described may be one, two, and/or three-dimensional and may appear in any sequence.

Reading and Writing Three-Dimensional Arrays

An unsubscripted variable name can also be used to read or write an entire three-dimensional array. But, as with a two-dimensional array, extreme caution must be exercised because three-dimensional arrays are always stored internally as follows:

The first storage space is reserved for the element whose subscripts are all 1's. The value of the first subscript, representing the row, increases most rapidly; and the value of the last subscript, representing the rank, increases least rapidly. Thus, the 60–element array SPACES will be stored internally as follows:

1. SPACES(1,1,1)
2. SPACES(2,1,1)
3. SPACES(3,1,1)
4. SPACES(4,1,1)
5. SPACES(5,1,1)
6. SPACES(1,2,1)
   Etc. through:

7. SPACES(5,6,1)
   Then:
8. SPACES(1,1,2)
9. SPACES(2,1,2)
10. SPACES(3,1,2)
    Etc. through:
    SPACES(5,6,2)

Assume that the elements of the SPACES array are punched in 10 cards. The first five cards contain six elements each, as illustrated in the section on two-dimensional arrays, and indicate the receipts from parking lot number 1. The last five cards are in identical format but indicate the receipts from parking lot number 2.

The following partial program can be used to describe, read, and write two tables. The first table written will indicate the receipts for each column and row for rank 1, and the second for rank 2.

```
|12345|6|7
   98  DIMENSIØN  SPACES(5,6,2)
    4  FØRMAT(6F5.2)
       DØ 5 NUMRNK=1,2
       DØ 5 NUMRØW=1,5
       READ(1,4)(SPACES(NUMRØW,NUMCØL,NUMRNK),
    1    NUMCØL=1,6)
    5  CØNTINUE
       DØ 6 NUMRNK=1,2
       DØ 6 NUMRØW=1,5
       WRITE(3,4)(SPACES(NUMRØW,NUMCØL,NUMRNK),
    1    NUMCØL=1,6)
    6  CØNTINUE
```

Note that three DØ's are used for reading and for writing in this routine (two DØ statements and an "implied DØ").

Illustrative Routines

Any routine used for one or two-dimensional arrays can also be used for three-dimensional arrays if adjustment is made for the multiple subscripts. Variations of the routines used to illustrate two-dimensional arrays are used in this section to illustrate three-dimensional arrays; it is assumed that the SPACES array is dimensioned and read as indicated in the preceding section.

The following routine will compute the average of the six elements in row 3, rank (lot number) 1:

```
|12345|6|7
       NUMRNK=1
       NUMRØW=3
       SUM=0.0
       DØ 7 NUMCØL=1,6
    7  SUM=SUM+SPACES(NUMRØW,NUMCØL,NUMRNK)
       AVE=SUM/6.0
```

The following routine will compute the average of all the 10 elements in column 6, ranks 1 and 2:

```
|12345|6|7
         NUMCØL=6
         SUM=0.0
         DØ 7 NUMRNK=1,2
         DØ 7 NUMRØW=1,5
         SUM=SUM+SPACES(NUMRØW,NUMCØL,NUMRNK)
      7  CØNTINUE
         AVE=SUM/10.0
```

This next routine will compute the combined average receipts of only the interior parking spaces for both lots:

```
|12345|6|7
         SUM=0.0
         DØ 7 NUMRNK=1,2
         DØ 7 NUMRØW=2,4
         DØ 7 NUMCØL=2,5
         SUM=SUM+SPACES(NUMRØW,NUMCØL,NUMRNK)
      7  CØNTINUE
         AVE=SUM/24.0
```

Before concluding the discussion on three-dimensional arrays, it should be emphasized that they are very powerful and have many applications. For example, the SPACES array can be changed so that the rank indicates the receipts for each day of the week, month, or year. (Basic FORTRAN IV does not permit an array to exceed three dimensions, so it is impossible to "build" one with rows, columns, lots, and days.)

The examples in this chapter were designed to illustrate what two- and three-dimensional arrays are, how they work, and when they might be used. The programming logic can be quite complex when these types of arrays are used. Before attempting to work with them, a programmer should have considerable experience and a thorough familiarity with arrays of one dimension. Because this book is designed for beginning programmers, rather than for the expert, no problems are included in this chapter.

CHAPTER
10

SUBPROGRAMS

$\mathbb{T}$ HE first five chapters in this book covered the basic statements required to write complete source programs and explained how the computer can be used to translate these programs into the unique language it is designed to understand and obey. Chapters 6 and 7 covered progressively more sophisticated programming techniques and various shortcuts available to the programmer. Chapters 8 and 9 illustrated and explained how to tell the computer to assign a unique variable name to each element in an array or, in effect, to write portions of statements. This powerful concept of causing the computer to help write the program will now be developed further. This chapter illustrates and explains how the computer can be used to write a minor or even a major portion of a program.

Many programs include various mathematical functions (such as the trigonometric sine of an angle) which can require an arithmetic statement with a long and/or complex expression when written with the five arithmetic operators ($+$, $-$, $*$, $/$, and $**$). This type of arithmetic statement must sometimes be repeated in several places in one or more programs. Furthermore, many programs include various routines which require a rather long series of statements (such as a routine for sorting, computing compound interest, or generating random numbers). These routines must sometimes be repeated several times in one program and are frequently required in many different programs.

To avoid writing or rewriting long and/or complex program segments, a *subprogram* can be used. A subprogram is defined as a set of instructions which perform a specific task under the control of another program. It is usually used for frequently repeated tasks and must be written only once. The computer can be told to include an available subprogram at almost any point in any program. Subprograms provide an obvious convenience to the programmer and, frequently, are relatively easy to use.

It should be noted that a subprogram is designed to solve only part of a problem. One or more of these parts are combined with other parts to form a larger and whole program designed to solve the problem. The various parts are "called for" and joined in proper order by a *calling program*. The calling program that creates the whole program is sometimes called the "main-line program." Subprograms can also be used as calling programs, but there must always be one main line. Long programs are often written as a series of subprograms which are individually tested and debugged, then joined to form a complete program. This technique makes it possible to assign several programmers to one problem and thus reduce the time required to complete the job. In this case, the main-line program may be a sort of "skeleton" program which calls for many subprograms of considerable size which, in turn, may call for other subprograms.

A subprogram is usually written only once, as previously indicated. Fortunately, the individual programmer is not required to write most subprograms he requires because they have already been written for him. Basic FORTRAN IV provides many subprograms, some of which are illustrated in this chapter. Most computer centers have a library of subprograms which have been written by their staff or obtained from other computer centers. Before attempting to write a long complex program, programmers should always check with their computer center to determine which subprograms are available locally or can be obtained from various sources. Unless the problem to be solved is very unusual, someone has probably already written, tested, and debugged the various routines required. In fact, complete programs may be available which require few, if any, changes to solve the problem. Many computer centers belong to one or more organizations which may have hundreds of complete programs and subprograms available for a wide variety of applications.

The two basic types of subprograms covered in this chapter are *function subprograms* and *subroutine subprograms*.

FUNCTION SUBPROGRAMS

There are three types of function subprograms. One type is supplied by FORTRAN, and the other two are supplied by individual programmers. All three types are discussed and illustrated in the sections which follow.

FORTRAN-Supplied Mathematical Function Subprograms

Basic FORTRAN IV provides many "built-in" subprograms. Many of these are of interest only to experienced programmers or to those who must solve complex mathematical problems. Selected examples of mathematical function subprograms are included in this section to illustrate a few of the many available; a complete list is given in Appendix E. No attempt will be made to enter into a full discussion of mathematical functions. Such a discussion is reserved for a course in mathematics. This section does, however, explain and illustrate how a mathematical function subprogram is used in FORTRAN. Because this is the only type of subprogram included in this section, for convenience, it will be referred to simply as a "subprogram."

General Description. Subprograms are already compiled and ready to go. Each has been assigned a unique variable name which follows the regular rules of variable names previously covered in this book. To "call for" a subprogram, the programmer uses the appropriate variable name in a statement. A variable name which refers to a subprogram is sometimes called an "arithmetic function," a "function variable name," or simply a "function." The latter term will be used throughout the remainder of this section.

Most functions require a set number of "arguments," usually either one or two. An *argument* is defined as an arithmetic expression, the current value of which is used by the subprogram to compute the result.

Using Subprograms. To use a subprogram, the programmer simply writes the function followed by one or more arguments enclosed in parentheses and separated by commas. For instance, one subprogram is designed to extract square root; the function is SQRT, and one argument is required. The use of this subprogram is illustrated by the following arithmetic statement:

```
|12345|6|7
 101   ANSWER=SQRT(144.0)
```

When a function is included in an arithmetic expression, the computer executes the subprogram, using the argument(s) supplied by the programmer; and the result of the computation becomes the current value of the function. The computer then returns to the "calling program" and continues on, using the current value of the function in the same manner as if it had been written in the expression as a constant. In the preceding illustrated statement, the current value of the function will replace, or initialize, the current value of ANSWER. In the following statement, the current value of the function will be added to the current value of ALPHA; and the resulting sum will replace, or initialize, the current value of ANSWER:

```
|12345|6|7
 102   ANSWER=SQRT(BETA)+ALPHA
```

In the following paragraph, the above statement is used to illustrate the difference between functions, other types of variable names, and pro-grammer-supplied constants.

Functions are variable names but are not handled by the computer in the same manner as other types of variable names appearing in expres-sions. To illustrate, the current value of ALPHA and BETA remain un-changed and are available for later use in the program. But the current value of the function SQRT is not available for later use because it refers to a subprogram rather than to a symbolic address where the current value of a variable name is stored. The current value of the function SQRT is handled by the computer in the same manner as if it had been written in the expression as a constant. But a function is not identical to a program-mer-supplied constant which always has the same current value each time a statement is executed; because the current value of BETA can change each time the subprogram is executed, the current value of the function can also change. Thus a subprogram may yield a different result each time it is executed.

The first letter of a function, like any other variable name, always im-plies the mode. Thus, SQRT implies that the current value of the function will be established in floating point rather than in integer mode.

Because the current value of SQRT will be handled by the computer like a programmer-supplied constant, an obvious question is whether the computer will yield a single-precision (real) or double-precision constant. If a programmer writes a constant, he can specify it to be a double preci-sion by writing a decimal value of 8 through 16 digits in length, or by using the D code to specify double-precision exponential form. But, if a subprogram yields a constant, the function used by the programmer de-termines the type. All subprograms are designed to establish the current value of a function in only one specific mode (integer, real, or double pre-cision). The subprogram "called for" by the function SQRT is specifically designed to yield a single-precision (real) constant. If a double-precision current value is desired, the programmer may use a DØUBLE PRECI-SIØN specification statement or, more conveniently, use a different func-tion. (In this case, he would use DSQRT.)

An argument is an arithmetic expression, so it may be a constant, a variable name, or various combinations of constants and/or variable names separated by operational signs. But, there are restrictions as to the mode of arithmetic expressions used as arguments. Each subprogram requires a specific mode of argument (integer, real, or double precision). If an argu-ment is in mixed mode, the rules of hierarchy determine the specific mode as in the case of any other arithmetic expression. (Programmers must al-ways be cautious when using mixed mode expressions.)

Also, each subprogram has specific requirements as to the number of arguments which can be used with a function; most must have either one or two; but some must have two or more.

Subprograms are easy to use; but because each has special requirements, they must be selected with care.

Illustrative Examples. Following are a few examples of FORTRAN-Supplied Subprograms. Each requires one single-precision argument and establishes a single-precision current value to the function. Each example has a double-precision counterpart.

Function	Calls Subprogram to Compute:
SIN	Trigonometric Sine
CØS	Trigonometric Cosine
ATAN	Arctangent
TANH	Hyperbolic Tangent
ALØG	Natural Logarithm
ALØG10	Common Logarithm
ABS	Absolute Value
SQRT	Square Root

Functions can be used in any arithmetic expression; they are not limited to arithmetic statements. An arithmetic expression may contain one or more functions; the same function may appear more than once in the same expression; and an expression may contain one or more nested functions. The following statements illustrate some valid expressions containing one or more functions:

```
┌12345│6│7
    103    IF(SQRT(A+B))7,8,8
           B=SIN(A)/CØS(A)
           C=SQRT(A*2.0)+SQRT(B)
           D=SIN(SQRT(A))
           E=SIN(SQRT(ALØG(A*A)))
```

Note that a nested function is actually an argument of another function. In any arithmetic expression, parentheses can be used to control the sequence of evaluation. Thus, with nested functions, the innermost function is evaluated first.

It might be questioned why a subprogram is provided to extract square root because either of the following statements will apparently produce the same results, but the second requires a longer expression.

```
┌12345│6│7
    104    RØØT=A**.5
           RØØT=SQRT(A)
```

The reason for providing a square root function is simply because it is faster than the exponential function. It is recommended that the subprogram be used to calculate square root.

All subprograms presented previously in this section required only one argument and also required that the function and argument be in the same mode. FORTRAN also provides some subprograms which require two or more arguments and several different combinations of function and argument modes. (It should be noted that when more than one argument is required for a particular subprogram, all arguments must be in the same mode.) To demonstrate this type, five very useful subprograms for determining the largest value in a series of arguments are presented next.

Function	Mode of Current Value Established for Function	Required Mode of Argument
MAX0	Integer	Integer
AMAX1	Real	Real
DMAX1	Double Precision	Double Precision
MAX1	Integer	Real
AMAX0	Real	Integer

The following statements demonstrate how these functions can be used in expressions:

```
|12345|6|7
 105    NUMBIG=MAX0(I,J,K,L,M,N)
        BIGNUM=AMAX1(A,B)
        HUGE=DMAX1(U,V,W,X)
        M=(MAX1(A,B,C))+(N*7)
        A=(AMAX0(J,K,L))+(B*7.0)
```

It should be noted that the last two statements illustrated above do *not* contain mixed mode expressions. The computer handled the arguments in the mode indicated when selecting the largest value which is then converted to a different mode before establishing the current value of the function. Because the function is consistent in mode to other elements in the expression, the expression is not in mixed mode.

It is emphasized again that only a few selected examples of FORTRAN-Supplied Subprograms are included in this section. Many more are available (see Appendix E) which perform a wide variety of functions including some which can be used to select the smallest number from a series, transfer the sign from one value to another, or determine if an integer is odd or even.

One-Statement Mathematical Function Subprograms

The previous section covered subprograms which have already been written by someone other than the programmer. This section covers one type of subprogram which can be written in FORTRAN by the programmer himself for his own special applications. This type of subprogram is "called for" the same as a FORTRAN-Supplied Subprogram. Because the programmer writes his own subprogram, he must supply the variable name called a "function" and also decide how many arguments he will require. Before he can use his subprogram, he must explicitly describe it to the computer. The statement used to describe his subprogram is a special type of arithmetic statement sometimes called a "function-defining statement." It indicates the programmer-supplied function name and the calculations to be performed. It must follow any specification statements but must precede all executable statements in the calling program.

General Description.   The general form of a function-defining statement is:

```
|12345|6|7
nnnnn    function(darg₁,darg₂,...dargₘ)=ae
```

Legend:

nnnnn	Any unique one- to five-digit integer which specifies the statement *number*. It is never required but may be used at the programmer's option.
function	A variable name selected by the programmer as the unique name of his subprogram.
(darg₁, ... dargₘ)	One or more nonsubscripted variable names enclosed in parentheses and separated by commas. They are selected by the programmer to serve as *dummy arguments*.
=	A required separator.
ae	Any *arithmetic expression* which must include each independent variable name that serves as a dummy argument (subscripted variable names are not permitted). It specifies the operation to be performed when the function is referenced in the main program.

Dummy Arguments.   The arguments in a function-defining statement are called "dummy arguments." They are used to indicate how many arguments are required when the subprogram is "called for" by the main program. Each dummy argument must be unique in the statement in which it appears but may be used as a dummy argument in more than one function-defining statement or even as a variable name outside the function-defining statement. When a subprogram is "called for," actual arguments are substituted for the dummy arguments. The actual and dummy arguments must correspond in number, mode, and sequence.

The calling program and subprogram transfer values to each other. The current value of an actual argument in the calling program is transferred to the subprogram where it becomes the current value of a dummy argument. After the subprogram has completed its job, the current value of the function is transferred back to the calling program.

Illustrative Examples.   To illustrate, assume that John Smith is writing a long program which requires three very similar IF statements. Each must appear many times in different places in the program. The arithmetic expressions required for the three IF statements are:

$$(A+Q+R+S+T+U+V+W)$$
$$(B+Q+R+S+T+U+V+W)$$
$$(C+Q+R+S+T+U+V+W)$$

Further assume that each time the IF statements appear in the program, the variable names have different values. Rather than prepare many long IF statements, he could prepare his own subprogram with the following statement:

$\overline{1\,2\,3\,4\,5\,|\,6\,|\,7}$

    106   SMITH(X)=X+Q+R+S+T+U+V+W

The function (programmer-supplied name) of the subprogram is SMITH. The dummy argument is X, and it appears first in the series of variable names instead of A, B, or C. The function, followed by an actual argument substituted for the dummy argument, is used to "call for" the subprogram. For example:

$\overline{1\,2\,3\,4\,5\,|\,6\,|\,7}$

    107   IF(SMITH(A))...
           IF(SMITH(B))...
           IF(SMITH(C))...

In the first IF statement, the current value of the actual argument (A) will be substituted for the current value of the dummy argument (X) in the subprogram expression. Thus, the current value of the function SMITH will be evaluated as follows:

$$A+Q+R+S+T+U+V+W$$

Similarly, B and C will be substituted for the dummy argument in the other examples.

A function-defining statement may include one or more other functions. A partial program which includes three dummy arguments in one FORTRAN-supplied function is illustrated below:

$\overline{1\,2\,3\,4\,5\,|\,6\,|\,7}$

           ...
    108   SMITH(X,Y,Z)=Y+R*SQRT(X**4.0)*(Y/(6.0+Z))
     2   ZAP=X+SMITH(A,B,C)

When statement number 2 is executed, the current values of the actual arguments A, B, and C will be substituted for the current values of the dummy arguments X, Y, and Z respectively. Thus, ZAP will be computed by evaluating the following arithmetic expression:

$$X+B+R*SQRT(A**4.0)*(B/(6.0+C))$$

Because the dummy argument X may be used as a variable name *outside* the function-defining statement, it may appear in statement number 2. Note, however, that A is substituted for X only where it appears in the subprogram expression.

A programmer may prepare as many of his own One-Statement Mathematical Function Subprograms as he desires, within the capacity of the computer. He may include these subprograms in any program he writes, but they must always be located in the proper position which is following any specification statements but preceding all executable statements in the calling program.

Declared-FUNCTIØN Subprograms

A one-statement mathematical function subprogram, covered in the previous section, is included as part of the calling program. The unique form of this statement *implies* that it is a one-statement subprogram.

The type of subprogram covered in this section is a separate subprogram rather than a part of the calling program. It may contain many statements and is similar in appearance to a complete independent program, so the computer must be told that it is a subprogram. The statement used to make this declaration is the FUNCTIØN statement. A subprogram which includes this statement is technically termed a "FUNCTIØN Subprogram." To distinguish it from a one-statement function subprogram, which is *implied* to be a subprogram, a more descriptive term might be "Declared-FUNCTIØN Subprogram." Like the two types of subprograms previously described, it is "called for" by a unique variable name (function) and is designed to return one value to the calling program.

General Description. A general description of a Declared-FUNCTIØN Subprogram follows.

1. It is written in FORTRAN. The programmer must select a unique variable name to serve as the function. The function must appear in the subprogram as well as in the calling program which references it. The programmer must also specify one or more dummy arguments. Actual and dummy arguments must agree in number, mode, and sequence.
2. It may include a whole series of statements designed to compute one result which becomes the current value of the function in the calling program. In fact, it is almost the same as a complete and independent program.
3. The first statement must be a FUNCTIØN statement. The key word "FUNCTIØN" declares it to be a separate subprogram rather than a complete independent program.

4. When control passes to a subprogram, it executes independently of the calling program. Thus, the variable names and statement numbers may be the same as those in the calling program. (They must, of course, be unique within the subprogram.)

5. It may include subscripted variable names and dummy arrays. Because it operates independently of the calling program, the dummy arrays must be defined and dimensioned. DIMENSIØN statements should appear at the beginning of the program following the FUNCTIØN statement which must always be first.

6. It must include a statement that sets the current value of the function to the desired result before control is returned to the calling program.

7. The mode of the current value returned to the function in the calling program can be specified in two ways: (1) implicitly by the first letter of the variable name which serves as the function, or (2) explicitly, by preceding the key word FUNCTIØN, in the first statement of the subprogram, with the specification INTEGER, REAL, or DØUBLE PRECISIØN.

8. Because the number of statements is not set, but can vary, the computer must be told when to terminate execution of the subprogram and return the result to the calling program. The STØP statement is the last statement executed in a complete independent program. But instead of a STØP, a counterpart called a RETURN statement is used in this type of subprogram (one RETURN statement is required but more than one may be included). The RETURN statement terminates execution of the subprogram and returns control to the calling program. One or more STØP statements may also be included in a subprogram. In fact, they are sometimes required by the program logic. Execution of a STØP statement will, of course, terminate execution of the main line as well as all related subprograms.

9. The subprogram is compiled independently of the calling program; and because it does not have a set number of statements, the terminal point must be indicated by an END statement.

Two special types of statements are required for this type of subprogram. A general description of each type follows.

The FUNCTIØN Statement. A Declared-FUNCTIØN Subprogram must begin with a FUNCTIØN statement. The general form is:

|12345|6|7

nnnnn   type FUNCTIØN function($darg_1, darg_2, \ldots darg_m$)

Legend:

nnnnn	Any unique one- to five-digit integer which specifies the statement number. It is never required but may be used at the programmer's option.
type	May be used at the programmer's option to specify the

mode of the current value returned to the function of the calling program. It is omitted if the mode is implied by the first letter of the function. The type may be either INTEGER, REAL, or DØUBLE PRECISIØN. If the mode is not implied, it must also be indicated in the calling program by an explicit specification statement. The calling program and subprogram operate independently, but both use the same function name; thus, it must be implicitly or explicitly specified in both.

FUNCTIØN — A key word which specifies a Declared-FUNCTIØN Subprogram.

function — A variable name selected by the programmer to serve as the unique name of his subprogram. It must also be included in some other statement in the subprogram which sets the current value of the function to the desired result before control is returned to the calling program. Like any other unique variable name, it may appear more than once in the subprogram.

$(darg_1, \ldots darg_m)$ — One or more nonsubscripted variable names enclosed in parentheses and separated by commas. They are selected by the programmer to serve as dummy arguments.

The RETURN Statement. A RETURN statement terminates execution of the subprogram and returns control to the calling program which may be another subprogram or the main line. When control is returned to the calling program, one value is also returned. The calling program then continues executing. The RETURN statement indicates the logical terminal point in the subprogram; and if it is omitted, no value can be returned. A STØP statement can also be included in a subprogram, but the execution of a STØP statement terminates the execution of the main line as well as all related subprograms. Because the usual purpose of a Declared-FUNCTIØN Subprogram is to perform some type of calculation and then return the result to the calling program, it ordinarily does not contain a STØP statement.

The general form of a RETURN statement is:

```
|12345|6|7
nnnnn   RETURN
```

Legend:

nnnnn — Any unique one- to five-digit integer which specifies the statement number. It is required only if referenced by another statement in the subprogram. It may always be used at the programmer's option.

RETURN — A key word specifying the type of statement.

Illustrative Examples. To start with an elementary example, a subprogram to multiply pi (3.14159265) times a variable name appearing in the calling program is used to demonstrate the general structure of a Declared-FUNCTIØN Subprogram:

```
|12345|6|7
109   FUNCTIØN SMITH(X)
```

SMITH=X*3.14159265
RETURN
END

The function (programmer-supplied variable name) of the subprogram is SMITH. The dummy argument is X which is also included in the arithmetic statement that establishes the current value of the function before control is returned to the calling program. Note particularly that the dummy argument must appear in the arithmetic statement to the right but not to the left of the equal sign. This should be compared to the type of subprogram illustrated in the previous section.

The function, followed by an actual argument, is used to "call for" the subprogram. For example, the calling program might use the following statement:

| 12345 | 6 | 7 |

1010   IF(SMITH(A))...

The current value of A (the *actual* argument) in the calling program will be substituted for the current value of X (the *dummy* argument) in the subprogram. Thus, the current value of the function SMITH will be evaluated as follows:

$$A*3.14159265$$

After the evaluation is completed, the result will be stored at the function SMITH in the subprogram. Next, the RETURN statement will cause this result to be transferred back to the calling program where it will become the current value of the function SMITH. Then the calling program will continue executing statements in the normal manner. Note again, as discussed in the preceding section, that the calling program and the subprogram transfer values to each other.

The preceding example is not very practical because it is easier to solve the problem by including the constant 3.14159265 directly in the calling program. It is presented to illustrate the difference between a Declared-FUNCTIØN Subprogram and the one-statement subprogram covered in the preceding section. A more practical illustration is presented next.

The following subprogram (named "TØTAL") will compute the sum of all values stored in an array. Because the subprogram operates independently of the calling program, the dummy array must have its own DIMENSIØN statement. (If two- or three-dimensional arrays are used, the actual and dummy arrays must be specified to contain the same number of elements.)

| 12345 | 6 | 7 |

1011   FUNCTIØN TØTAL(ARRAY,NUMELM)

```
        DIMENSIØN  ARRAY(500)
        TØTAL=0.0
        DØ  7  INDEX=1,NUMELM
     7  TØTAL=TØTAL+ARRAY(INDEX)
        RETURN
        END
```

Now suppose the calling program has several actual one-dimensional arrays, all properly dimensioned and established. It is desired to compute the sum of an array named ZEBRA which contains 100 elements and to compute the average (arithmetic mean) of an array called CAMEL which contains 300 elements. The following partial calling program can be used:

```
|12345|6|7
        . . .
   1012  KØUNT=100
         NUMBER=300
         SUM=TØTAL(ZEBRA,KØUNT)
         AVE=TØTAL(CAMEL,NUMBER)/300.0
```

How does the subprogram dummy array (ARRAY) get the current values of the elements in the two actual arrays (ZEBRA and CAMEL)? They are automatically supplied by the calling program. Remember, the current value of an argument is always sent to a subprogram; if the argument is an array variable name, the entire array is sent. Note that the subprogram can receive many values, but it can return only one.

The Declared-FUNCTIØN Subprogram has only two basic restrictions. It cannot contain a SUBRØUTINE statement (covered in the next section), and it cannot have more than one FUNCTIØN statement. Thus, it can be used for almost any purpose including reading and writing.

It is emphasized again that it may not be necessary for the programmer to write his own subprograms. The computer center may have many that have already been written by someone else and which might be used to the programmer's advantage.

SUBRØUTINE SUBPROGRAMS

Like the Declared-FUNCTIØN Subprogram, the type of subprogram covered in this section is not a part of the calling program. The computer must be told that it is a subprogram rather than an independent program. The statement used to make this declaration is the SUBRØUTINE statement. A subprogram which includes this statement is technically termed a "SUBRØUTINE Subprogram." Because it is not *implied* to be a subprogram, a more descriptive term might be "Declared-SUBRØUTINE Subprogram."

Declared SUBRØUTINE Subprograms

There is only *one* type of subroutine subprogram. To distinguish it from the three types of function subprograms, and as a matter of convenience, it will simply be called a *subroutine*.

General Description. When any of the three types of *function* subprograms are used, the calling program sends values via arguments and receives values back via functions. When a *subroutine* is used, the calling program also sends values via arguments, but it receives values back via arguments instead of via functions.

A subroutine, like the other three types of subprograms is identified by a unique name which must follow the same rules of length and composition as a regular variable name. But no values are ever associated with this name, so there is no implied mode and no restrictions on the first letter. Because this name performs no function, other than to identify a subroutine, it will not be called a "function" but simply a subroutine *name*.

A subroutine is very similar to a Declared-FUNCTIØN Subprogram, but it differs in three major respects. It starts with a SUBRØUTINE statement; it is "called for" by a CALL statement; and, most important, it is not limited to returning one value to the calling program. Because values are returned via arguments instead of via a single function, it may return as many values as there are arguments. However, it is not limited to returning one value per argument. Because array names are permitted as arguments, it may send back perhaps hundreds or thousands of values for each argument (one for each array element). On the other hand, if a value is not changed by the subroutine, it will return the same value it received. Thus, in effect, it may return no values.

The SUBRØUTINE Statement. Only one SUBRØUTINE statement is permitted in a subroutine, and it must be the first. The general form is:

```
|12345|6|7
nnnnn    SUBRØUTINE name(darg₁,darg₂,...dargₘ)
```

Legend:

nnnnn	Any unique one- to five-digit integer which specifies the statement number. It is never required but may be used at the programmer's option.
name	The programmer-supplied subroutine name.
SUBRØUTINE	A key word which specifies a Declared-SUBRØUTINE Subprogram.
(darg₁, ... dargₘ)	One or more optional nonsubscripted variable names enclosed in parentheses and separated by commas. They are selected by the programmer to serve as dummy arguments. They may be omitted in some types of subroutines.

The CALL Statement. This statement is required in a calling program to "call for" a subroutine. The general form is:

```
|12345|6|7
nnnnn    CALL name(arg₁,arg₂,...argₘ)
```

Legend:

nnnnn	Any unique one- to five-digit integer which specifies the statement number. It is required only if referenced by another statement in the calling program. It may always be used at the programmer's option.
CALL	A key word specifying the type of statement.
name	The subroutine name.
(arg₁, ... argₘ)	One or more optional arguments enclosed in parentheses and separated by commas. Arguments may be any type of arithmetic expression, but only independent and array variable names are illustrated in this section.

Illustrative Examples. To start with an elementary but practical example, suppose a company has several programs which require the same message or header line to be printed. Instead of including the same FØRMAT and WRITE statements in several programs, one subroutine can be written to do the job. The following subroutine will write a header line:

```
|12345|6|7
 1013    SUBRØUTINE HEADER
    7    FØRMAT(T11,'NAME',T27,'AMOUNT')
         WRITE(3,7)
         RETURN
         END
```

All programs requiring this subroutine could include the following statement:

```
|12345|6|7
 1014    CALL  HEADER
```

When the CALL statement is executed, the subroutine will write the header line then return control to the calling program. Notice that no arguments are used, and no values are exchanged in this example.

Array routines included in Chapter 8 will be used as subroutines in the next two illustrative examples.

The following subroutine exchanges values with the calling program. It is designed to initialize all elements in the calling program array to zero:

```
|12345|6|7
 1015    SUBRØUTINE ZERØ(ARRAY,N)
         DIMENSIØN  ARRAY(100)
         DØ  7  I=1,N
    7    ARRAY(I)=0.0
         RETURN
         END
```

The name of the subroutine is ZERØ. The subroutine is designed to work with floating point values; but because the name assumes no value, it may start with any letter. Thus, the name could be MIKE, but a more descriptive term is preferred. The current values of the dummy arguments ARRAY and N are established by the calling program. Note that this subroutine will change each nonzero element in ARRAY, but it will not change the current value of N which is used as a test value for the DØ statement.

Suppose a calling program has a 100–element array, properly dimensioned, called GRAPES. It contains single-precision floating point data which the computer has completed processing, so the values of the individual elements need not be saved. It is desired to use the previously illustrated subroutine to replace the data with zeros. The following two statements in the calling program will perform the desired task:

```
|12345|6|7
 1016   NUMELM=100
        CALL ZERØ(GRAPES,NUMELM)
```

When the CALL statement is executed, 101 current values will be transferred from the two actual arguments to the two dummy arguments. Because GRAPES is the name of a 100–element array, this one argument will transfer 100 current values to the subroutine. On the other hand, NUMELM is an independent variable name, so it will transfer only one current value. When the subroutine RETURN statement is executed, the current value of each element in the dummy array (ZERØ) will be transferred back to the actual array (GRAPES) in the calling program. The current value of the other dummy argument will also be transferred back, but in this case it is unchanged so, in effect, only the array values are exchanged. Notice how the arguments are a sort of "two-way street;" they transfer values back and forth to each other.

Now assume that a calling program has a DIMENSIØN statement which specifies three arrays named ARRAY1, ARRAY2, and ARRAY3; lengths are 300, 200, and 100 respectively. Single-precision (real) data has been read into all elements in ARRAY3, but no data has been placed in the elements of the other two arrays. A DIMENSIØN statement reserves space for an array, but it does not initialize the elements within the array to any specific value. Thus, ARRAY1 and ARRAY2 contain "garbage." Suppose it is necessary to create two duplicates of ARRAY3, and the other two arrays are to be used to store the duplicate data.

The following subroutine is designed to create two duplicates of an array:

```
|12345|6|7
 1017   SUBRØUTINE  DUPTWØ(ARRAY,DUP1ST,DUP2ND,N)
        DIMENSIØN  ARRAY(1),DUP1ST(1),DUP2ND(1)
```

```
      DØ 7 I=1,N
      DUP1ST(I)=ARRAY(I)
   7  DUP2ND(I)=ARRAY(I)
      RETURN
      END
```

The following two statements in the calling program will solve the problem:

```
┌─────────────
│12345│6│7
   1018   N=100
          CALL DUPTWØ(ARRAY3,ARRAY1,ARRAY2,N)
```

This problem is designed to illustrate several points:

1. There is no conflict caused by the use of the same variable name (N) to specify the number of elements in the dummy and actual arrays because the calling program and the subroutine operate independently of each other.
2. Two of the arrays in the calling program contain "garbage," but the first 100 elements in each will be duplicates of ARRAY3 when the subroutine has finished its job.
3. The dummy arrays are specified to contain only one element, but they work with three arrays containing 100 elements each. Actual arrays must be dimensioned large enough to accommodate all elements in an array, but this is not required for one-dimensional dummy arrays. The purpose of a DIMENSIØN statement in a subroutine, or other type of subprogram, is only to specify that the variable names are array names. Thus, dummy arrays may be specified as minimum size. It is beyond the scope of this book to explain the details of what happens within the computer, but essentially the calling program passes the beginning address and length of the actual arrays to the subprogram which then works with the actual arrays. In other words, instead of actually transferring values, the calling program tells the subroutine where these values are located. Thus, less processing time and less storage space is required because less data is transferred and the values of the actual and dummy arrays share the same storage locations. (If multiple-dimension arrays are used, they must be dimensioned the same in the calling program and in the subprogram.)

THE CØMMØN STATEMENT

In previous sections of this chapter, arguments were used to transfer values to and receive values from subprograms. As stated, the purpose of an argument is to make data available to a called subprogram by explicitly indicating an independent or array variable name which specifies the location of the data the subprogram is to work with. When arguments are used to pass values back and forth, the actual transfer takes place at *execution* time.

If a program includes several programmer-supplied subprograms which each require the transfer of many values, repeatedly listing long strings of arguments can be tedious and subject to error. To eliminate the necessity of listing arguments each time a subprogram is called, FORTRAN provides another shortcut. A CØMMØN statement can be used to tell the subprogram at *compilation* time where the data will be located when the subprogram is called. Because it already "knows" the data location at execution time, arguments to provide this information are neither required *nor allowed.* In effect, the arguments are *implied.* When a CØMMØN statement is used, a program will execute faster because argument data are not passed back and forth at execution time.

The CØMMØN statement is a nonexecutable specification statement. It must precede any executable statements in the program or subprogram in which it appears. Its general form is:

| 12345 | 6 | 7
---

nnnnn   CØMMØN $vn_1(ne_{1a},ne_{1b},ne_{1c}),\ldots vn_m(ne_{me},ne_{mb},ne_{mc})$

Legend:

nnnnn	Any unique one- to five-digit integer which specifies the statement number. It is never required but may be used at the programmer's option.
CØMMØN	A key word which identifies the type of statement.
$vn_1,\ldots vn_m$	One or more independent or array variable names which this statement will assign to a special common block of storage in the order in which they are listed.
$(ne_{1a},\ldots ne_{1c})$	One, two, or three unsigned integer numbers representing the *number of elements* in a one-, two-, or three-dimensional array. These numbers are omitted when an independent variable name is used. They are also omitted when an array variable name is used if the array has been dimensioned by a preceding DIMENSIØN or explicit specification statement.

As previously stated, the same variable name, such as DEMØ, may be used in two or more different subprograms without conflict because the compiler will assign a different *actual* storage location to DEMØ for each subprogram in which it appears. But, the programmer can tell the compiler that DEMØ has a common meaning and should be assigned the same actual storage location by including the following statement in *each* subprogram in which DEMØ appears:

| 12345 | 6 | 7

      CØMMØN DEMØ

Like the EQUIVALENCE statement (discussed in Chapter 8), the CØMMØN statement causes storage to be shared; but these two statements are used for different situations. EQUIVALENCE is used when two or more different variable names in the *same* program or subprogram are to share the same storage location. CØMMØN is used when two or more variable names in *different* subprograms (or in the main line and one or more different subprograms) are to share the same storage location. The special storage area reserved by the CØMMØN statement is sometimes called the "CØMMØN block."

More than one variable name may be listed in a CØMMØN statement. For example, if the following statement is included in *each* of two different subprograms:

12345	6	7

          CØMMØN ABLE,BAKER

ABLE in one subprogram will be assigned the same area in the CØMMØN block as ABLE in the other; and, likewise, BAKER in one will share storage with BAKER in the other. The same results will be obtained if the sequence of the variable names is reversed:

12345	6	7

          CØMMØN BAKER,ABLE

The sequence of the variable names in the CØMMØN statement must be the same in both subprograms, in this case, because the compiler associates the first variable name in one subprogram to the first in the other and, likewise, the second to the second.

The preceding examples illustrated cases in which storage space was to be shared by the *same* variable names. The CØMMØN statement can also be used to cause storage to be shared by *different* variable names. For example, assume that the first subprogram includes this statement:

12345	6	7

          CØMMØN A,B,C

and the second subprogram this one:

12345	6	7

          CØMMØN X,Y,Z

The preceding two statements specify that the variable names A, B, and C in the first subprogram are to share storage with X, Y, and Z in the second; A will share with X, B with Y, and C with Z. It should be noted that the first subprogram may include the variable names X, Y, and Z in other statements without conflict. Because these variable names are not specified in the CØMMØN statement of the first subprogram, they will *not* share storage with X, Y, and Z in the second. They can be made to share storage with X, Y, and Z in the second as well as A, B, and C in the first, by including an appropriate EQUIVALENCE statement in the first subprogram.

A CØMMØN statement may include independent and/or array variable names. If an array name is included, it must either be dimensioned in this statement or in a preceding DIMENSIØN or explicit specification statement. (As a general rule, an array must be dimensioned in the first statement in which its name appears. The only exception to this rule is that the name of a dummy array must appear in a FUNCTIØN or SUBRØU-TINE statement before it is dimensioned.) The following two statements:

```
|12345|6|7
        DIMENSIØN  ARRAY(100)
        CØMMØN  ARRAY
```

can be replaced by this single statement:

```
|12345|6|7
        CØMMØN  ARRAY(100)
```

The programmer may elect to use different statements to dimension different arrays as illustrated below:

```
|12345|6|7
        DIMENSIØN  X(50)
        REAL  N(100)
        CØMMØN  A(200),N,X
```

Now, the effects of the CØMMØN statement will be illustrated by an elementary example. Assume the following main-line program:

```
|12345|6|7
        CØMMØN  A,B,C
        B=1.0
        C=2.0
        CALL  SUB
        Z=C*2.0
        WRITE(3,99)Z
   99   FØRMAT(F4.1)
        STØP
        END
```

and the following subprogram:

```
|12345|6|7
        SUBRØUTINE  SUB
        CØMMØN  A,Y,Z
        A=3.0
        Z=A+Y
        RETURN
        END
```

If the CØMMØN statements were omitted in the preceding illustration, it would be necessary to include the arguments A, B, and C in the CALL statement and A, Y, and Z in the SUBRØUTINE statement. Note that B

and C in the main line as well as Y and Z in the subprogram are initialized
by arithmetic statements in the main line. But, A in the main line and A
in the subprogram are both initialized in the subprogram. Execution of the
second arithmetic statement in the subprogram ($Z = A + Y$) will cause the
current value of Z in the subprogram and C in the main line to be changed
to 4.0, but Z in the main line is not affected because it does not share storage with any other variable name. Likewise, execution of the final arithmetic statement in the main line ($Z = C*2.0$) will initialize Z in the main
line to 8.0 but will not change the current value of Z in the subprogram.

The preceding illustration included only one CALL statement, so the
programming convenience of using CØMMØN statements (instead of arguments) to pass information back and forth was not clearly demonstrated.
But, it should be obvious that the CØMMØN statement can provide quite
a shortcut when many calls are made.

In all previous illustrations in this section, an equal number of variable
names was always listed in the corresponding CØMMØN statements.
That is, if three variable names were specified as CØMMØN in the main
line, for example, three were also specified as CØMMØN in the subprogram. This practice was followed because it was assumed that the data
sharing storage was always the same type. It is possible to store different
types of data in the same place (but not at the same time) in which case
the number of variable names in the corresponding CØMMØN statements
will not necessarily be equal. Before illustrating this point, the manner in
which data are stored will be briefly reviewed.

The CØMMØN statement reserves a special area of storage called a
"CØMMØN block." Data are stored in this CØMMØN block in the sequence in which the independent variable names appear in the CØMMØN
statement. As pointed out in Chapter 3, a double-precision floating point
value is represented by 64 contiguous bits, but a single-precision (real) or
integer value is represented by 32. Internal storage is divided into groups
of bits; each group of eight bits is called a "byte;" and each byte is considered to be one storage location because it is the smallest addressable unit
of storage. So, stated another way, a double-precision value is stored in
eight contiguous locations, but a single-precision or integer value is stored
in only four.

To illustrate how integer data are stored in a CØMMØN block, assume that I and J are independent variable names and K is a four-element
array. The following statement:

12345	6	7

CØMMØN I,J,K(4)

will reserve 24 storage locations in the CØMMØN block. I will be assigned
the first four locations, J the next four, the first element of the K array the
next four, the second element the next four, etc.

Now that the necessary background has been developed, a more complex application will be illustrated. Assume that a CØMMØN block is reserved by a calling program and its three subprograms. The following statements appear in the calling program:

| 12345 | 6 | 7 |

DØUBLE PRECISIØN X,Y
CØMMØN X,Y

the following in the first subprogram:

| 12345 | 6 | 7 |

DØUBLE PRECISIØN Z
CØMMØN Z,A,B

the following in the second subprogram:

| 12345 | 6 | 7 |

REAL I,J
CØMMØN C,D,I,J

and the following in the third subprogram:

| 12345 | 6 | 7 |

CØMMØN K(3),L

Figure 10–1 illustrates the manner in which the CØMMØN block will be shared.

FIGURE 10–1
Illustrative CØMMØN Block Shared by a Calling Program and Its Three Subprograms

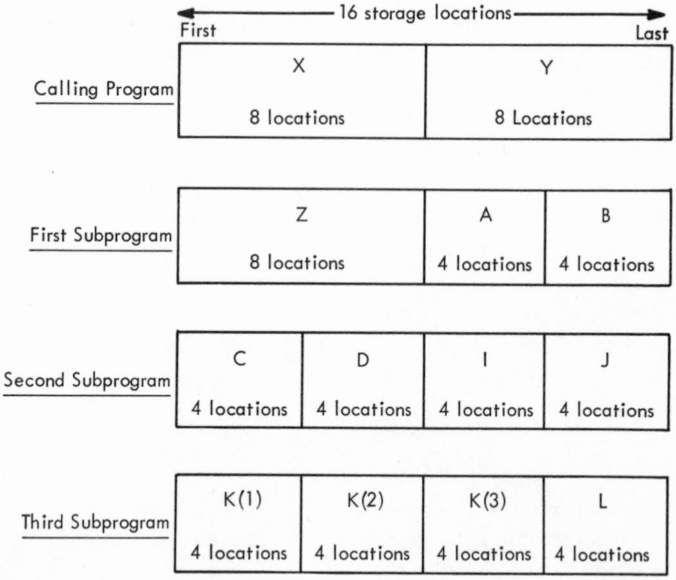

Note that X in the calling program shares storage with Z in the first subprogram, with C and D in the second, and with K(1) and K(2) in the third. The calling program may validly reference X or Z; but even though C and D, as well as K(1) and K(2), share the same storage, they cannot be referenced by the calling program. Variable names sharing the same storage can be validly referenced only by a program or subprogram which use corresponding locations to store the *same types of data*. Thus, in these preceding illustrations, the calling program can reference X, Y, and Z, the first subprogram can reference A and B, as well as I and J (which were included in a REAL statement), etc.

As illustrated, the CØMMØN statement is very powerful, but it must be used with caution. When a change is made in a CØMMØN statement, either directly or indirectly (such as a change in a DIMENSIØN, explicit specification, or EQUIVALENCE statement), extreme care must be taken to see that all corresponding CØMMØN statements are changed accordingly.

THE POWER OF SUBPROGRAMS

The first section of this chapter covered the "built-in" subprograms provided by FORTRAN. As indicated, these subprograms are already compiled and ready to go. They are usually stored on a high-speed external device such as a magnetic disk drive where they are almost instantaneously available to a calling program. It is emphasized that other types of subprograms can also be stored on magnetic disk, for example, where they are available to any calling program similar to the "built-in" subprograms provided by FORTRAN. This makes it possible for a very short "skeleton-type" main program to call a subprogram which will solve a complete problem.

For instance, a program to compute the weekly payroll can be written as a subprogram which performs the complete job, then compiled and stored so it is available to a short calling program. Subprograms can also be used as calling programs. To carry this almost to the extreme, each Friday a short calling program can call a subprogram named FRIDAY which, in turn, can call other subprograms which will execute several or all jobs required for that day. This is not as simple as it may appear, but it demonstrates the power of subprograms.

Finally, this book is designed to serve as both a text and reference manual for beginning FORTRAN programmers. No attempt has been made to include all there is to be known about the language. It is recommended that the manufacturer's manuals, *Basic FORTRAN IV Language* and *Basic FORTRAN IV Programmer's Guide*, be referred to for more advanced applications.

APPENDIX
A

DEBUGGING TECHNIQUES

ETECTING and correcting programming errors is a process called "debugging." Fortunately, the programmer can get substantial help from both the compiler and the computer system in locating any errors which are encountered during compilation or execution. A program may have to be rerun several times before it is completely "checked out." Reruns may save hours of debugging, but it is the programmer's responsibility to be sure each run will be helpful. The purpose of this Appendix is to discuss the debugging process in general and to explain and illustrate various debugging techniques.

THE DEBUGGING PROCESS

If the control cards (see Appendix D) include OPTION LIST, the source program will be listed (printed) by the high-speed printer. Any violation of the rules of FORTRAN will cause compilation to terminate, but the compiler will cause diagnostic messages and error summaries to also be listed. These messages and summaries should be used by the programmer to detect the type of error and its exact or general location within each listed statement. After any and all errors encountered during compilation are debugged, the source program can be compiled into an object program and storage maps listed on the printer. The compiler's job is now complete, and control will pass from the compiler to the computer system. If the program is to be compiled and executed in the same run, it will be "linkage edited" and ready for the next processing step, which is execution of the object program.

An object program can be terminated during execution in several ways. For example, it may be terminated by power failure, machine malfunction, operator intervention, or by an automatic timing device. It can also be terminated automatically as a result of a programming error which makes it impossible for the computer to execute the object program. When this latter type of error is encountered, the computer system (and the compiler) will generate and list an error code indicating the reason for the termination. This error code should be used to detect both the type of error and the type of statement being executed at the time the program failed. After any and all errors encountered during execution of the object program are debugged, the program can be executed.

After the program has been executed, the programmer must carefully examine the output to determine if it provides the correct solution to the problem to be solved. Even though the program has been compiled and executed, it may require more debugging. The programmer may not have allowed for all possibilities or may have committed other logic errors. Errors in programming logic can cause a variety of results. For example, the output may be from the wrong device or it may contain incorrect data; it is also possible that no output can be produced by the program. Correcting logic errors can be the most difficult step in the debugging process.

To summarize, the debugging process requires locating and correcting, in order, any:

1. Errors terminating compilation.
2. Errors terminating execution.
3. Errors in programming logic.

Each of these three types of programming errors will be discussed and illustrated in turn in the pages that follow.

ERRORS TERMINATING COMPILATION

If the programmer violates the rules of FORTRAN, the compiler will flag all incorrect statements and cause diagnostic messages to be included in the program listing. The messages are brief but self-explanatory. They vary according to the compiler used but are illustrated here to indicate what to look for. Two types of messages can be generated, statement error messages and summary messages.

Statement Error Messages

If a statement violates a rule of FORTRAN, both the type and general location of the violation are indicated within the program listing.

On the line below a violation, the compiler used for the illustrations in this Appendix causes a dollar sign to be printed which acts as a pointer to indicate where the violation was encountered by the compiler. The actual error of omission or commission will usually be found in the exact location or immediately preceding or following the location indicated by the dollar sign.

On the line below the dollar sign pointing to the general location of the violation, a diagnostic message will be printed indicating the type of error encountered by the compiler.

The compiler scans the statements from left to right searching for violations of the rules of FORTRAN. It should be noted that it will always detect and indicate the first violation in a statement but may not indicate any or all additional violations. It should also be noted that detection of the first *violation* does not necessarily mean detection of the first *error*. For example, suppose the statement:

$\overline{\lceil 12345 \lvert 6 \lvert 7}$

    READ(1,7)A,B,C,D,E,F,G

was incorrectly written with five of the six required commas omitted:

$\overline{\lceil 12345 \lvert 6 \lvert 7}$

    READ(1,7)A B C D E F,G

Embedded blanks are permitted in variable names so no violation has occurred thus no error would be indicated. But, if the sixth comma was also omitted, there would be a violation; the compiler would cause a dollar sign and the statement error message NAME LENGTH to be listed.

Because the compiler may indicate only the *first* violation, any statements with error indications should be carefully checked for additional violations and errors.

Summary Messages

All summary messages appear at the end of the program listing. They identify errors which the compiler cannot associate with any particular statement. For example, a valid statement within the program may reference another statement such as statement number 17. If no statement in the program is numbered (labeled) 17, the compiler cannot determine which statement the programmer intended to reference. In this case, the diagnostic summary message UNDEFINED LABELS will appear at the end of the program listing. This message is followed by a list of all undefined labels referenced in the program.

Debugging Illustration Program—First Run

The program which follows (Figure A–1) contains a variety of errors which might be encountered by the programmer. This same program, after debugging, is illustrated again (Figure A–2 and A–3) in the last section of this Appendix. The illustrative program is supposedly designed to compute:

1. The regular, bonus, and total pay for each of 10 employees,
2. The total pay for all employees, and
3. Print the output complete with descriptive columnar headings.

The input deck contains 11 cards. The first 10 contain the integer code 1, 2, or 3 to indicate the amount of bonus for the individual employee:

Code	Amount of Bonus
1	Double the regular pay
2	Equal to the regular pay
3	One-half the regular pay

The last card in the input deck contains the integer code 4. This card is used to cause a branch to statement number 22 which will WRITE the total pay for all 10 employees.

Statements numbered 111, 112, 113, 114, and 115 are not related to the problem. They are included only for the purpose of illustrating additional errors in the program. An explanation of each error message immediately follows Figure A–1.

FIGURE A–1
Illustrative Debugging Program Containing Error Messages

```
          C    DEBUGGING ILLUSTRATION PROGRAM
          C         *** 1ST RUN ***
          C
          C      THIS  1ST RUN  ILLUSTRATES
          C      SOME OF THE MANY DIAGNOSTIC
          C      ERROR MESSAGES WHICH CAN BE
          C      GENERATED BY THE COMPILER.
          C      BECAUSE THIS PROGRAM CONTAINS
          C      ERRORS,IT CAN NOT COMPILE AND
          C      THUS CAN NOT EXECUTE OR
                 PRODUCE ANY OUTPUT.
                 $
   01) SYNTAX
          C
                 1 FORMAT(//4X,'EMP',T29,'REGULAR',
                 1T47,'TOTAL')
                 2 FORMAT(7H     NO.,T10,'HOURS',T17,
                 1'RATE',T23,'CODE',T30,'PAY',T38,
                                                  $
   01) SYNTAX
                 'BONUS',T48,'PAY'/)
                 $
   01) SYNTAX
                 3 FORMAT(I5,2F6.2,I2)
                 4 FORMAT(I6,T9,F6.2,T15,F6.2,T24,I2
                 1,T28,F7.2,T37,F7.2,T46,F7.2)
```

FIGURE A-1—*Continued*

```
                      5 FORMAT(T33,'GRAND TOTAL',T45,F8.2)
                      6 WRITE(3,1)
                      7 WRITE(3,2)
                      8 FINALTOT=0.00
                          $
    01) NAME LENGTH
                      9 KOUNT=0
                     10 READ(1,333),NUMEMP,HOURS,RATE,KODE
                          $
    01) SYNTAX
                     11 REGPAY=HOURS*RATE.
                          $
    01) SYNTAX
                     12 GO TO(13,15,17,22)KODE
                          $
    01) COMMA

                     13 BONUS=REGPAY*2.00
                    A14 GO TO 18
                       $
    01) SYNTAX
                     15 BONUS=REGPAY
                     21 GO TO 18 NOW
                          $
    01) SYNTAX
                        BONUS=REGPAY/2.00
                       $
    01) LABEL
                     18 TOTPAY=REGPAY+BONUS
                     19 WRITE(3,444)NOEMP HOURS,RATE,KODE
                          $
    01) NAME LENGTH
                      1REGPAY,BONUS
                          $
    01) NAME LENGTH
                     20 FINTOT+TOTPAY=FINTOT
                          $
    01) SYNTAX
                     21 GO TO 10
                       $
    01) DUP. LABEL
                     22 WRITE(3,5)FINTOT
                    111 FORMAT(F7.1
                          $
    01) SYNTAX

                    112 FORMAT(F7.1 F9.0)
                          $
    01) SYNTAX
                    113 FORMAT(15,F6.2,E6.2,D7.5,1234E+04))
                          $
    01) SYNTAX
                    114 UP=DOWN
                    115 GO TO 1
                          $
    01) ILLEGAL LABEL
                     12 STOP
                        $$
    01) DUP. LABEL        02) NO END CARD


                                UNDEFINED LABELS


    00333        00017        00444
```

Explanation of Error Messages. The Debugging Illustration Program (Figure A–1) contains, in sequence, the following statement errors:

Statement Number	Cause of Error Indication
None	Column 1 does not contain the letter "C" to indicate this is a *comment* rather than a statement.
2, Continuation 1	Close (rightmost) parenthesis is missing.
2, Continuation 2	No continuation character in column 6. This also caused the preceding error indication.
8	FINALTØT exceeds six characters in length.
10	Comma not allowed preceding first variable name.
11	Period (or decimal point) not allowed.
12	Comma omitted preceding KØDE.
A14	Alphabetic letter not permitted in statement number.
21	Variable name not permitted following a completed statement.
None	Any statement following an unconditional GØ TØ, IF, RETURN, or STØP statement must have a number (label) or it cannot be referenced or executed. *LABEL is a statement error message which does not terminate compilation.* It serves as a warning that the program contains a statement which cannot be executed.
19	Comma omitted between variable names. Because embedded blanks are permitted in variable names, the computer assumes only one name which exceeds six characters in length.
19, Continuation 1	Comma omitted following KØDE on first line of statement number 19. Computer assumes REGPAY is a continuation of KØDE thus the variable name exceeds six characters in length.
20	Arithmetic statement in improper form (reversed).
21	This statement number (label) has appeared earlier in the program.
111	Close (rightmost) parenthesis omitted.
112	Comma omitted between format codes.
113	This is a "tricky" error to detect. The first format code begins with the number "one" instead of the letter "I." This statement contains additional violations which were not indicated by the compiler.
114	No error is indicated because the statement is correctly written. It is included here to indicate that a meaningless statement in the program is not detected by the compiler if it is in proper form.
115	Statement number (label) 1, references a FØRMAT statement instead of an executable statement.
12	Two errors are indicated: (1) statement number (label) 12 has appeared in a previous statement in the program, and (2) the program does not contain an END statement.

Following the program listing, one summary message appears. It indicates that statement numbers 333, 17, and 444 were referenced in the program but no statements are numbered as such.

ERRORS TERMINATING EXECUTION

Errors causing termination of a program at the time of *compilation* were covered in the preceding section. This section is limited to errors causing termination at the time of *execution.*

If a program is automatically terminated because of an error occurring during execution of a FORTRAN program, the compiler will cause a COMPUTATION TERMINATED . . . message to be written on SYSLST (printer). Immediately following this message, an execution error code will be printed indicating the reason for the termination. The explanation for these error codes indicates both the type of error and the type of statement being executed at the time the program failed. The error code message appears as IJTnnnI where nnn indicates the error code number.

Error Codes

A complete written list of execution error codes with explanations should be available at any computer center using Basic FORTRAN IV language. The error codes probably most often encountered by beginning programmers are:

Code Number	Type of Error	Explanation
212	data	The computer has been instructed to read more characters from a record than it actually contains. If cards are used for data input, the FØRMAT statement specifies more than 80 positions. This error often occurs as a result of miscounting when X instead of T format codes are used to ignore input fields.
216	program	The computer has been instructed to read from a device that can be used for output only. Check READ statements. The device number specified is assigned to a printer, punch, or other output-only device.
217	program	The computer has been instructed to write on a device that can be used for input only. Check WRITE statements. The device number specified is assigned to a card reader or other input-only device.
218	program	The specified device number of a FORTRAN logical unit is not between 1 and 15 inclusive. Check READ and WRITE statements. Possibly device number and FØRMAT number are reversed.
219	data	An end-of-file condition has occurred on an input device. The computer has been instructed to read a record but has found no record in proper format in the input device. Check programming logic for loop control. Computer may have returned to a READ command after all records have been read. If program specifies the number of times to return to the READ, perhaps some data cards are missing. If "header card" or "trailer card" technique is used, perhaps header or trailer card contains incorrect data or the data is not contained in the fields indicated by the FØRMAT statement.
220	data	This is an unusual error code for beginning programmers. If encountered, check control cards sequence. Perhaps a /* immediately follows a // EXEC and immediately precedes input data cards.
223	data	An input or output record contains an invalid character according to the FØRMAT specification. Perhaps the error is in the FØRMAT statement specification rather than in the data.

Code Number	Type of Error	Explanation
225	data	An interruption has occurred during execution of an arithmetic statement. Check arithmetic statements. Perhaps a variable name has been misspelled or has been improperly initialized. Maybe mode of input data does not agree with input format codes.
241	data	The computer has been instructed to perform an exponentiation and has found the base equal to zero or has found the exponent to be negative or zero. Examine arithmetic expressions containing an integer base raised to an integer power.
242	data	The computer has been instructed to perform an exponentiation and has found the base equal to zero or has found the exponent to be negative or zero. Examine arithmetic expressions containing a single-precision (real) base raised to an integer power.
243	data	The computer has been instructed to perform an exponentiation and has found the base equal to zero or has found the exponent to be negative or zero. Examine arithmetic expressions containing a double-precision base raised to an integer power.
244	data	The computer has been instructed to perform an exponentiation and has found the base equal to zero or has found the exponent to be negative or zero. Examine arithmetic expressions containing a floating point (real) base raised to an integer power.
245	data	The computer has been instructed to perform an exponentiation and has found the base equal to zero or has found the exponent to be negative or zero. Examine arithmetic expressions containing a double-precision base raised to a floating point (real) power.

ERRORS IN PROGRAMMING LOGIC

After a program has been debugged of all errors indicated by the compiler, it can be compiled; after it has been debugged of all errors indicated by the computer system, it can be executed. But, after it is executed, the output may not provide a proper solution to the problem to be solved. The program may require more debugging to correct and eliminate logic errors committed by the programmer. This can be the most difficult step in the debugging process. The problem to be solved, the source program, and the output produced (if any) must be carefully analyzed to determine the cause of the invalid output. This requires an understanding of the effect of each statement in the source program as well as some sound reasoning by the programmer.

Detecting Logic Errors

If an executed program produces no output, the first step should be to examine the source program to determine why a WRITE statement was not executed. Whenever a WRITE statement containing a literal and/or a list of variable names referenced to a valid FØRMAT statement is executed, there will always be some output even though it may be "garbage."

If invalid output is produced, the first step should be to check the input data deck, if any, to determine if it contains complete and correct data (as the saying goes: "garbage-in, garbage-out"). Next, the input data deck should be compared to the appropriate READ and FØRMAT statements to determine if they agree. After the programmer is assured that valid input was properly read in, the next step should be to examine the program logic.

The variety of reasons why an executed program can produce invalid results is almost infinite. In general, the program may (1) include incorrect, incomplete, or improper statements, (2) include improperly sequenced statements, and (3) omit required statements. Perhaps the best approach to use in detecting logic errors is first to carefully examine the output and then to determine why it was produced via examination of the source program.

If the output is supposed to contain several fields, it is usually preferable to debug one field at a time. For example, assume that the output statement was WRITE (3,100)A,B,C,D,E; and all output fields contained invalid data. One of the fields, for example A, should be selected to be debugged first. The programmer should use the source program to follow the sequence of execution of all statements containing the variable name A. Some programmers prefer to work "backwards" through the program, starting with the WRITE statement. All nonexecutable statements describing the A field should also be examined. After debugging the A field error, the other fields should be selected one at a time and similarly debugged. Quite often, the correction of one source of error will correct several or all additional errors, but occasionally it can create other problems.

The reason for some output errors can be quite obvious. For example, if the output was written by the wrong device, the WRITE statement referenced the incorrect device number; if a series of output fields are in improper sequence, the FØRMAT and/or WRITE statements are incorrect; if printed output drops the first character and/or line spacing is incorrect, the FØRMAT statement does not provide proper line spacing control.

The computer system can help the programmer detect some types of logic errors. For example, an asterisk will appear in each column of an output field if the format code does not provide sufficient field length for the output or if the WRITE statement contains an undefined variable name.

Most logic errors are not easy to detect, particularly those occurring in arithmetic and control statements. Typical arithmetic statement errors include improper operational signs, improper sequence of operations, and an incorrect or incomplete formula for the problem to be solved. Typical control statement errors include not allowing for all possibilities, improper branching, and improper loop control. If a bug is particularly difficult to find, someone should be asked for help. Quite often a programmer becomes so involved with a problem that he overlooks an obvious cause of the trouble.

To summarize, the compiler can be used to detect all violations of the rules of FORTRAN; the computer system will detect all errors occurring during execution; but the programmer must detect logic errors. Good programming comes from experience, and experience—well, that comes from poor programming!

Debugging Illustration Program—Second Run

To illustrate the effect of logic errors, the same program used to illustrate compiler-generated error messages in the first section of this Appendix (Figure A–1) will now be used again. The "Second Run" of this program (Figure A–2) has been debugged of all violations of the rules of FORTRAN, and all unnecessary statements have been removed. The program has been compiled and executed but contains invalid output. An explanation of each logic error causing the invalid output immediately follows Figure A–2.

Correcting Logic Errors. The following step-by-step explanation illustrates one method of locating and correcting the logic errors which caused the invalid output in Figure A–2:

1. All 10 lines of the "Employee No." output field contain an asterisk in each of the five columns of the field.
   A. An examination of the input data reveals it is complete and correct. The employees are numbered consecutively 1 through 10, and the input data were properly read in.
   B. The output format code (I6) indicates a field length of five columns because the first character of the first field is dropped when a printer is used for output. This field length is more than adequate for the output data.
   C. The WRITE statement uses NØEMP as the variable name. The only other statement in the program using the employee number is the READ statement where the variable name is spelled differently (NUMEMP). Thus, the output is invalid because the WRITE statement includes an undefined variable name. Stated another way, the computer does not know the current value of NØEMP because it hasn't been told by the program.
   This error can be corrected by changing the variable name to NUMEMP in the WRITE statement, by changing the variable name

FIGURE A–2
Illustrative Debugging Program Containing Logic
Errors

```
C   DEBUGGING ILLUSTRATION PROGRAM
C          *** 2ND RUN ***
C
C      THIS   2ND RUN   HAS BEEN
C      DEBUGGED OF ALL   1ST RUN
C      ERRORS INDICATED BY THE
C      COMPILER AND UNECESSARY
C      STATEMENTS REMOVED. IT WILL
C      COMPILE AND EXECUTE BUT
C      OUTPUT WILL BE INVALID
C      BECAUSE OF PROGRAMMING
C      LOGIC ERRORS.
C
    1 FORMAT(//4X,'EMP',T29,'REGULAR',
   1T47,'TOTAL')
    2 FORMAT(7H     NO.,T10,'HOURS',T17,
   1'RATE',T23,'CODE',T30,'PAY',T38,
   2'BONUS',T48,'PAY'/)
    3 FORMAT(I5,2F6.2,I2)
    4 FORMAT(I6,T9,F6.2,T15,F6.2,T24,I2
   1,T28,F7.2,T39,F5.2,T46,F7.2)
    5 FORMAT(T33,'GRAND TOTAL',T45,F8.2)
    6 WRITE(3,1)
    7 WRITE(3,2)
    8 FINTOT=0.00
    9 KOUNT=0
   10 READ(1,3)NUMEMP,HOURS,RATE,KODE
   11 REGPAY=HOURS*RATE
   12 GO TO(13,15,17,22),KODE
   13 BONUS=REGPAY*2.00
   14 GO TO 18
   15 BONUS=REGPAY
   16 GO TO 18
   17 BONUS=REGPAY/2.00
   18 TOTPAY=REGPAY+BONUS
   19 WRITE(3,4)NOEMP,HOURS,RATE,KODE,
   1REGPAY,BONUS
   21 GO TO 10
   20 FINTOT=FINTOT+TOTPAY
   22 WRITE(3,5)FINTOT
   23 STOP
      END
```

Output from Above Program

EMP NO.	HOURS	RATE	CODE	REGULAR PAY	BONUS	TOTAL PAY
*****	40.00	2.00	1	80.00	*****	
*****	40.00	2.00	2	80.00	80.00	
*****	40.00	2.00	3	80.00	40.00	
*****	38.50	4.74	2	182.49	*****	
*****	41.25	6.00	2	247.50	*****	
*****	36.00	2.00	1	72.00	*****	
*****	18.50	1.30	1	24.05	48.10	
*****	40.50	2.00	3	81.00	40.50	
*****	32.00	3.50	3	112.00	56.00	
*****	20.00	1.00	1	20.00	40.00	
				GRAND TOTAL		0.0

to NØEMP in the READ statement, or by changing both the READ and WRITE statements to include the same, but differently spelled, valid integer variable name such as NUMBER. As a matter of practicality, it is easier to change one statement than two; in this case, it is easier to change the WRITE statement because, as indicated later, it requires another change as the result of another error.

2. The "Bonus" field also contains an asterisk in each of the five columns of the output field (F5.2) but only in 4 of the 10 printed lines.

   A. An examination of the output reveals that the amount of BØNUS is correct for 6 of the 10 printed lines. The next step is to determine why four lines contain invalid output.

   B. An analysis of the problem and the source program indicates that any employee with a bonus code of 1 should earn a $100.00 bonus if his regular pay is $50.00. The output reveals that the four lines containing invalid data each correspond to an employee who earned in excess of $100.00 in bonus. Thus, the error is in the format code (I5) because it does not provide adequate space for output which exceeds 99.99 (five positions).

   This error can be corrected by changing the format code. (It should be noted that changing one format code may require several others to be changed including the format codes for the column "headings." In this case, only one format code requires a change.)

3. The "Total Pay" field contains no output data for any of the 10 employees. An examination of the WRITE statement immediately reveals the reason; the last name in the WRITE list is BØNUS. This error can be corrected by adding the variable name TØTPAY to the end of the WRITE list.

4. The "Grand Total" is also invalid.

   A. An examination of the output indicates that the WRITE statement was executed because the literal GRAND TØTAL and the value 0.0 were printed.

   B. A careful examination of the source program reveals that FINTØT was initialized to zero but was not incremented as each employee's card was processed. This error was caused by an unconditional GØ TØ statement preceding the arithmetic statement which was to do the incrementing.

   This error can be corrected by simply changing the sequence of two statements; statement number 20 should precede rather than follow statement number 21. The programmer should be extremely cautious when the sequence of a statement in the source deck is changed because one such change may necessitate many more changes in other statements. In some cases, a whole series of statements may have to be renumbered, and control statements may have to be changed to reference different statements.

Debugging Illustration Program—Final Run

Figure A–3 illustrates the same program used throughout this Appendix after all logic errors have been debugged. The resulting output provides the correct solution to the problem to be solved.

FIGURE A–3
Illustrative Debugging Program after Final Debugging

```
C     DEBUGGING ILLUSTRATION PROGRAM
C          *** FINAL RUN ***
C
C     THIS  FINAL RUN HAS BEEN
C     DEBUGGED OF ALL LOGIC ERRORS
C     CONTAINED IN THE  2ND RUN.
C     THE OUTPUT WILL BE CORRECT.
C
   1 FORMAT(//4X,'EMP',T29,'REGULAR',
    1T47,'TOTAL')
   2 FORMAT(7H     NO.,T10,'HOURS',T17,
    1'RATE',T23,'CODE',T30,'PAY',T38,
    2'BONUS',T48,'PAY'/)
   3 FORMAT(I5,2F6.2,I2)
   4 FORMAT(I6,T9,F6.2,T15,F6.2,T24,I2
    1,T28,F7.2,T37,F7.2,T46,F7.2)
   5 FORMAT(T33,'GRAND TOTAL',T45,F8.2)
   6 WRITE(3,1)
   7 WRITE(3,2)
   8 FINTOT=0.00
   9 KOUNT=0
  10 READ(1,3)NUMEMP,HOURS,RATE,KODE
  11 REGPAY=HOURS*RATE
  12 GO TO(13,15,17,22),KODE
  13 BONUS=REGPAY*2.00
  14 GO TO 18
  15 BONUS=REGPAY
  16 GO TO 18
  17 BONUS=REGPAY/2.00
  18 TOTPAY=REGPAY+BONUS
  19 WRITE(3,4)NUMEMP,HOURS,RATE,KODE,
    1REGPAY,BONUS,TOTPAY
  20 FINTOT=FINTOT+TOTPAY
  21 GO TO 10
  22 WRITE(3,5)FINTOT
  23 STOP
     END
```

Output from Above Program

EMP NO.	HOURS	RATE	CODE	REGULAR PAY	BONUS	TOTAL PAY
1	40.00	2.00	1	80.00	160.00	240.00
2	40.00	2.00	2	80.00	80.00	160.00
3	40.00	2.00	3	80.00	40.00	120.00
4	38.50	4.74	2	182.49	182.49	364.98
5	41.25	6.00	2	247.50	247.50	495.00
6	36.00	2.00	1	72.00	144.00	216.00
7	18.50	1.30	1	24.05	48.10	72.15
8	40.50	2.00	3	81.00	40.50	121.50
9	32.00	3.50	3	112.00	56.00	168.00
10	20.00	1.00	1	20.00	40.00	60.00
					GRAND TOTAL	2017.63

APPENDIX B

FLOWCHART SYMBOLS

THE following program flowchart symbols are substantially those recommended by the American National Standards Institute, Inc. (ANSI/X3.5–1968). Any descriptive comment or explanatory note may be written inside these symbols.

Symbol	Represents
	PROCESSING General processing operations (such as arithmetic operations) not represented by other symbols in the flowchart.
	INPUT/OUTPUT A general symbol for any operation of an input/output device.
	DECISION Alternate branches to two or more different points in a flowchart.
	PREDEFINED PROCESS Operations not indicated in a particular flowchart (such as a subroutine).
	TERMINAL A starting or stopping point in a program.
	FLOWLINE Direction of flow between the various action symbols

Symbol	Represents
	in the flowchart. If arrowheads are omitted, flow is assumed to be from left to right or top to bottom.
◯	CONNECTOR An exit to or an entry from some other part of the flowchart. Substituted for a flowline when the direction of flow is broken.
▭	ANNOTATION An optional descriptive comment or explanatory note. Broken line is connected to the appropriate location.

APPENDIX
C

OPERATING AN IBM
"KEYPUNCH" MACHINE

THE machine used to punch cards is officially called a "card punch" but more commonly, a "keypunch." The more popular term is used throughout this Appendix.

The major portion of this Appendix covers the general description of the IBM Model 29 keypunch and presents step-by-step procedures which can be used to punch FORTRAN program cards and a few data cards. If many data cards (perhaps 50 or more) are to be punched as one job, the IBM reference manual for this machine should be read. It includes a description of a keypunch program card which can be used to automatically control spacing, duplicating, shifting, and printing.

The latter portion of this Appendix briefly covers the IBM Model 26 keypunch and the differences in operation between this model and Model 29. It also illustrates the different special character codes produced by these two models and discusses the types of coding acceptable to the Basic FORTRAN IV Compiler.

MODEL 29

The most popular keypunch machine used to punch cards to be processed on IBM System/360 and System/370 is Model 29. In addition to alphabetic letters and decimal numbers, it can be used to punch about two dozen special characters which are required for the various source program languages which can be processed by System/360 and/370.

The 29 keypunch and the keyboard and switch panel, with keyboard diagram are illustrated in Figures C–1 and C–2, respectively and should be referred to while reading the discussion which follows.

FIGURE C–1
IBM Model 29 Keypunch Machine

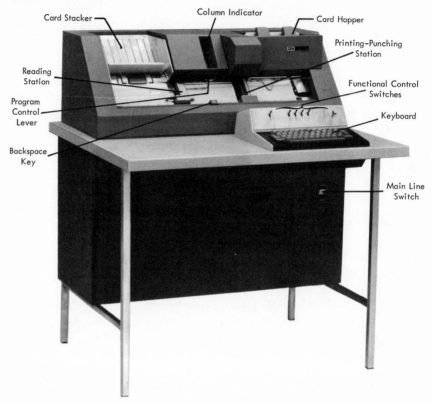

Photo courtesy of IBM Corp.

General Description (Figure C–1)

The *Main-Line Switch* is located below the keyboard on the right-front side of the machine. Model 29 requires no "warm-up period"; it is ready to go immediately after the switch is turned on.

The *Card Hopper* is located on the upper-right side of the machine. It is "loaded" with cards to be punched (usually "blanks"). A pressure plate must be released to place cards in the hopper, then reset to press against the cards. Cards are placed in the hopper face-forward, 9–edge down, and are fed front card first.

FIGURE C-2
Functional Switches, Keyboard, and Keyboard Diagram

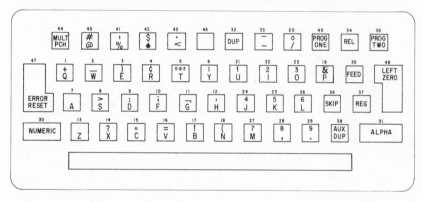

Photo courtesy of IBM Corp.

The cards enter the "card bed" from the *Card Hopper,* 9–edge first. They move across the card bed 1–edge first (from right to left) column by column until all 80 columns have passed each station. Punching and printing occurs at the first of the two stations, the *Printing-Punching Station.* After passing this station, the card enters the *Reading Station* which is used for any duplication required. Finally, after passing this station, the processed cards enter the *Card Stacker.* When removed from the Card Stacker, cards are in the sequence in which they were punched.

The operator can determine the exact location of the cards at the Reading and/or Printer-Punching Station by use of the *Column Indicator,* which denotes the next column to be processed. Beginning operators are sometimes confused by the Column Indicator, which tells where the card is, not where it has been. If the Column Indicator is on 28 and the letter "A" on the keyboard is depressed, for example, the card at the Printing-Punching Station will be punched in column 28, not column 29. It should be noted that the Column Indicator is always synchronized with the location of the cards at both stations.

The *Program Control Lever* should be turned to the right to place it in "off" position. This automatically places the machine in "alphabetic mode" which will be discussed later. This lever should be turned to the left or "on" position only if the program drum contains a keypunch program card (which controls the operation of the keypunch and should not be confused with a FORTRAN program card). A keypunch program card is required only if many cards are to be punched. As indicated previously, preparation of keypunch program cards is not included in this Appendix.

The *Backspace Key* has the same function on a keypunch as on a typewriter, but it should be noted that it is not located on the keyboard. It is below the card bed between the two stations. When it is held down, cards at both stations continue to backspace until column 1 is reached. Cards should not be backspaced if the Column Indicator is on 79 or 80; in no case should cards be backspaced more than 20 columns or future punching may not be properly aligned.

Keyboard Switch Panel (Figure C-2)

Six "functional control" switches are located on this panel.

The CLEAR switch is held in "off" position by an internal spring. It is turned "on" (lifted up) to clear all cards from the card bed without feeding additional cards from the hopper; the internal spring automatically restores this switch to "off" position.

The PRINT switch is normally placed in "on" position to activate the printing mechanism. This causes the characters to be printed (interpreted) directly above the 12 row in the column in which the character is punched. Printing and punching occur simultaneously.

The AUTO FEED switch is ordinarily turned "on" when more than one or two cards are to be punched. It is used to cause automatic feeding, registering, and stacking. It is discussed in more detail in a following section.

The other three functional control switches are inoperative when the program control lever is in "off" position and may be ignored.

Keyboard (Figure C-2)

A keypunch keyboard is similar, but not identical, to a standard typewriter keyboard. Most keys are used to punch alphabetic, numeric, and special characters; some are used for card control; and a few are special purpose keys which will be ignored. The discussion which follows assumes that the Program Control Lever is in proper ("off") position for punching a few cards, as previously indicated; and the machine is therefore locked in alphabetic mode.

Alphabetic Characters. Keys numbered 1 through 19, 21 through 27, and the unnumbered space bar at the bottom of the keyboard are identical in arrangement to a standard typewriter. They are operated like typewriter keys and have a "touch" similar to an IBM electric typewriter. Because the keypunch is in alphabetic mode and only uppercase (capital) letters can be punched in Hollerith Code, no shifting is required. It might be noted that key number 31 is the alphabetic shift key, but it may be ignored because this key is, in effect, "locked" down because of the Program Control Lever position. When any alphabetic key is depressed, the corresponding Hollerith Code is punched in the column denoted by the Column Indicator; the card then automatically advances to the next column. To omit punching and printing in a column, the space bar is depressed.

Numeric Characters. Keys numbered 20 through 29 are used to punch numbers. Particular note should be made of the arrangement of these keys which permits a rapid "three-finger touch system" to be used. Beginning keypunch operators who are experienced in the use of a standard 10–key adding machine may experience some difficulty because of the similar but sort of reversed arrangement of these numeric keys compared to that with which they are accustomed.

Beginning operators are particularly cautioned to distinguish between the letters I and O, and the numbers one and zero; they are similar in appearance, and all appear on the numeric keys.

Because the machine is in alphabetic mode and there is no "shift lock," the numeric shift (key number 30) must be manually held down when numbers are punched. The numeric shift is located so it can be held down with the left hand while punching with the right. When a numeric key is depressed, the corresponding Hollerith Code is punched in the column denoted by the Column Indicator. The card then automatically advances to the next column. The space bar can be used to omit punching and printing in any column.

Special Characters. Note that most keys have two characters. Alphabetic characters are indicated on the lower half of the key, numeric characters on the upper half; but special characters are indicated on either the upper, lower, or both. When the machine is in alphabetic mode, all keys numbered 1 through 29, 33, and 40 through 43 will always punch the character indicated on the lower half; to punch characters indicated on the upper half, the numeric shift (key number 30) must be held down. Beginning operators are cautioned to be sure the numeric shift is *fully* depressed before striking the numeric keys.

The dollar sign is considered an alphabetic letter in FORTRAN IV but was not mentioned in the section on "Alphabetic Characters" because it is indicated on the upper, rather than lower, half of key number 42. Because of its location on the key, the numeric shift must be depressed to punch this character.

Card Control Keys.   Only a brief description of card control keys is given in this section; they are covered in more detail in the "Punching Operations" section later in this Appendix.

Card Duplicate (Key Number 32).   The DUP key is used to reproduce or duplicate data punched in the card at the Reading Station into the card at the Printing-Punching Station.

Card Release (Key Number 34).   The REL key is used to advance a card located at any position in the Printing-Punching and/or Reading Station past these stations to the next position in the card bed.

Card Feed (Key Number 35).   The main purpose of the FEED key is to transfer a card from the Card Hopper into the card bed. It can also be used to "register" a card at the Printing-Punching Station.

Card Register (Key Number 37).   The REG key can be used to advance a card in the card bed so that column 1 is properly positioned for punching and printing and/or for reading. It can also be used to advance a card into the Card Stacker from a position which follows the Reading Station.

Punching Operations

This section covers step-by-step procedures which can be followed to punch one or more cards. Before covering these detailed procedures, two recommendations are made.

First, beginning operators often run into trouble because of a "locked" keyboard. A variety of operator errors can cause this problem, and there are several methods of correction. It is recommended that whenever a key is depressed and nothing happens, the ERROR RESET key should be depressed. If this does not solve the problem, the operator should depress the REL (release) key and begin again.

Second, on rare occasions a card becomes "jammed" at one of the two stations. If this occurs, it is recommended that an experienced operator be called. No attempt should be made to pull the card out by hand because serious damage can result, not only to the card, but also to the machine. The card can be removed only if the pressure roll release lever is depressed. This lever is unmarked and hidden under a cover near the Column Indicator, but an experienced operator knows where it is and how to use it.

Punching One Card Only.   The following steps can be used to punch one card:

1. Turn the Main-Line and PRINT switches "on;" turn the Program Control Lever and AUTO FEED switches "off."
2. "Load" the Card Hopper with a deck of several "blanks." If only one card is placed in the card Hopper, it may not feed properly.
3. Depress the FEED key. This will transfer one card from the Card Hopper to the card bed. The card will be positioned slightly to the right of the Printing-Punching Station which is called the "preregistered position."

Note: An alternative to steps 2 and 3 is to manually insert one card into the card bed to the right of the Printing-Punching Station. The card must be carefully placed under the several card guides and kept tight against the bottom of the card bed. It should not be pushed against the hidden card stop; if it is, it should be pulled back slightly to the "preregistered position." If it is not properly positioned, the next step cannot be completed. In this case, the card has to be readjusted and/or the REL (release) key depressed. It is usually more convenient for inexperienced operators to machine feed than to hand feed.

4. Depress the REG (register) key. This will advance the card so column 1 is properly positioned for punching. The card is now "registered" and synchronized with the Column Indicator.
5. Depress the various keys to punch the desired data into the card. Don't forget to hold the numeric shift down when punching characters indicated on the upper half of the key. To omit punching in any column, depress the space bar. It should be noted that if punching is completed before column 80 is encountered, for example if the last data field ends in column 50, it is not necessary to use the space bar to pass over each of the unused columns. When the last data field has been punched, go to the next step.
6. Lift (turn "on") the CLEAR switch. This will cause the punched card to move across the card bed and into the Card Stacker. The operation is now complete.

There is an alternative procedure to step number 6. It is recommended to beginning operators as an exercise for learning the functions of the Card Control Keys. Because it is less convenient, it is generally not used by experienced operators except in the rare (but not unheard of) case when the CLEAR switch malfunctions. The alternative steps are:

1. If punching is completed before column 80, depress the REL (release) key. This will cause the remaining columns to be passed over without being punched or printed and will advance the card to the right of the Reading Station in the "preregistered position." If column 80 is punched

or passed over by the space bar, the card is automatically released and positioned as indicated; thus this step may be omitted.

2. Depress the REG (register) key. This advances the card so column 1 is properly positioned at the Reading Station. The card is now "registered" for reading and synchronized with the Column Indicator. (In this case, no reading is desired because only one card is to be punched.)

3. Depress the REL (release) key. This releases the card from the Reading Station and advances it to a position near the left side of the card bed.

4. Depress the REG (register) key. This moves the card into the Card Stacker. The operation is now complete.

Punching Two or More Cards.   If two or more cards are to be punched, obviously the procedure for punching one card can be repeated as many times as required. But, if several cards are to be punched, the following procedure is recommended because it is more convenient:

1. Turn the Main-Line, PRINT, and AUTO FEED switches "on;" turn the Program Control Lever "off."

2. "Load" the Card Hopper with a deck of "blanks."

3. Depress the FEED key *twice*. The first time it is depressed, one card will enter the feed bed and be placed in the "pre-registered position" to the right of the Printing-Punching Station. The second time it is depressed, the first card will be registered at the Punching Station. At the same time, another card will enter the card bed and be placed in the "unregistered position."

4. Punch the desired data in the first card. If punching is completed before column 80, depress the REL (release) key. When column 80 is passed (as a result of punching, spacing over with the space bar, or releasing with the REL key), several things happen automatically because the AUTO FEED switch is "on":

   A. The first card is released from the punching station and registered at the Reading Station.

   B. The second card is registered at the Printing-Punching Station.

   C. A third card enters the card bed and is placed in "preregistered position."

5. Punch the desired data in the next card. When column 80 is passed, all card movement is fully automatic including releasing the card at the Reading Station and placing it in the Card Stacker.

6. If more than two cards are to be punched, repeat step 5 until the job is completed. When the last card has been punched, lift (turn "on") the CLEAR switch. The operation is now complete. It might be noted that the CLEAR switch removes all cards from the feed bed so the last two cards placed in the stacker will be "blanks." It should also be noted that as a matter of "good housekeeping," and as a courtesy to the next op-

erator who will use the machine, all cards should be removed from the card bed when a job is completed.

Observe that use of the AUTO FEED switch eliminates the necessity of depressing the register key. The FEED key is depressed twice to begin the operation but is not used on any subsequent feedings. The release key may be used as necessary. When the machine is set for automatic feeding, the operator, in effect, need only concern himself with punching.

Card Duplication. As previously indicated, the DUP (duplicate) key can be used to duplicate data in the card at the Reading Station into a card at the Printing-Punching Station. It should be noted that no shifting is required when the DUP key is used; all punch holes in the card being read will automatically be duplicated in corresponding locations in the card at the Printing-Punching Station. This is an extremely useful feature of the machine and can be used in several ways.

Suppose an incorrect punching key is depressed, in column 60 for example, and the operator is aware of the error. Of course, a hole in a card cannot be erased; so a new card must be punched. If the duplication feature is used, it is unnecessary for the operator to repunch each of the first 59 columns. The first step should be to depress the REL (release) key. This will cause the card containing the error to be registered at the Reading Station, and a blank card to be registered at the Printing-Punching Station (registering is automatic when the AUTO FEED switch is "on"). Next, the DUP (duplicate) key should be held down until the data in the first 59 columns is duplicated into the card at the Printing-Punching Station. The operator can then continue punching each of the remaining columns in the normal manner.

It should be noted that in this example the DUP key should be held down until the Column Indicator is on 60, not 59. When the Indicator is on 60, the next punching key depressed will cause punching in column 60. As previously emphasized, the Column Indicator tells which column will be punched next. If the operator holds the DUP key down until the Indicator has passed 60, he has also duplicated the error so the cycle must be repeated.

The DUP key can also be used to advantage when the same data is to be punched in the same columns in two or more sequential cards. For example, suppose each card in a data deck contains a field for the current date. The operator can key this data into the first card only and then use the DUP key to transfer it into each following card. This procedure is recommended because it is faster and eliminates the possibility of keypunching errors.

The DUP key is also useful when making minor corrections. For example, suppose at debugging time a programmer discovers a card has been incorrectly punched with a 3 instead of a 4 in one of the card columns. Instead of keypunching the entire card, he should manually insert the error card at the "preregistered position" of the Reading Station and a blank card at the "preregistered position" of the Printing-Punching Station. Both cards should then be registered and duplicated through the column preceding the error. The correct character should then be punched and the remainder of the card duplicated. It is emphasized again that when cards are inserted manually, they should not be pushed against the card stop or they may not be registered properly.

A rather common error of some beginning programmers is to omit a character on their coding sheet. The resultant statement card will thus contain a blank instead of the desired character. There are three ways to prepare a corrected card. First, the entire card can be keypunched column by column, which is usually inefficient unless the card contains relatively few characters. Second, the card containing the omitted character can be registered at the Printing-Punching Station, spaced over to the proper column, the character punched, and the card cleared. This method is not recommended because of the time required to space over to the desired column as well as the possibility that data might accidentally be punched in the wrong column thus creating an additional error in the original card. A third and preferred method is to duplicate the correct portion of the error card and make the necessary correction as described previously. Thus, if another error is made in the correction process, the original card remains unchanged and is available for another try.

Punching a Numeric Data Deck.   If many data cards (perhaps 50 or more) are to be punched at one time, it is recommended again that the IBM reference manual for this machine be read and that a keypunch program card be prepared. Without getting into the details of how a keypunch program card is prepared, how it operates, and what it can do, one little "trick" is covered in this section which can be useful when punching numeric data only.

If a blank card is placed on the program drum and the Program Control Lever is turned "on" instead of "off," the machine will be locked in numeric instead of alphabetic mode. Thus, numeric data can be punched without the necessity of holding down the numeric shift key. Key number 43 instead of 29 should be used if decimal points are punched because it eliminates the problem of shifting. When the machine is locked in numeric mode, only symbols on the upper half of a key can be punched unless the alphabetic shift (key number 31) is held down.

Beginning operators should *never* attempt to place a card on a program drum except under the supervision of an experienced operator. It only takes a few seconds; but unless it is done properly, the machine can be damaged.

MODEL 26

Some computer centers have Model 26 keypunches. (They may also use

Model 24 which is essentially identical, except it does not have a printing mechanism, so it will be ignored in this section.) This machine differs from Model 29 in very few ways which are of importance to beginning operators.

Operating the Machine

This machine operates the same as Model 29, previously described in detail, except for a few minor differences.

One difference is the location of the Main-Line Switch. On Model 26 it is located on the left side of the machine near the top of the Card Stacker. The location is such that when the Card Stacker is full, the cards automatically force the switch into "off" position.

Another difference is that the REL (release) key must be depressed after the Main-Line switch is turned on; this causes a mechanical release cycle indicating the machine is ready to go. (Incidentally, this machine requires about 30 seconds to "warm up.")

A more major difference is that this machine does not have the convenient CLEAR switch. As a result, the alternative method of clearing the card bed (previously described) must be used. Also, the AUTO FEED must be turned "off" before the card bed can be cleared.

Aside from these differences, Model 26 can be operated similarly to Model 29 as previously described in detail.

Special Character Codes

One of the major differences between this machine and Model 29 is the number of special characters which are available and their assigned codes.

Model 29 provides unique codes for about two dozen special characters which are required for various symbolic languages, other than FORTRAN, which can be processed on IBM System/360 and/370.

Model 26 provides codes for only about one dozen special characters, some of which are "dual codes." For example, the Ampersand (&) and Plus (+) are coded identically. It provides all the special characters required for FORTRAN but does not provide all special characters used in some other symbolic languages such as COBOL.

Models 29 and 26 use identical punching codes for the 27 FORTRAN IV alphabetic characters (standard Hollerith coding for the 26 letters, and 11–8–3 punches for the dollar sign). They also use identical punching codes for the 10 numeric characters and the decimal point (standard Hollerith coding for the numbers, and 12–8–3 punches for the decimal point). Thus, either model may be used for punching numeric data cards in I, F, E, or D format, or for punching alphabetic data.

However, the punching codes used for some of the 11 special FORTRAN characters are not identical as indicated below:

Special FORTRAN Characters	Model 29 Punching Codes	Model 26 Punching Codes
blank	no punch	no punch
plus	12–8–6	12
minus	11	11
asterisk	11–8–4	11–8–4
slash	0–1	0–1
equal	8–6	8–3
decimal point	12–8–3	12–8–3
comma	0–8–3	0–8–3
apostrophe	8–5	8–4
open parenthesis	12–8–5	0–8–4
close parenthesis	11–8–5	12–8–4

Because of the different special character codes used by these machines, FORTRAN source programs punched on Model 26 will obviously not be the same as those punched on Model 29. Fortunately, Basic FORTRAN IV Compilers will accept source programs punched on either machine. *But* if the source program contains some statements punched on one model and some statements punched on the other, invalid results may be produced. Stated simply, use one model or the other, but don't use both. At locations where both models are available, programmers must be cautious at debugging time to punch correction cards on the same model used for the original program. It should be noted that some installations have more powerful FORTRAN IV Compilers which will accept statements with mixed coding.

APPENDIX
D

SYSTEM CONTROL STATEMENTS

F ORTRAN statements direct the compiler, but system control statements direct the computer and have their own unique format requirements. System control statements (commonly called "control cards" or "control statements") indicate the action the computer is to take. They are required regardless of the language used (such as FORTRAN, COBOL, RPG, PL/1, etc.). System/360 operates on a "job" basis. A job consists of all cards between a "JOB card" and an "end-of-job card" including all control statement cards, input data cards, and source program cards. No attempt will be made to describe each of the many control statements recognized by System/360; only those most useful to beginning FORTRAN programmers are included in this section.

The reader is cautioned to consult with his instructor or computer center supervisor to determine any special control statement requirements before submitting jobs for processing. For example, installations with a timing device may use the typewriter console to print a *log* (record of performance) of all jobs processed and may require specific comments on the JOB card. The typewriter console log consists of data from the JOB card (such as name of job, user-account number, and name of programmer), time in (in hours, minutes, and seconds), and EOJ (end of job) notation with time out and job duration time. If an automatic job accounting routine is used, a unique format may be required for the JOB card. It should be noted that some installations use a special type of compiler to process jobs submitted by beginning programmers. A special complier may require special control cards rather than the standard ones described in this Appendix.

JOB STATEMENT

The first card in any job deck must be a JOB control statement or "JOB card." It indicates to the computer that a new job is starting through the computer. The format of the JOB card is as follows:

/ / JOB jobname comments

1. The two slashes must be in columns 1 and 2.
2. These slashes must be followed by at least one blank column.
3. The word JOB must appear after the blank column(s).
4. At least one blank column must follow the word JOB.
5. A symbolic name from one to eight alphameric characters in length must follow the blank column(s). This symbolic name is not restricted to the FORTRAN character set. It may be composed of any combination of numbers, letters, or special characters compatible to the computer system (except the "blank" which serves as a delimiter). If eight blanks are used for the symbolic name, the computer will automatically assign the symbolic name NO NAME to the job.
6. If desired, the programmer may place any combination of alphameric "free-form" comments in the JOB card provided he leaves at least one blank space following the symbolic name. Any comment should end before column 72. Many installations have unique format requirements for the comments field such as:
   A. User-account number must be punched in columns 17 through 24.
   B. Programmer's name must be punched in columns 26 through 45.
   C. Comments, if any, may begin in column 46.

Following is an example of a JOB card:

/ / JOB PAYROLL   765–3100 DONALD H. FORD   WRITTEN 1/4/71

OPTION STATEMENT

Each installation selects certain options regarding listing and punching as standard. If no OPTION statements are included in a job, the standard options for the installation apply. To use other options for a particular job, OPTION statements must be included in that job.

It may appear redundant, but it is permissible to include options in a job which are standard for the installation; in fact, it has certain advantages. The programmer may wish to keep his job "device-independent" so it can be run at different installations with different standard options. Also, computer centers may occasionally change their standard options. If the job deck includes all OPTION statements required for execution of that job, the programmer avoids the necessity of determining current standard options each time his job is run. OPTION statements remain in effect until a contrary option is encountered within the job or until the end of the job, whichever occurs first. The required format for the OPTION card is:

$$// \text{ OPTION option}_1,\text{option}_2,\dots$$

1. The two slashes must be in columns 1 and 2 and must be followed by at least one blank column.
2. The word OPTION must follow the blank column(s), and this word must be followed by at least one blank column.
3. One or more options must follow the blank column(s). If more than one option is specified, they must be separated by commas. Options may appear in any order. Some of the options available are as follows:

DUMP	Causes a "core dump" of the registers and main storage to be written on SYSLST (printer) if the program terminates abnormally. This core dump indicates the contents of all addresses in hexadecimal numbers. Ordinarily used only by expert programmers for debugging difficult programs.
NODUMP	Specifies no core dump is desired if the program terminates abnormally. Used by most beginning programmers.
LINK	Specifies that the job is to be both compiled and executed in the same run. Causes the computer to write compiler output in a special disk area called SYSLNK where it is available to the linkage editor immediately after compilation is complete. It should precede the EXEC LNKEDT and EXEC FORTRAN statements. Used in most programs.
NOLINK	Specifies that the job is to be compiled but not executed. Causes the LINK option to be ignored and the object deck to be written on SYSPCH (card punch). Infrequently used.
LIST	Causes the source program, diagnostic messages, error summaries, and storage maps to be written on SYSLST (printer). Used in most trial runs.
NOLIST	Causes LIST option to be ignored.
LOG	Causes listing of all job control statements on SYSLST (printer). This option aids the programmer to detect control card problems caused by keypunching errors or by locating control cards in the incorrect position in the job deck.
NOLOG	Suppresses LOG option.

EXEC STATEMENT

The beginning of each "job step" is specified by an EXEC (execute) statement. Examples:

// EXEC FORTRAN	Tells the computer to load and begin executing the FORTRAN compiler. Must immediately precede the FORTRAN source deck.
// EXEC LNKEDT	Calls in linkage editor and executes program
// EXEC	immediately after being linkage edited when these two consecutive statements immediately precede the data deck. One of the functions of the linkage editor is to join subprograms to the calling program.

/* STATEMENT

The "end-of-job step" statement consists of a slash in column 1 and an asterisk in column 2. It is required at the end of each job step in the program with minor exceptions.

/& STATEMENT

The "end-of-job" statement consists of a slash in column 1 and an ampersand in column 2. This statement terminates the job. *It must be the last system control statement in every job.*

JOB DECK COMPOSITION

Following is an illustration of a typical elementary job deck:

```
//  JOB PAYROLL   765–3100 DONALD H. FORD
//  OPTION  LIST,LINK,NODUMP,LOG
//  EXEC FORTRAN
              {
              {
        FORTRAN source deck terminated by END card.
              {
              {
  /*
//  EXEC LNKEDT
//  EXEC
              {
              {
        Input data deck
              {
              {
  /*
  /&
```

Following is an illustration of a more complex job deck which includes two programmer-supplied FORTRAN subprograms:

```
// JOB PAYROLL   765–3100 DONALD H. FORD
// OPTION LIST,LINK,NODUMP,LOG
// EXEC FORTRAN
```

        Main-line program terminated by END card.

```
 /*
// EXEC FORTRAN
```

        Subprogram terminated by END card.

```
 /*
// EXEC FORTRAN
```

        Subprogram terminated by END card.

```
 /*
// EXEC LNKEDT
// EXEC
```

        Input data deck

```
 /*
 /&
```

APPENDIX
E

BUILT-IN MATHEMATICAL FUNCTIONS

Ⅰ HERE are two types of built-in mathematical function subprograms. *In-line* functions are part of the FORTRAN compiler. Those listed in this Appendix are common to *all* installations. *Out-of-line* functions are not part of the compiler but, for programming purposes, are treated as if they were. They are stored in a library and are common to *most* installations. Specific installations may remove from their library some of those in the basic list.

In-line functions are identified by key words and out-of-line functions by other FORTRAN-supplied variable names. A function of either type is called by using its unique variable name as explained in Chapter 10.

The following tables include all mathematical function subprograms which are supplied by Basic FORTRAN IV.

TABLE E–1
In-Line Mathematical Functions

Name of Function	Explanation	Number of Arguments	Type of Argument	Type of Value Returned
IABS ⎫ ABS ⎬ DABS ⎭	Absolute value of argument	1 1 1	Integer Real Double Precision	Integer Real Double Precision

Name of Function	Explanation	Number of Arguments	Type of Argument	Type of Value Returned
FLØAT ⎫ DFLØAT ⎭	Convert integer to real or to double precision	1 1	Integer Integer	Real Double Precision
IFIX ⎭	Convert real to integer	1	Real	Integer
ISIGN ⎫ SIGN ⎬ DSIGN ⎭	Transfers sign of second argument to absolute value of first	2 2 2	Integer Real Double Precision	Integer Real Double Precision
IDIM ⎫ DIM ⎭	Difference of arguments made positive	2 2	Integer Real	Integer Real
SNGL ⎭	Most significant part of double precision argument made real	1	Double Precision	Real
DBLE ⎭	Real argument made double precision	1	Real	Double Precision

TABLE E–2
Out-of-Line Mathematical Functions

Name of Function	Explanation	Number of Arguments	Type of Argument	Type of Value Returned
EXP ⎫ DEXP ⎭	Natural anti- logarithm of argument (e raised to the argument power)	1 1	Real Double Precision	Real Double Precision
ALØG ⎫ DLØG ⎭	Natural logarithm of argument	1 1	Real Double Precision	Real Double Precision
ALØG10 ⎫ DLØG10 ⎭	Common logarithm of argument	1 1	Real Double Precision	Real Double Precision
ATAN ⎫ DTAN ⎭	Arctangent of argument in radians	1 1	Real Double Precision	Real Double Precision
SIN ⎫ DSIN ⎭	Trigonometric sine of argument in radians	1 1	Real Double Precision	Real Double Precision
CØS ⎫ DCØS ⎭	Trigonometric cosine of argument in radians	1 1	Real Double Precision	Real Double Precision

Name of Function	Explanation	Number of Arguments	Type of Argument	Type of Value Returned
SQRT ⎱ DSQRT ⎰	Square root of argument	1 1	Real Double Precision	Real Double Precision
TANH ⎱ DTANH ⎰	Hyperbolic tangent of argument in radians	1 1	Real Double Precision	Real Double Precision
MØD ⎫ AMØD ⎬ DMØD ⎭	Modular arithmetic —value of first argument modulus the second (remaindering)	2 2 2	Integer Real Double Precision	Integer Real Double Precision
INT ⎫ AINT ⎬ IDINT ⎭	Sine of argument times absolute value of largest argument (truncation)	1 1 1	Real Real Double Precision	Integer Real Integer Integer
MAX0 ⎫ MAX1 ⎪ AMAX0 ⎬ AMAX1 ⎪ DMAX1 ⎭	Largest value of the arguments	2 or more 2 or more 2 or more 2 or more 2 or more	Integer Real Integer Real Double Precision	Integer Integer Real Real Double Precision
MIN0 ⎫ MIN1 ⎪ AMIN0 ⎬ AMIN1 ⎪ DMIN1 ⎭	Smallest value of the arguments	2 or more 2 or more 2 or more 2 or more 2 or more	Integer Real Integer Real Double Precision	Integer Integer Real Real Double Precision

INDEX

*This book has been set in 10 and 9 point Cale-
donia, leaded 2 points. Chapter numbers are
in 30 point Spire #377 and 36 point Corvinus
Bold. Chapter titles are in 24 point Corvinus
Bold #237. The size of the type page is 27 by
45½ picas.*